D'Arcy McNickle's

The Hungry Generations

D'Arcy McNickle's
The Hungry Generations

The Evolution of a Novel

Edited by
Birgit Hans

UNIVERSITY OF NEW MEXICO PRESS • ALBUQUERQUE

©2007 by the University of New Mexico Press
All rights reserved. Published 2007
PRINTED IN THE UNITED STATES OF AMERICA

11 10 09 08 07   1 2 3 4 5 6 7

LIBRARY OF CONGRESS CATALOGING-IN-PUBLICATION DATA

Hans, Birgit, 1957–
    D'Arcy McNickle's "The hungry generations" :
the evolution of a novel / Birgit Hans.
        p. cm.
    Includes a reprinting of the original manuscript of
McNickle's novel The surrounded.
    Includes bibliographical references.
    ISBN-13: 978-0-8263-3862-4 (cloth : alk. paper)
    1. McNickle, D'Arcy, 1904–1977. Surrounded.
    2. McNickle, D'Arcy, 1904–1977—Manuscripts.
    I. Title. II. Title: Hungry generations.
        PS3525.A2844S8734 2007
        813'.52—dc22

                        2006031025

Book and jacket design and type composition by Kathleen Sparkes
This book was typeset using Sabon 10.5/13, 26P
Display type is Helvetica Neue and Rage Italic

Contents

Acknowledgments   vii

Introduction   1

The Hungry Generations
by D'Arcy McNickle   45

Part One
Montana   47

Part Two
Paris   151

Part Three
Montana   263

Acknowledgments

I WOULD LIKE TO THANK THE NEWBERRY LIBRARY IN CHICAGO, WHICH generously gave me access to the D'Arcy McNickle Papers as a graduate student and later on granted me permission to work on this very important early version of McNickle's novel *The Surrounded*. Hopefully, others will find "The Hungry Generations" as exciting and insightful as I have.

I would also like to take this opportunity to thank Larry Evers and Mary Jane Schneider for their patience and encouragement over many years. They were always willing to listen. There are others as well to whom I owe a debt of gratitude. Foremost among them are my parents, Lieselotte and Guenter Hans, and my sister Ursula Hans who encouraged me throughout. Merry Ketterling provided technical support.

Introduction

> Indians, of course, have never accepted the idea that they had
> to become White men. No people ever voted itself out of
> existence, and so the Indians never had. There have been
> individual Indians who have tried to make it in the White
> world, often times paid a very high price in the way of
> discrimination in seeking jobs, advancement.... But in spite of
> these losses and alterations, I have the impression that the
> simple core of Indian life persists. The family and kinship lines
> still function. Values and belief systems still function. There's
> still respect for the individual; there's still a quality of sharing;
> there's still identity with Whites. (McNickle, Northwest Indian
> Education Conference, 1977, McNickle Collection)

CONSIDERING THE 1936 PUBLICATION DATE OF *The Surrounded*,
McNickle certainly belongs to that group of early Native American nov-
elists comprised of Mourning Dove, John Joseph Mathews, John Milton
Oskison, and others. In fact, *The Surrounded* was followed by thirty years
of silence in the literary field and only with the publication of N. Scott
Momaday's *House Made of Dawn* in 1968 did Native American literature
gain momentum once more. Novel quickly followed novel, and innova-
tive and powerful writing distinguished these fictions from other literatures.
The canon has grown rapidly ever since, and a number of Native American
writers have become an integral part of the American literary canon as
well. The richness of contemporary writings has unfortunately pushed the
earlier novels by Native American writers into the background and, frequently, they are read only for their historic interest.

2　|　Introduction

McNickle does not fit comfortably into this early group of Native American writers though, as his non-assimilationist plot, writing style, and technique set *The Surrounded* apart from novels such as *Co-ge-we-a* (1927) and *Sundown* (1934). A look at "The Hungry Generations," an earlier, handwritten manuscript version of *The Surrounded* in the McNickle Papers at the Newberry Library that is presented here, shows clearly what a triumph *The Surrounded* really was. "The Hungry Generations" is a frontier romance that echoes *Co-ge-we-a* and, on the whole, would have fitted very comfortably into the group of early novels if McNickle had managed to get it published before he started serious revisions in 1934. The revisions resulted in an entirely different novel, and, while the plot generally remained the same and continues to revolve around the death of the game warden, the characters assume an entirely different kind of life in their respective cultural contexts that naturally lead the novel in a different direction. *The Surrounded* is much more complex, disturbing, and accomplished than "The Hungry Generations" and anticipates very clearly the novels of the Native American Renaissance that began with Momaday's *House Made of Dawn* thirty years after its publication.

While *The Surrounded* is McNickle's outstanding literary achievement, "The Hungry Generations," despite its elements of frontier romance, is a fascinating social document that provides insight into Indian-white marriages, the life of the mixed-blood children of these marriages, and the pressures of assimilation brought to bear on them. The novel has strong autobiographical traits and can easily serve as a mirror of McNickle's own growing up and coming of age on and near the Flathead Reservation in Montana. In fact, "The Hungry Generations" provides a unique insight into McNickle's personal struggles as well as those that he experienced as a writer. It may also be time to rethink his place in Native American literature.

McNickle's Life

McNickle's Native heritage came to him through the family of his mother, Philomene, who was a half-blood Cree from the Duck Lake area in Saskatchewan, Canada. Her parents, Angelique (or Judith) La Plante

Parenteau and Isador Parenteau, were Métis, that is, mixed-blood descendants of Native American women and white fur traders. As a result of the 1885 Riel Rebellion, many Métis, who had fought to secure their lands and their distinct identity, were forced to flee across the international border into the United States and into exile.[1] Isador Parenteau seems to have been deeply involved in the political struggle, and he and his family fled to Montana when Philomene was about three years old. McNickle's daughter Antoinette told me that the flight across the border was her grandmother's earliest childhood memory. It must have been a confusing time for Philomene; her parents would have continued their Métis traditions, and she would have grown up in that heritage. At the same time she would have been aware that other Native peoples around them regarded her, her family, and other Métis as very marginal Native people—an attitude engendered, on the one hand, by the Métis' long tradition of intermarriage with whites and, consequently, a mixing of the two cultural traditions and, on the other hand, by the Canadian Métis' insistence on defining themselves as a group distinct from both Native peoples and whites. In addition, Philomene became a student at the Ursuline convent school on the Flathead Reservation at an early age and struggled with Catholicism and white cultural traditions.

Philomene was born in 1882 and, when she entered school, federal policy advocated complete assimilation of Native peoples, including the Métis. The commissioner of Indian affairs summarized the intent of the government's educational policy in his annual report in 1887:

> It is believed that if any Indian vernacular is allowed to be
> taught by the missionaries in schools on Indian reservations,
> it will prejudice the youthful pupil as well as his untutored
> and uncivilized or semi-civilized parent against the English
> language, and, to some extent at least, against Government
> schools in which the English language exclusively has always
> been taught. . . . It is also believed that teaching an Indian youth
> in his own barbarous dialect is a positive detriment to him.
> The first step to be taken toward civilization, toward
> teaching the Indians the mischief and folly of continuing
> in their barbarous practices, is to teach them the English

4 | Introduction

language. . . . If we expect to infuse into the rising generation
the leaven of American citizenship, we must remove the
stumbling blocks of hereditary customs and manners, and
of these language is one of the most important elements.
(Prucha 1975, 176)

Surrounded by two different Native cultures, that is, her family's
Métis culture and the Salish culture of the people that they had settled
among, as well as the demands of white culture in boarding school,
Philomene must have been confused as a child and teenager, struggling
to find her identity.

Considering her experiences, it is not surprising that Philomene
Parenteau married a white man, William McNickle, in 1899; at the time
she was seventeen years old and her husband was eleven years her sen-
ior. Their three children were born within the next five years: Ruth
Elizabeth in 1900, Florence Lea in 1902, and William D'Arcy in 1904.
At this point neither Philomene nor her children were legally recognized
as American Indians as they were not enrolled members of a federally
recognized tribe, and they certainly had no rights as such. However, the
year after McNickle's birth this was to change, giving him a tribal connection different from that of his ancestors but a cultural heritage more
familiar to him than any other.

The reasons for Philomene's decision to apply for adoption into the
Salish Kootenai Confederated Tribes (Flathead) can only be speculated
on. Her husband seems to have held a number of different jobs, but
farming was his most constant endeavor. Antoinette McNickle Vogel,
McNickle's older daughter, once told me that William McNickle urged
the adoption because it would establish a land base for farming through
allotment. Under the General Allotment Act or Dawes Act of 1887, each
enrolled member of a tribe was to be allotted 160 acres that were to be
held in trust for twenty-five years; so-called surplus lands, that is, the
reservation lands not needed for allotment, were to be returned to public domain and opened for homesteading.[2] If his wife and children were
adopted, the four allotments would provide land for farming. These economic considerations most likely led to Philomene's application to the
Flathead Tribal Council to be adopted. In the Council Proceedings she is

Introduction | 5

listed as a half-blood Cree; consequently, her children had one-fourth Cree blood and were also eligible for enrollment. They legally became members of the Flathead Tribe in 1905, the year after McNickle's birth, and were assigned allotments.

Adoption and the secure legal status do not seem to have solved Philomene's or her children's confusion about their cultural identity. Philomene, culturally marginalized during her growing up and taught to regard her Native American heritage as inferior in school, strove to raise her children "white." After her divorce from William McNickle and her marriage to another white man, Gus Dahlberg, she wrote a letter to the commissioner of Indian affairs in Washington that states her intent clearly:

> [T]hat Morgan had sent him [D'Arcy]—to Chemawa school
> and as for the circumstances I don't know what they are and
> would like to find out there is no reason what aver for Morgan
> to take that child way from me I am marrd [sic] with a good
> respectable man we have a good home for him and want to
> raise him as white man . . . he has [not] got eneght Indian
> blood for them schools in the first place, my children are
> only one 8 Indian my wishis is to raise them as white children.
> (Letter from Mrs. Gus Dahlberg to the Commissioner of
> Indian Affairs, 1914, McNickle Collection)

Distraught at the loss of her three children who had been sent to the federal boarding school in Chemawa, Oregon, Philomene denies that the three have the necessary blood quantum for enrollment. The passage reads like a last desperate bid to reclaim her children, especially her son. Enrollment, which was supposed to have provided economic stability, had made her vulnerable in other areas. Since her children were legally Indian, the superintendent of the Flathead Reservation had the legal power to remove them from the care of a mother whom he regarded as immoral and incapable of properly caring for them. The letters that Philomene wrote to the commissioner of Indian affairs are the only ones by her that are part of the McNickle Papers at the Newberry Library, and they reflect the anguish of a mother caught between the need to deny her Indianness and her rejection as white.

6 | Introduction

The divorce of Philomene Parenteau McNickle and William McNickle in 1913 was acrimonious as it involved custody of the three children and, through them, control over their allotments. Fred Morgan, superintendent of the Flathead Reservation, clearly felt that William McNickle would make the best use of the children's allotments by farming them and also expressed doubts about Philomene's morals as she had a hired man living in the house (Letter from Fred. C. Morgan to Commissioner of Indian Affairs, 22 July 1913, McNickle Collection). Very quickly after her divorce, Philomene married this hired man, Augustus Dahlberg, another white man. The marriage did not give her respectability in Morgan's eyes though, and he advocated against returning the children to her care.

McNickle did not see the papers pertaining to his parents' divorce until 1974 at the age of seventy, and, in a letter thanking Robert Bigart for the materials, he comments on the event:

> I was too young to know what was going on between my
> parents, although I was aware of a great deal of mud slinging
> both ways. It is interesting to discover, what might be expected,
> that the pillars of respectability—the church, the agency
> personnel—sided with the male white man and ascribed all
> the bad things to the mixed-blood woman. It was a hell of a
> society to grow up in. (15 October 1974, McNickle Collection)

There is no evidence among McNickle's papers that he had a relationship of any kind with his father after his parents' divorce. The fact that he would not even use his father's last name in everyday life until 1934 indicates that he was deeply affected by both the divorce and the custody battle, even though, as he points out in the above quotation, he was too young to really understand the issues. At the urging of his mother he used his stepfather's name and was known as D'Arcy Dahlberg, and even his first passport, still extant among his papers, identifies him as "William D'Arcy McNickle, aka D'Arcy Dahlberg." He was also identified as D'Arcy Dahlberg when he published some short poems in a student publication at the University of Montana.

However, it was not only the divorce that caused confusion for McNickle. Legally, he was a member of the Salish Kootenai Confederated

Introduction | 7

Tribes, and even though he grew up on the Flathead Reservation or close to it, he was prevented from full participation in the Salish culture by his mixed-bloodedness, but, unlike his mother, he had no other Native cultural tradition to draw on. Even at age seventy McNickle harbored bitter feelings about the cultural exclusion he suffered while growing up.

> My recollection of that point in my life is that we knew so little and tried to ignore what we did know, since it was not a source of pride. As "breeds" we could not turn for reassurance to an Indian tradition, and certainly not to the white community. (Letter to Karen C. Fenton, 15 October 1974, McNickle Collection)

McNickle's dilemma was not a unique one, though. In 1914 the secretary of the interior sent out a questionnaire to prominent members of various tribes to determine how the "Indian problem" could be solved. The *Flathead Courier* picked up on the story and quoted some of the responses of a Flathead and his signature: "[T]he effort of a true-reared Indian, trying hard to think as a white man, the failure of which will prove the impossibility of anyone to be both at the same time" (vol. 5, no. 6). McNickle, however, did not even have a choice. Without a Native cultural tradition to draw on and influenced by his mother, he must have seen assimilation into white culture as the only way open to him, a decision that would certainly have been reinforced during the four years that he was a student at Chemawa Indian School in Oregon.

His sisters, caught in the same dilemma, reacted in similar ways. Parker points out in *Singing an Indian Song* that "D'Arcy's sister Florence never told her own children that Chemawa was an Indian boarding school. All they knew was that the boarding school their mother had attended was a very good school and she had enjoyed it" (1992, 19). It is not surprising that Florence enjoyed boarding school; some students did as we know from autobiographical accounts and life histories. Chemawa probably provided the stability that her parents' rocky marriage and their messy divorce could not. However, McNickle's sister also denied that the family was "Indian" enough for enrollment, which indicates that boarding school had done its job well and had stripped her

D'Arcy McNickle at the Newberry Library.
Courtesy of the Newberry Library.

completely of her Native cultural heritage. All in all, there seems to have been little contact between McNickle and his sisters after their time in Chemawa and, apart from mentioning them once or twice in the early New York journals, McNickle did not refer to them at all. It could easily be that McNickle's own growing awareness of his Flathead cultural ties resulted in severed contact with them.

Introduction | 9

McNickle's formal education was marked by the same kind of set-backs that plagued him in everyday life. He attended Chemawa from 1913 to 1917 and was then permitted to return to his mother and her husband to attend public schools. After his graduation from high school in Missoula, he enrolled at the University of Montana, possibly as the first Native American student, in 1921 (figure 1). He completed 134 of the 154 credits required for graduation; he thought that it would have taken him another two semesters to graduate. Fifty-two of his credits were in English and thirty-one were in Greek and Latin. Even though he took nine credits of history, its formal pursuit was not yet one of his priorities, but in 1934 he wrote in his employment application to the Bureau of Indian Affairs: "In history I have made greatest progress since leaving the University. I had a course in American history at Columbia but in addition I have read rather widely in that field under my own guidance" (Exhibit B, Application to BIA, 1934, McNickle Collection). His interest in history was ever present during the remainder of his life, and he contributed three well-received volumes of Native American history to the field—*They Came Here First* (1949), *Indians and Other Americans* (1959) with Harold Fey, and *The Indian Tribes of the United States: Ethnic and Cultural Survival* (1962)—as well as countless articles. McNickle was unusual in that he could write history and fiction with equal facility. In his application to the Bureau of Indian Affairs he explained his early choice of fiction as his medium of expression:

I am writing of the West, not of Indians primarily, and certainly not of the romantic West which best-selling authors have exploited to the detriment of a rational understanding of the meaning of the West, the Frontier in American life. I have chosen the medium of fiction, first of all because I understand the storytelling art, and in the second place I know by rationalization that fiction reaches a wider audience than any other form of writing; and if it is good fiction it should tell a man as much about himself as a text combining something of philosophy and psychology, a little physiology, and some history and should send him off with the will to make use of his best quality, which is his understanding. (Exhibit C, Application to BIA, 1934, McNickle Collection)

10 | Introduction

Fiction to McNickle, then, was more than a story, skillfully told and expertly crafted, to be enjoyed by the reader. Fiction was to educate the reader in a number of areas, to make him or her aware of complex situations in the everyday life of real people. He set his sights high. He must have found the strict disciplinary approach of history restricting at times when dealing with the past records of peoples that were based on oral traditions. It is not surprising then that he maintained his interest in fiction throughout his life and that his journals continue to mention work on one or the other short fiction piece or the revision of a second novel that he had begun to write before *The Surrounded* was published in 1936. In 1954 he published another kind of fiction; his juvenile novel *Runner in the Sun* was set in prehistoric times and revolves around the importance of maize. Finally, his second novel, *Wind from an Enemy Sky*, was accepted for publication several years before McNickle's death in 1977 but was published posthumously in 1978. After a long, full life that had brought him an incredible range of experiences, McNickle reaffirmed his youthful theory that fiction provided the best possible framework, the greatest flexibility, to write about the Native American experience.

McNickle's education at the University of Montana ended in 1925 when he was suspended for a semester for spending more time reading in the library and writing poetry than working in the classroom. He decided to finish his education abroad, sold his allotment on the Flathead Reservation, and left for England to attend Oxford University. After a semester he realized, however, that it would take him at least two years to finish a degree, which exceeded his financial resources, and he left to spend another six months in France before returning to the United States in 1926. His time at Oxford was not wasted, though, as it taught him an awareness of the English language and fine craftsmanship, two elements that distinguish his fiction. Certainly, "The Hungry Generations" that he was already working on at that time shows indications of the same facility with language, the ability to make each word count, that *The Surrounded* does. Oxford did start him on the path that made him a superior craftsman, and he continued to hone his writing skills throughout a long life. McNickle spent May to September 1931 at the University of Grenoble in France and took courses at Columbia University in 1933 as well as the New School for Social Research in New York

City, but he was not to complete the academic requirements for an undergraduate degree. Not surprisingly though, the University of Colorado acknowledged his scholarly attainments and the respect that he commanded in the national scholarly community and conferred an honorary doctorate on him in 1966.

His formal education gave McNickle the tools that he used so successfully throughout his life, but it also continued to encourage his complete assimilation. The literature he studied in school and at the various institutions of higher learning that he attended would have been that of the British and American canons, and the history books would have been written from the Euro-American point of view. The Native part of his heritage would have been completely denied in the educational process. As his journal entry of 23 August 1932 shows, McNickle had internalized the need for individualism and capitalism, two main values of the mainstream Euro-American culture: "Through long repetition, I had been led to assume that only the practical, the engineer-trained, the extrovert, the 'smart,' the super-salesman had any chance or any right to survive" (McNickle Collection). McNickle left Montana in 1925, but it would take another nine years for him to rethink the Euro-American cultural values he had striven to accept as his own and to accept his mixed-bloodedness as well as the Cree element of his heritage.

On his return from England and France in 1926, McNickle settled in New York City, convinced that he had to write and that, ultimately, he would be successful and publish his fiction. Meanwhile, he was employed as an editor and writer in the publishing field. In 1928 he even worked in Philadelphia on the trade journals for seven months. He continued to write fiction from 1926 to 1936 and, even though he was accumulating rejection slips, he never lost hope. He knew that what he had to say was worth saying and went from publisher to publisher, trying to sell "The Hungry Generations." In 1926 he also married his first wife, Joran, who had been a fellow student at the University of Montana during his time there.[3] She had accompanied him to Europe. Their economic situation was stable, even comfortable, and McNickle enjoyed life in New York City: the libraries, music, theater, sports, and so forth. He considered himself part of that urban culture, and others then and later also saw him as a cosmopolitan.

The first inkling of financial disaster occurred in 1932 when, as a result of the Great Depression, his salary was cut by 10 percent without warning. It was the beginning of a financial struggle that would become increasingly more difficult for the next three years. At times McNickle, his wife, and later their daughter Antoinette were almost destitute as work in the publishing field became less and less dependable. It was during this time of upheaval that McNickle experienced significant personal growth, a growth that changed the course of his life. To begin with, the economic crisis that America experienced shook McNickle's faith in those values of white culture he had worked so hard to make his own. What happened to self-reliant individuals in a crisis like the present one? What happened to the culture of materialism that he had subscribed to when there was no opportunity for employment? Secondly, with the birth of his daughter Antoinette on 3 January 1934 McNickle had to make a decision that brought him face to face with the problems of his youth; he had to decide which last name he wanted to use permanently—McNickle or Dahlberg.[4] He decided on his biological father's name and, from then on until his death, was known as D'Arcy McNickle. And, finally, during these painful years in New York City, he learned a fundamental truth: it was impossible to deny or abandon his Native American heritage at will. It was an integral part of who he was (figure 2).

Outwardly, the most significant events in this regard were his acceptance of his father's name and his getting in touch with his mother, which required some effort on his part as he did not even have her address. He had cut himself off completely from everything painful in his childhood when he had left Montana nine years earlier in 1925. Accepting his mixed-blood heritage also made it possible for him to apply for employment to the Bureau of Indian Affairs in 1934, a decision made easier by the new government policy to respect and value Native American cultures. The new emphasis on acculturation rather than assimilation was part of the Indian Reorganization Act of 1934, which, in turn, was part of the New Deal for all American people. Furthermore, McNickle embarked on the most thorough revision of his manuscript novel "The Hungry Generations," a revision that would turn the main character's, Archilde's, rejection of all things Indian into an acceptance of Flathead culture.

*D'Arcy McNickle in 1958.
Courtesy of the Newberry Library.*

McNickle was hired by the Bureau of Indian Affairs in 1936, after a very brief stint in the Federal Writers' Project in Washington DC. From then on, his career was intimately connected with the political and economic struggles of Native American peoples. He held various positions in the Bureau of Indian Affairs during the next sixteen years, among them field representative, assistant to the commissioner, and director of tribal relations. In 1952, with termination looming on the horizon, McNickle resigned as the policy negated everything that he had worked for, that is, a delicate balance between the old and the new that had attracted him to the Collier administration in the first place. During the last twenty-five years of his life, McNickle called Boulder, Colorado, and Albuquerque, New Mexico, his homes, except for the four years that he spent in

Saskatchewan, Canada. His growing national reputation obliged him to travel extensively. From 1952 until 1966 McNickle was headquartered in Boulder, working on education projects on the tribal and national level for American Indian Development as well as conducting summer workshops for Native American students at the University of Colorado, Boulder. His resignation letter to the other board members of American Indian Development makes it clear that he felt that some positive changes had occurred as a result of their efforts: "It is with astonishment that I look up at times and realize what changes have struck the climate in which Indian affairs are discussed. I believe we have contributed to that" (Letter to Royal Hassrick, 16 March 1964, McNickle Collection). In 1966 McNickle accepted a position as chair of the newly established Department of Anthropology at the University of Saskatchewan, Regina Campus. The next four years were dedicated to developing a curriculum as well as organizing and running the department. Interestingly, McNickle did not visit the Duck Lake area in Saskatchewan from which his grandfather Isador Parenteau had fled to Montana in 1885. His papers indicate though that he did check the provincial archives for information on the Parenteau family. It was a fruitless search.

His most important writing project during that time was a biography of Oliver La Farge who had been a writer, archaeologist, and politician. The book *Indian Man* was well received when it was published in 1971, even though some readers pointed out that it was less the story of Oliver La Farge's life than the story of federal Indian law and policy in which La Farge had played an important role as the one-time president of the influential Association on American Indian Affairs. McNickle readily admitted this shortcoming of his biography and explained in a letter that it had been one way of dealing with his dislike of the man without belittling his achievements and contributions:

> I find that I am beginning to admire the guy a great deal,
> which was not the case when I began to dig into his
> background. I still don't like his attitude toward Indians,
> in spite of what he accomplished in their behalf and the
> undoubted sacrifices which his Indian work required of
> him. . . . But he was fearless, faithful and a hell of a hard

worker. One can settle for that. (Letter to Pamela Cragun, 15 February 1969, McNickle Collection)

The La Farge biography was McNickle's last major new writing project. His retirement years were devoted to the revision of *The Indian Tribes of the United States*, originally published in 1962 and republished in a revised edition in 1973 as *Native American Tribalism: Indian Survivals and Renewals*, and the revision of the manuscript of his second novel, *Wind from an Enemy Sky*, published posthumously in 1978. He also agreed to edit the first volume of the *Handbook of North American Indians* for the Smithsonian series; the volume was to be a collection of essays on the history of federal Indian policy. Unfortunately, he died before completing this task.

After four years in Saskatchewan, McNickle retired and moved to Albuquerque with his third wife, Viola, whom he had married in 1969. In addition to his writing he continued to be involved in conferences and other professional activities. He was named director of the Center for the History of the American Indian at the Newberry Library in Chicago, which honored him posthumously by naming the center for him. McNickle enjoyed his busy retirement that, nevertheless, left him time for gardening, bird watching, spending time with his daughters and their families, and visiting old friends in the area (figure 3). The last years of his life were marred by having to watch his wife succumb to Alzheimer's. Viola died in July 1977, just three months before McNickle himself suffered a massive coronary in October.

When McNickle accepted an invitation to speak at the Northwest Indian Education Conference in 1977, his life came full circle. Even though he had been to Montana and had worked with the Salish Kootenai Confederated Tribes in his professional life, this was his coming home. He went to look at his erstwhile allotment for the first time since he had sold it to finance his year of study in Europe. He had come to terms with growing up in two cultural contexts, and he was accepted within the Native American community as well as in the white scholarly community, but, as he points out in the quotation at the beginning of this section, he was one of those who had "paid a very high price." His mother's and his own experiences while growing up had excluded him from everyday participation

D'Arcy McNickle, far left. Courtesy of the Newberry Library.

in the Flathead community, but he had also found that the culture he grew up in could not be simply dismissed, that "the simple core of Indian life persists.... Values and belief systems still function" (McNickle, Northwest Indian Education Conference, 1977, McNickle Collection). He devoted his life to changing things in the political and educational arenas to ensure that there would be no need for future Native American children to deny any part of their cultural heritage.

The Manuscript—"The Hungry Generations"

Fortunately, a number of McNickle's journals covering his life in New York City from 1926 to 1935 and a publisher's manuscript report of "The Hungry Generations" still exist at the Newberry Library. These materials provide some insight into the evolution of the manuscript.

The journals indicate that McNickle was working on his first novel by the late 1920s at least. Some of the journal entries made during his

Grenoble stay in 1931 reflect passages of the manuscript as well as refer to passages that he had just written. The manuscript underwent numerous revisions and had at least three working titles: "The Hungry Generations," "Dead Grass," and "The Surrounded." The manuscript at the Newberry Library has no title page, but internal evidence suggests that it must be one of the earliest versions under the first working title. The journal entry of 7 June 1934 talks about the most thorough revision undertaken yet: "This time I began on p. 47 and from then on everything is refocused. Unessential details have been pared away more rigorously than ever before . . . wordiness excised . . . incidents pointed up" (McNickle Collection). This revised draft was named "Dead Grass." The manuscript report on this version, which talks about the Catholic theme, the skeletal nature of the plot, the whites as "unmitigated villains," and the ending of the novel that has Archilde going to jail for a murder that he has not committed, is definitely not about the manuscript novel still extant (23 October 1934, McNickle Collection). These elements fit *The Surrounded* but not the manuscript at the Newberry Library; therefore, the manuscript presented here must be one of the versions called "The Hungry Generations."

McNickle submitted versions of the manuscript to publishers for years. Despite the rejection slips he collected, he never lost faith in his novel. Occasionally, a publisher's interest would raise his hope, as in 1934–35 when it seemed for several weeks that Corvici-Friede might take it on. The novel was finally accepted for publication by Dodd, Mead in November 1935 when McNickle had begun to work for the Federal Writers' Project. However, Dodd, Mead would not pay an advance, thereby requiring the author to share some of the risk of publication. Sales of *The Surrounded* were disappointing indeed. Even though McNickle noted that fact in his journal, it is clear that his mind was occupied by the new challenges of his position in the Bureau of Indian Affairs. While he was certainly disappointed, he was not devastated.

Both "The Hungry Generations" and *The Surrounded* revolve around the same plot: the murder of the game warden by the protagonist's mother. Interestingly, the plot seems to be based on an actual occurrence. On 16 October 1908, a party of eight Flathead—consisting of three men, one boy, three women, and one girl—was hunting off the reservation on state land at a place called Holland Prairie where they encountered the game warden in company with another white man. The Flathead had a hunting permit. After harassing and threatening the party, the deputy state game warden shot at the Flathead. It remains unclear in the account that I have read whether his white companion took part in the shooting, but the Flathead claimed that he did. The upshot was the death of the three Flathead men and the boy as well as the death of the deputy state game warden who was shot by one of the women. The women and the girl escaped. There are two depositions by the Indian women in the Montana Historical Society Archives, one dated 25 October 1908, about a week after the shooting, and the other 15 November 1955. While the second description is more detailed, it is remarkable how similar the details are in the two accounts, despite the almost fifty years that had passed. There can be no doubt that McNickle was familiar with the event, as it would have become a part of the oral tradition and been told and retold many times in all the surrounding American Indian and Euro-American communities. Even in 1913 official letters about the incident were still exchanged between the Bureau of Indian Affairs and various agencies on and off the reservation. The second white man disappeared and was never apprehended and brought to trial (US Interior Department, Flathead Agency, Records 1908–15, 1955). What such a trial might have been like McNickle describes in "The Hungry Generations," when Archilde is tried for the murder of the game warden at the end of the novel.

"The Hungry Generations" consists of three distinct parts: part one is set in Montana and follows roughly the events in *The Surrounded* to Archilde's reconciliation with his father; part two takes place in Paris where Archilde meets Claudia and her family, learns to recognize the destructive nature of ambition, and receives word of his mother's death; part three depicts Archilde as a farmer, his arrest and trial for the murder of the game warden, and his renewed interest in farm life. The element of romance is added by Archilde's growing attraction to Claudia in Paris and by her letter announcing her arrival at the end of the novel.

The manuscript version of "The Hungry Generations" at the Newberry Library is a handwritten one that also shows corrections and additions in McNickle's hand. I merely transcribed the text and made some

Plot Summary of *The Surrounded*:
manuscript version and published version

Montana (Flathead Reservation)
- Archilde's return to his father's ranch
- Harvest
- Hunting trip with his mother; death of Louis and the game warden
- Father Grepilloux's death
- Archilde's arrest and release
- Reconciliation

Manuscript version	*Published version*
Paris • Archilde practicing on his violin, his interest in history, the city • "Friendship" with several young American musicians and Claudia Burness • Memories of Chemawa • Confrontation with Mrs. Burness about her sons, who are among his new friends • Death of Archilde's mother • Departure for Montana	
Montana • Archilde's unsuccessful attempts to make his nephews into white farmers after their return from Chemawa • Trouble with the storekeeper Moser • Archilde's arrest for murder of the game warden • Kangaroo court and weeks in jail • Trial with lengthy speeches of the prosecuting and defense attorneys • Archilde's acquittal and return to the ranch • Announcement of Claudia's arrival	Montana • Recollections of missionaries' arrival by Archilde's mother • Return of his nephews from school • Dance and "covering the fault with the whip" • Relationship with Elise • "Badlands" episode • Death of Archilde's mother • Flight to the mountains to escape arrest for game warden's murder • Arrest in mountains after Elise has killed the sheriff

(The chart is from Hans 1986, 227.)

20 | Introduction

minor editorial changes to ensure consistency in names, spellings, punctuation, and so forth. On a few occasions I have been unable to decipher a word; those words are identified by question marks in the text.

Even though I initially felt that the middle part of "The Hungry Generations" set in Paris might be too lengthy and drawn out, I decided against editorial intrusion. Though slightly distracting to the plot, it is going to be important to scholars interested in McNickle's development as a writer as well as those with an interest in the so-called Lost Generation. No journals survive that describe McNickle's experiences in Oxford, and the journals dealing with his sojourn in France are very sparse as well. The Paris part of "The Hungry Generations" implies, however, that he had some encounters with American writers and musicians there. After all, Paris was not a city that could be bypassed by anyone with literary aspirations traveling in Europe during the first three decades of the twentieth century. As Fitch points out: "Paris had traditionally called to the American heart—from Benjamin Franklin to Henry James. If art is truly international, as James and T. S. Eliot believed, then its cultural capital in the twenties was Paris" (1983, 162). McNickle's protagonist, Archilde, struggles with ideas of art and nationality, art and identity, Paris as a "cultural capital," artistic ambition, and the male and female writers of the Lost Generation in Paris. Though Archilde aspires to an education in this city that is regarded as the pinnacle of civilization, the arbiter of artistic taste, it causes physical and mental lethargy for Archilde and brings him face to face with the destructive nature of blind ambition. In the end he is glad to turn his back on Paris and to return to Montana. He embraces the Protestant work ethic and the mechanized American world instead.

There is a certain irony in the reflection that McNickle's original plot might have appealed more to the general reader in the 1930s than the one of *The Surrounded* did and that it may actually have had more financial success than the published version. Artistically speaking, the revisions that McNickle undertook made the novel into a gem that anticipated the novels of the so-called Native American Renaissance by thirty years. However, the manuscript version of "The Hungry Generations" can stand on its own and shows many of the traits for which critics value *The Surrounded*.

The Social and Historical Context

Mr. and Mrs. Gus Dahlberg and son Dorsey, of Missoula,
are making their home on their ranch two miles east of
town. They expect to go into the dairy game. (*St. Ignatius
Post*, 25 May 1923, vol. 11, no. 46)

Among the local men who were called to Kalispell this
week were G.H. Beckwith, J.R. Smock, Max H.
Lowenstein, Jos. Grenier Jr., Wm. Orville, Bert Lish,
Dr. Becker, W.H. Meglasson, Wm. McNickle, W.F. Fellows
and J.D. Buckhouse. (*St. Ignatius Post*, 17 November
1922, vol. 11)

The "local news" section of the *St. Ignatius Post* provides one of the rare
glimpses of McNickle, his mother, and his stepfather as well as of his
father in the years after the divorce in 1913. The newspaper entry indicates that McNickle returned to the area where he had lived before his
four-year residence in Chemawa and that he did acquire firsthand
knowledge of the ranch and farm life to be used so extensively and interestingly in "The Hungry Generations." Neither Mrs. Dahlberg nor her
son are identified as mixed-bloods, which is not unusual for the local
papers during that time period. Only if there were negative things to be
reported, for instance drinking, bootlegging, divorce, and so forth,
would the paper mention the offender's American Indian background.
After leaving Montana McNickle began to keep a journal and some of
the volumes have survived. However, very little is known about his life
before 1925 and even the journals dealing with his time in Europe are
sparse and, in fact, consist of little more than sporadic entries. "The
Hungry Generations," however, reflects the social environment of
McNickle's growing up so accurately that it can provide additional
insights into what it meant to be a mixed-blood growing up in Montana
during the first two decades of the twentieth century.

The local newspapers, even though they did publish world and
domestic news, emphasized local events and news, as was to be expected.

22 | Introduction

Like the "moccasin telegraph" of Native peoples, they disseminated information to people living on isolated ranches and farms as well as to people in towns. Looking closely at these local newspapers can provide at least an inkling of how Native peoples and the mixed-bloods were regarded by their Euro-American neighbors. I will concentrate on the local papers of towns closest to the Flathead Reservation—*St. Ignatius Post, Lake Shore Sentinel, Flathead Courier, Lake County Vista*—and on the years that McNickle was growing up in that area. McNickle was an avid newspaper reader throughout his life, and it stands to reason that he also read the papers while growing up, especially since they contained so much local information.

Considering the time frame of the newspapers looked at, 1909–25, it is surprising that editors, on the whole, seem so nonjudgmental in regard to American Indian activities and followed the rules of so-called objective reporting. Common stereotypes are evident, especially in the vocabulary used; for instance, a 1910 headline of the *Lake Shore Sentinel* reads "Charlot, Hereditary Chief of the Flathead Indians, Crosses the Divide and Enters Happy Hunting Grounds" (14 January 1910). The article emphasizes the eighty-year-old chief's bitterness at the loss of the Bitterroot Reservation without touching on the fact that Charlot's signature was added to the treaty by whites without his consent. The description of his appearance and demeanor continues the stereotypical perception indicated by the "happy hunting grounds":

> In marked contrast to Chief Charlot's outward appearance,
> he being almost repulsive in his darkened mood and surly
> manner, it has been learned through officials at the agency
> and some of his Indian friends that he was at heart a man truly
> good and that his labors for the welfare of his people were
> from pure and unselfish motives. (*Lake Shore Sentinel*,
> 14 January 1910, vol. 1, no. 19)

In the same newspaper's speculations on the possible successor of Charlot as chief of the Flathead, the stereotypes shift to those of Charlot as the wise old leader of his people, setting him apart from other elders who are considered useless:

But there are not many of the old men who are fitted for the place; they are old and they are a thousand years behind the times; they have not the intellect of Charlot and will not be able to advise as well as he did. (*Lake Shore Sentinel*, 4 February 1910, vol. 1, no. 22)

Throughout history it has been possible to romanticize those American Indians who represent a bygone era while their living descendants and friends are treated as unworthy of any regard. Therefore, the description of Chief Martin Charlot who is elected by the men of the band to succeed his father returns to the warrior stereotypes: the warrior who has outworn his usefulness by reasons of age and his inability to adjust to the demands of whites:

He figured quite prominently with his tribe and his father in the early fights with the Sioux, Crow and Blackfeet Indians, but since the civilization of the tribe was commenced he has not been conspicuous in its affairs and his life has been uneventful. (*Lake Shore Sentinel*, 11 February 1910, vol. 1, no. 23)

No attempt is made to understand why the Flathead would choose an elder for this position or what the cultural significance and standing of elders is in the tribe. Since all papers consistently emphasize the aggressive cultivation of the land, including the reservation lands, those who are part of that movement become the heroes and those who hold back or oppose it are dismissed as living in an unproductive past. An article published in the *Flathead Courier* in 1914 reassures Euro-Americans that "The North American Indian is a disappearing race" (11 June 1914, vol. 5, no. 10) and uses the case of the Crow to illustrate the point. The writer of the article points out that the Crow people, who would be extinct within the next thirty-five years, only cultivate 5 percent of their seventy-eight-thousand-acre reservation and that it would make economic sense to take their land and to pension them off. The concluding argument of the article follows naturally from the so-called evidence: "Surely we have treated them generously in the past. If they cannot adapt

24 | Introduction

themselves to new conditions, then they must fall by the way" (*Flathead Courier*, 11 June 1914, vol. 5, no. 10). Nine years later the issue was revisited in the *St. Ignatius Post* in an article titled "Montana Indians Best as Farmers." Here the writer claims that the Blackfeet have made more progress than any other tribe in the United States in achieving self-support within "their civilized confines of reservation life" (28 December 1923).

Most of the articles on Native peoples published in the local papers under discussion here deal with some aspect of reservation lands, especially Flathead Reservation lands, as these papers were published in the reservation's immediate vicinity. Some of the topics are irrigation water, jurisdiction, boundary questions, and claims to surplus lands. Needless to say, the newspapers make no attempt to look at these issues from the Native point of view. Those who fall in with the agricultural dream of Euro-Americans are praised for their superior intellect; those who do not are dismissed as the old men of the Flathead were dismissed. The mixed-bloods, the writers feel, were more likely to fall in with the plans that the Euro-Americans had made for the state. For example,

> The numerous mixed-bloods, or "breeds" as they are called, are mainly the descendants of these Britishers and French Canadians. Most of the farming is done by them. Some are quite wealthy, having large, well kept farms and herds of live stock, with good, substantial buildings, supplied with many modern conveniences and luxuries. (*Lake Shore Sentinel*, September 1909, vol. 1, no. 1)

These ethnocentric ideas of an agrarian paradise, "a veritable Eden" (*Lake Shore Sentinel*, 9 September 1909), and the disappearing Indian are ever present and also appear in McNickle's fiction. In fact, in "The Hungry Generations," the main mixed-blood character, Archilde, in keeping with the popular ideas of McNickle's early life, becomes a model farmer and descriptions of wheat and alfalfa fields as well as an expanding dairy business abound in the last third of the novel. Archilde also defines his standing in the Euro-American community by his success in farming and in the dairy game. It becomes a means to set himself apart from his shiftless brothers whose failures as farmers are defined by their broken-down

Introduction | 25

machinery and their refusal to accept the white man's definition of success. The description of Archilde's brother's house and "farm" is certainly in stark contrast to the meticulously taken care of property that Archilde lives on:

> Pete's home was built hastily out of rough, unpainted boards. It had been built less than two years ago and it was already dark and weather stained. Dark brown streaks marked the rows of nails. The roof was covered with tar paper that was becoming loose and torn in places. In the yard everything was confusion and dirt. Two mowing machines and a wagon, new only the year before, were backed under a large pine tree. They had been standing there all winter—and the summer before that. A hay rake stood by the barn, there was no more space under the tree; it was heavily rusted. The barn was built of straw stuffed between poles that were placed close together; the roof was also of straw. This had not been repaired for a year or so, and large holes began to appear where the wind had carried away some of the straw or where the cattle had eaten holes during the winter. . . saddles and bridles lay on the ground where they had been pulled from the horses. A set of harness lay across the tongue of the wagon, stiff and cracked with weathering.

The tone of the local newspapers changes when the articles move away from Native peoples' participation in the agrarian paradise and, instead, deal with traditional cultural values and beliefs. An article in the *Flathead Courier* describes a recent traditional tree burial of an Indian child that had been discovered by some whites. The writer lets the description of the burial suffice without commenting on the beliefs behind it (3 September 1914, vol. 5, no. 22). The situation is different in, for example, the *Lake Shore Sentinel*'s description of a powwow in 1910:

> For some time the Indians have been holding frequent dances on the west side of the river opposite Polson and the sound of the drums and the shrill cries of the participants, plainly heard

26 | Introduction

across the intervening water, has attracted many of the
palefaces to cross over and view the weird dancing and listen
to the still weirder music of the aborigines. The Indians are
adorned in savage splendor, some of their costumes being
valued in the hundreds. (13 May 1910, vol. 1, no. 36)

Later accounts continue to use words like "weird" and summarize
powwows as follows: "These creepy seances are a part of the red man's
sacred tribal ceremonies." (*St. Ignatius Post*, 29 June 1923, vol. 40,
no. 51). The same vocabulary is used by the *St. Ignatius Post* to describe
the vision of a medicine man as a "dance and trance" (1 June 1923).
Native American spirituality is reduced to the level of a parlor trick, a
public exhibition that cannot command respect from Euro-Americans.

Not surprisingly, Flathead spirituality is conspicuously absent in
"The Hungry Generations." Only once in the novel, when Archilde considers himself an outcast of Euro-American society during his time in
jail, does he acknowledge that his mother's people must have had some
spiritual beliefs before the coming of the Jesuit missionaries:

He stood arm in arm with his mother those days, breathing
the unhealthy mist of a hundred generations before his day.
Inhabitants of a bleak world into which the sunlight had not
yet penetrated, there were his people. They gazed into the sky
and scanned the earth, picking their food from under the rocks
and in the meadows. They feared the passing shadow of a
bird overhead, they stood in awe before a blasted tree, they
worshipped the wind that howled at night. They murdered
their enemies, who were no more than their brothers, casually.
They wrought hideous distortions on their own bodies in
deference to savage pride. On all these faces, not a laugh or
smile. They walked grim faced through life and passed out
amidst a burst of wailing. When opposition and adversity
overtook them and threatened death and starvation on the
snowy flats of winter, they sat in a huddle before a sick fire
and, with blank eyes, awaited the hand to fall. They fought
when the hand of the spirit pushed them forward—when it

Introduction | 27

turned against them, they bowed their heads before the wind of wrath. Dull, naked, savage, the breath of their nostrils was fatalism—these were the hundred generations who stood behind Archilde. In his sad days they came upon him and feasted on his strength, drawing his blood away and thinning the marrow of his bones.

Archilde sees Flathead spirituality in animistic terms, terms that require mindless reaction rather than thoughtful response. In his mind it encourages lethargy and indifference, which prevent any cultural development. The Flathead people will remain in this "savage" state until they renounce their arcane and outdated culture completely and accept the terms of civilization, that is, Christianity and farming based on the individual effort because the group, in Archilde's and Euro-Americans' minds, destroys the individual. The reader of "The Hungry Generations" gets some sense of the pressure that must have been brought to bear on Native communities in everyday life. Again, the previously published version, *The Surrounded*, shows a remarkably different picture of Flathead spirituality. Like the Archilde of "The Hungry Generations," the Archilde of *The Surrounded* initially rejects the values and beliefs of his mother's people. However, in the powwow scene he recognizes the healing power of the community, the dignity of the old men, and the spiritual nature of what the Flathead are doing. The white spectators see the dancing at the powwow in very similar terms to those quoted from the newspapers above. The juxtaposition of the different perceptions brings home to the reader how far Archilde has come in accepting the American Indian part of his heritage.

The first issue of the *Lake Shore Sentinel* describes the city of Polson and its surroundings, including the Flathead Reservation. The continuous friendship of the Flathead with the whites is touched on, but little else is said about these Native peoples and their culture before the advent of the Catholic missionaries; however, the article quotes Father Palladino's description of the Flathead:

Instead of a warlike, shiftless people, they are peaceful, kind, temperate, industrious, and stand in respectful fear of their

28 | Introduction

Maker. They read, they write, they till the soil, have their
orchards, their cattle and other domestic animals. Some live
in comfortable frame buildings; they wear the white man's
garb in large numbers; observe the laws of the land; are
comparatively free from all immoral practices, and
worship God with an unswerving faith and devotion.
(9 September 1909, vol. 1, no. 1)

Clearly for these Flathead who have accepted Christianity and see
the need for agriculture the powwows should be no more than aberra-
tions, remnants of a spirituality that has been replaced with Christianity.
The *St. Ignatius Post* (1923–24) ran a series of lengthy articles on Indian
history but stayed away from Montana Native peoples completely in
this series as well as from American Indians as contemporary peoples
with complex, viable cultures. Admiration and respect, especially for
spiritual values, can only be given to Native cultures of the past, prefer-
ably those that have disappeared.

Interestingly, crimes committed by the Flathead are given no more
attention than those of Euro-Americans in the newspapers. Offenders
are identified as Indian or "half-breed," but that does not seem to have
had a bearing on the way in which crimes were reported. "Criminals"
are judged as individuals and no generalization as to their community
takes place. This might be different in other local papers surrounding
other reservations in Montana, as there seems to have been a general
feeling that the Flathead were fundamentally different from other tribes
within the state. They had invited the Jesuits, the Black Robes, among
them to be instructed in the Christian faith; they had a record of continuous friendship toward whites; and many of the mixed-bloods were successful agriculturists. Obviously, the Flathead understood the superiority
of civilization, Euro-Americans argued, and an "offender" would be seen
as an individual, an exception.

"The Hungry Generations" could serve as an illustration, a specific
example, for the articles in the local papers that McNickle must have been
familiar with. McNickle fully assumes this white point of view, and there
is little discernible evidence of a critical stance; social problems are seen as
grounded in the Flatheads' inability to let go of the past. However, the

Introduction | 29

manuscript version is full of local color and valuable examples of cultural and social history during that time.

History, of course Euro-American history, plays a central role in "The Hungry Generations" as well. The protagonist, Archilde, is portrayed as sitting in the lobby of a busy hotel in Paris, France, reading a history of the United States. Other American visitors to the city remark on the fact. However, Archilde's interest in history is the need to absorb the Euro-American point of view, an unreflecting acceptance that becomes an important point in the lawyer's defense of Archilde during the murder trial at the end of "The Hungry Generations": "I was bringing out the point that, contrary to the charge, the defendant has studied—in the east—in Paris—and at home. In his house he has a library that won't be matched in many homes in this county," and "I'll give the prosecutor ducks and drakes and wager that right at this minute the defendant can beat him in an examination in history." This knowledge of history raises Archilde above other mixed-bloods and Indians and makes him worthy to be included in the community of whites. His education, his struggle to improve the Leon ranch, and, most of all, his proven innocence of murdering a white man, cause the judge to praise him at the end of the trial: "Nor could he [Archilde] forget that the judge had shook his hand after the trial and commended his stolid qualities that would, no doubt, make him a splendid citizen. 'I commend you!' were the judge's words and as Archilde passed through the corridors packed with people, everyone paused to let him pass and smiles and pleasant words met him on every hand."

There is little evidence throughout "The Hungry Generations" that the Flathead have a history of their own to draw on, a history that extends beyond the arrival of the Jesuit missionaries to times immemorial. Again, this idea that nothing worth retaining existed before the advent of the Euro-Americans is one that McNickle would have encountered in his local newspapers, his early reading at the University of Montana, as well as in his independent readings.

Despite the fact that the Flathead are seen as distinct from other tribes, the popular images of Indians apply to them as well in histories and memoirs. To give an example, Kate Hammond Fogarty wrote in 1916:

The missionaries who came in the early forties made a great

30 | Introduction

difference in the life of the Indians. The Flatheads especially profited by the temporal help that Father DeSmet and his followers brought. Being hidden away beyond the mountains, they were beyond the game haunts and were more dependent than other tribes upon roots and berries; the introduction of grains and vegetables made their food supply more to be depended upon. The building of warm cabins took away the dread of winter. The spiritual benefits taught them to be more merciful to each other, taught the men to lighten the work of the women, and taught them all that there was a higher motive of life than war. (1916, 53)

Stereotypical images abound in this passage: Indians are improvident, Indian women are "beasts of burden," Indians love war, and Indians have no spiritual values of their own. The reader of Fogarty's *The Story of Montana* wonders how the Flathead could have survived all these hundreds of years without the help of the whites.

Major Ronan, longtime superintendent on the Flathead Reservation, quoted in *Historical Sketch of the Flathead Indian Nation* (1890) the opinion of a Mr. Cox:

The Flathead had fewer failings than any of the tribes he ever met. He described them as honest in their dealings, brave in the field, quiet and amenable to their chiefs, fond of cleanliness, and decided enemies to falsehood of any description. The women were excellent wives and mothers and their character for fidelity so well established that the early traveler and trader bears witness that he never heard of an instance of one of them proving unfaithful to her husband. (1890, 8)

These excellent characteristics do not validate Flathead culture as one equal to that of the whites though, but they are seen as a fertile ground in which to plant the seed of civilization and thereby, ironically, to replace the culture that could bring forth such excellent people.

Memoirs of immigrants to Montana convey a similar image of the Flathead as different and trustworthy; in many of these reminiscences

Introduction | 31

American Indians are an ominous presence, but there seem to have been relatively few violent encounters. For instance, in a long letter of Emily Meredith to her father, begun on 30 April 1863, she mentions the Flathead:

> Tonight I heard that a party of 60 Flatheads is camped not far off. If this crazy populace treat them well, they will be as good as a company of soldiers for their friendship for the whites is reliable, + they are mortal enemies of the Snakes + Bannocks. (Montana Historical Society Archives)

"Crazy" refers to her fellow settlers here, but this woman, newly arrived in Montana and unfamiliar with Native peoples, is absolutely convinced that this one tribe, the Flathead, is reliable and will even protect the settlers from other Native peoples.

Another common element in the histories and memoirs is that the root of all unpleasantness between Native peoples and white settlers lies in alcohol. There is many a caustic comment to be found about the Euro-Americans who sold the stuff to the American Indians to the detriment of all. However, none of these writers ever entertained any doubt that Euro-Americans had a right to claim what they saw as a "wilderness" and to transform it into a garden. It is telling that McNickle's protagonist, after his release from prison with its brief, tentative connection to the American Indian world of his mother, looks over the fields on his ranch and also sees nature in terms of cultivated earth:

> The road on which he walked was familiar. The fence posts along the way were not unknown; the hollows and high spots met recognition in his eyes. Now, as he came nearer his goal, his blood began to quicken. He had not expected it, he had not looked forward to the first glimpse of his fields, but as he mounted a rise after crossing a dried creek bed and saw his green land, the round hill beyond his house, he could scarcely breathe, so choked was his breast and so hot his blood. His eyes dimmed . . .
>
> As Archilde sat there with half-closed eyes he felt his strength mounting bit by bit. The far corners of his world

32 | Introduction

began to press upon him, faintly and indistinctly at first, but resolutely, like water washing in small wavelets to a river's edge. The blood within his body grew yet warmer. He hadn't looked forward to the homecoming; he did not know that there was magic in the earth beneath his feet. The hill beyond the house lay like a great dog fawning and crouching at his side. All this world would be his—when he had recaptured it again. He must march out soon and make a survey of everything, asserting his command once more. What had the chickens and hogs been living on? Had Tom milked the cows right? How was the water running in the fields and pastures? His was a large and complicated world; everything seemed to depend on what time of year he bred his cows.

In the final scene of "The Hungry Generations" Archilde and his nephews as well as the hired help are cutting hay. McNickle provides so detailed a description of the process that the reader can feel the sun beating down on the working men, smell the cut hay, and see the sweat on the mares pulling the machine. His writing brings the scene alive, a scene that sharply contrasts with the equally powerful descriptions of jail and the aimless, lethargic days that Archilde spent in there before his trial. The vivid, dense descriptions show McNickle's mastery of the material he worked with and the medium he chose to work in.

While "The Hungry Generations" reflects Euro-American history, McNickle manages to present the complete and complex history of Indian-white relations in the last version of the novel *The Surrounded*. He includes oral tradition as well as manages to show how writing history can be determined and hindered by the writer's or narrator's cultural assumptions. One of the most complex scenes of the novel is Father Grepilloux's arrival among the Salish; the reader learns about this encounter in a passage of the history that the priest Father Grepilloux is writing, a scene in which Chief Running Wolf attempts to surrender all power to the Jesuit priests:

Then he would have given over his Badge of Office, his Eagle Wing. When Ignace explained this offer, Father Lamberti simply bestowed his blessing on the Symbol of Power, and returned it to the Chief, explaining at the time that we would not interfere in temporal matters, and wished nothing of them but be allowed to minister to their Spiritual Health. I thought the people looked disappointed, and I have no doubt they would willingly have delivered themselves to us. They have the hearts of children. (1964, 47)

To the priest this was a moving event, the beginning of a better life for the Flathead. However, because he cannot see beyond his own cultural assumptions, Father Grepilloux does not understand how destructive, both physically and mentally, this encounter was for the Salish. The eagle wing that Running Wolf attempts to surrender to the Jesuits represents both spiritual and temporal power as the Salish, like other Native peoples, did not separate the two. By assuming responsibility for only one aspect of Salish life, the world is out of balance and developments in subsequent decades show that Christianity has not fulfilled its promise as a replacement for traditional Flathead spirituality. Faithful Catharine rejects the new faith in the end as it does not help her deal with her guilt for killing the game warden or save her sons from hell, and Archilde loses respect for the church when he finds the squalor behind the altar and realizes what missionary school has done to his nephew Mike.

In their physical life the Flathead live in poverty and have lost control over their children; one powerful example of reservation poverty is McNickle's description of the old woman pulling a child's wagon filled with the guts of slaughtered animals that will feed her family. Traditional ways of dealing with offenders, that is, covering the fault with the whip, are no longer permissible, and the community can no longer exert any control over any aspect of their lives. As the elder Modeste says in *The Surrounded*:

In the old days it [the whip] was a good thing because it kept the people straight. We knew our guilt and we told it; or, if we tried to forget, somebody would speak up and then it came out. When we were told to give this up, they said they would give us new laws. Well, they gave us those new laws and now

34 | Introduction

nobody is straight. Nobody will confess and nobody will go to
the white judge and say "My nephew has broken the law," or
"my relative over there on Crow Creek whipped his woman
and ought to go to jail." That's the way it goes now; the old
law is not used and nobody cares about the new. I am sorry
about this; the young people respect neither old nor new and
the old ones do not enjoy having nothing to say about right
or wrong. (1964, 207)

The Jesuits' separation of powers has torn the entire fabric of their
lives, the Salish world is out of balance, and all the people can do is
endure. Another issue Modeste addresses here is the loss of all temporal
power that Father Lamberti supposedly restored to them. Laws are made
by those from another culture and often make little sense in the context
of Salish culture. With Catharine's whipping to "cover the fault," the
spiritual and the physical laws are one again and, in the Leon family at
least, the healing process can begin. The skill as a writer that McNickle
had achieved is clearly evident here and, instead of inserting long
explanatory passages about the history of Salish-white relations in *The
Surrounded*, as McWhorter did in Mourning Dove's *Co-ge-we-a*, he
makes the reader work for that knowledge. He makes sure that the
reader understands that history is not universal and that historical events
need to be looked at from cultural perspectives. It is also a powerful
strategy because the reader can feel for both parties involved in the
Salish-white encounter. The Salish, convinced that Christianity is the
only way for them, cannot oppose those who bring the new beliefs as
they do not understand these ways yet, and the Jesuits, secure in their
conviction that they bring the only true faith, do what is right in their
minds. In a way, both groups are victims of their cultural perceptions;
however, the Salish manage to find their way back while the priests, in
the character of the new kind of priest, Father Jerome, become fossilized,
caught up in form and formula. It is a powerful way to write history.

One theme that McNickle explores in much greater depth than
either Montana histories or memoirs do is mixed-bloodedness. The published accounts of early life in Montana sometimes describe the casual
way in which settlers took full-blood or mixed-blood wives. Granville

Introduction | 35

Stuart, a prominent man in the early years of the state, includes his brother James's journal entry in *Forty Years on the Frontier*, which describes how he became a family man:

MARCH 1, 1862. Cold, nearly clear. Snow is drifting very bad. I brought with me the Indian woman ransomed from Narcisses, the Flathead. Powell's wife objected to having her and as we have no cook it seems to fall to my lot to take her and take care of her at least until we can turn her over to some of her own people, should she wish to go. I might do worse. She is neat and rather good-looking and seems to be of a good disposition. So I find myself a married man. (Phillips 1957, 1:198)

Full-blood and mixed-blood wives are mentioned repeatedly in Stuart's journal. Men seem to have been fond of their families and not until Euro-American women appear on the scene do they make value judgments. Stuart's description of balls during the winter months shows that Euro-American men took as much pleasure in their wives' beaded finery as the women did. However, Euro-American women did come and change these marriages and entire communities profoundly. Marriages that had once been acceptable were denied, and when the three monumental volumes of biographical sketches of Montana's prominent men and, very occasionally, women were published in 1913, not even a handful of subjects would admit to Indian ancestry. In fact, in several thousand pages and thousands of entries I could only find three cases: one was a trader who married a Crow woman, one was a mixed-blood Indian attorney who married a mixed-blood, and, finally, one was a mixed-blood descendant of a captive. On the whole, American Indian people in general are very rarely mentioned in these biographical sketches; about half a dozen entries mentioned participation in Indian wars, some subjects were government representatives on Indian reservations in Montana at some point in their lives, a few served briefly as teachers on Indian reservations, a few mentioned their American Indian neighbors who did not seem to have caused them much concern, and a few had trading interests that involved American Indians. Overall though, the presence of Native Americans in these

36 | Introduction

three very substantial volumes is negligible, and mixed-bloodedness remains unacknowledged (Sanders 1913).

There is always an exception, though. The *History of Montana, 1739–1885* contains an unusual story about a white-Métis marriage. At Colville the author found the first white woman in Montana married to a mixed-blood who is described as "a blue-eyed fellow with light hair" (1885, 858). The white woman had accompanied her mistress from Scotland to the Red River area in Canada where she had met her mixed-blood husband, Tom Brown. Despite opposition she had married him: "[B]ut the lady opposed the match, and it was not till after she was dead, and I had been offered a passage home, that I felt independent to do as I pleased, and we were married" (858–59). With unusual restraint the author does not comment on the marriage, except to point out that both mixed-blood daughters looked very Indian while neither of the parents did. As already mentioned, it is a very unusual account.

The mixed-blood issue is commented on much more revealingly and extensively in the manuscript of "The Hungry Generations" than in the published version of the novel where McNickle almost ignores it. Max describes his marriage to his Flathead wife, who remains nameless throughout the novel by the way, in the same casual terms in the manuscript version that Stuart uses in his journal. "Wives were makeshift too. A white man married a squaw in the same way that he put dirt on the roof of his cabin in place of shingles. That was how he married a squaw." There is nothing casual about his view of the mixed-blood children though:

> A squaw was all right until she gave you a child. There he lay in front of you, ugly and black. What could you do? Give him the best Christian name you could think of and let it go at that. Thus, Pedro, Umberto, Blasco, Luis—Archilde was a crazy name, he didn't know where it came from—these were the names of his sons, much good it did him. For his squaw, he had no harsh words. She worked, not hard and what she did was of little account, but she minded her own business and never asked for anything. But was she civilized? Was she a companion, friend, an equal? Could she sit at the head of his table? Not for a thousand years yet.

The color symbolism in connection with the Christian names creates very negative images of these children. They are literally children of the devil and are marked as such. From birth these mixed-blood children are doomed in Max's eyes to a life of degradation, evil, and uselessness. They cannot be "civilized." His Flathead wife, on the other hand, is merely useless but not necessarily evil as their children are. He feels deceived and victimized: "Never had he seen a white man who was happy with his Indian wife and family," but he never considers the suffering of the Flathead full- or mixed-bloods.

He could not think of that yard full of energetic youngsters without a shudder. In his mind's eye he saw them as they would be in ten or fifteen years. He saw the misery they would bring to themselves and such of their relatives as had any sense. They would all be a drain upon the community, for there would be but few who would earn their livings honestly. The community was at their mercy; it could never develop under such a handicap. Yet, it was a rich and beautiful valley in which they lived.

Max continues to believe in the possibilities of an agrarian paradise but excludes everyone who is not white from it. At the end of "The Hungry Generations" Archilde, formally accepted into Euro-American culture after the trial, shares his father's thoughts. He doubts that his nephews Mike and Narcisse have changed permanently, are willing to work and live like white men, and he is prepared to kick them out at the slightest infraction of the rules he has set. Archilde remains the exception, just as his name is different, "crazy," and while the mixed-bloods should strive to join civilization, they have almost no chance of succeeding.

McNickle paints a bleak but revealing picture of the mixed-bloods and their ambiguous place in Montana society in "The Hungry Generations." This is particularly interesting because *The Surrounded*, the last version of the manuscript, shifts the focus from the mixed-bloods to the full-blood Salish people, who were denied a strong presence in "The Hungry Generations." By including all three cultural groups in the published novel, McNickle creates a more complex story that no longer

38 | Introduction

moves along by defending the need for complete assimilation at all cost. When his novel was published in 1936, it was a novel that could be enjoyed by members of all three cultural groups as it presents a struggle that they were familiar with. Dusenberry, a resident of Ronan, wrote at least two letters to McNickle just after the novel was published, reporting a favorable reception of the novel by all, with one exception: "One thing more—and this is mere hearsay. It is reported that Father Taelman read your book and has stated he thinks you have gone completely mad. That is the only dissenting voice admid [*sic*] the cheers 'The Surrounded' has received. But after all, one would expect him to feel that way" (Letter from J. Verne Dusenberry, 3 June 1936, McNickle Collection).

On a national level the novel was also well received. It was reviewed, among others, by Oliver La Farge, who felt that McNickle "adds 'The Surrounded' to the small list of creditable modern novels using the first American as theme" (1936, 10). While "The Hungry Generations" is less complex than *The Surrounded*, it provides the reader with a fascinating fictional history of Montana during the first three decades of the century as well as provides glimpses of immigrant life earlier on. Its discussions of assimilation and the mixed-blood issues from a Euro-American point of view provide insights into what life must have been like for McNickle and the significant number of mixed-bloods growing up in Montana who were marginalized by both Native and Euro-American communities in the first three decades of the twentieth century. Furthermore, "The Hungry Generations" provides us with the rare opportunity to study the development of an American Indian writer. It will also be interesting to look at the early version of *The Surrounded* in the context of Native American writings by Mourning Dove and John Joseph Mathews, among others. "The Hungry Generations" is an important addition for those readers interested in McNickle and Montana and cultural history, as well as those interested in early Native American literature.

Introduction | 39

Notes

1. For a history of the Riel Rebellion, please see Howard's *Strange Empire* (1952).

2. For a history of federal Indian law and policy, see McNickle's *Native American Tribalism* (1973).

3. McNickle was married three times: Joran Birkeland (divorced 1936), Roma Kauffman (married in the late 1930s, divorced 1967), and Viola Pfrommer (married 1969, died 1977).

4. McNickle had a second daughter, Kathleen, with his second wife, Roma Kauffman. Kathleen was born in 1940.

Bibliography

The McNickle Collection is housed in the Newberry Library in Chicago. The uncataloged collection contains journals, letters, manuscripts, and so forth. Materials in the collection that were used in this introduction are marked as from the "McNickle Collection."

Fitch, Noel Riley. *Sylvia Beach and the Lost Generation: A History of Literary Paris in the Twenties and Thirties.* New York: W. W. Norton, 1983.

Fogarty, Kate Hammond. *The Story of Montana.* New York and Chicago: A. S. Barnes, 1916.

Hans, Birgit. "'Because I Understand the Storytelling Art': The Evolution of D'Arcy McNickle's *The Surrounded.*" In *Early Native American Writing: New Critical Essays,* edited by Helen Jaskoski, 223–38. Cambridge: Cambridge University Press, 1986.

History of Montana, 1739–1885: A History of Its Discovery and Settlement, Social and Commercial Progress, Mines and Miners, Agriculture and Stock-Growing, Churches, Schools and Societies, Indians and Indian Wars, Vigilantes, Courts of Justice, Newspaper Press, Navigation, Railroads and Statistics. Chicago: Warner, Beers, 1885.

Howard, Joseph Kinsey. *Strange Empire: A Narrative of the Northwest.* New York: William Morrow and Company, 1952.

40 | Introduction

La Farge, Oliver. "Half-Breed Hero." Review of *The Surrounded* by D'Arcy McNickle. *Saturday Review*, 14 March 1936, 10.

McNickle, D'Arcy. *The Hawk Is Hungry & Other Stories*. Edited by Birgit Hans. Tucson: University of Arizona Press, 1992.

————. *Native American Tribalism: Indian Survivals and Renewals*. New York: Oxford University Press, 1973. First published 1962.

————. *The Surrounded*. Albuquerque: University of New Mexico Press, 1964. First published 1936.

Meredith, Emily R. Undated letter. Family Papers, 1862–67. Montana Historical Society Archives, Helena.

Parker, Dorothy R. *Singing an Indian Song: A Biography of D'Arcy McNickle*. Lincoln: University of Nebraska Press, 1992.

Phillips, Paul C., ed. *Forty Years on the Frontier as Seen in the Journals and Reminiscences of Granville Stuart, Gold-Miner, Trader, Merchant, Rancher and Politician*. 2 vols. Glendale, CA: H. Clark, 1957.

Prucha, Francis Paul, ed. *Documents of United States Indian Policy*. Lincoln: University of Nebraska Press, 1975.

Purdy, John L., ed. *The Legacy of D'Arcy McNickle: Writer, Historian, Activist*. Norman: University of Oklahoma Press, 1996.

————. *Word Ways: The Novels of D'Arcy McNickle*. Tucson: University of Arizona Press, 1990.

Raymer, Robert George. *Montana: The Land and the People*. Vol. 3. Chicago: Lewis, 1930. Ronan, Peter. *Historical Sketch of the Flathead Indian Nation from the Year 1813 to 1890*. Helena, MT: Journal Publishing, 1890.

Sanders, Helen Fitzgerald. *A History of Montana*. Vol. 3. Chicago: Lewis, 1913.

US Interior Department, Bureau of Indian Affairs, Flathead Agency, Records 1908–15, 1955. Montana Historical Society Archives, Helena.

Pages 41–43: Manuscript pages of D'Arcy McNickle's "The Hungry Generations," courtesy of the Newberry Library.

of his cabin in place of shingles. That was how he
married a squaw. Father Grepillone praised him for
it. In his opinion, it was better than the preachings of
ten missionaries; it was simpler but more, much
more effective. There could be no misunderstanding such
an action. Possibly Grepillone had even thought of
putting aside the robe and living what he thought
was more powerful than the word. His vision was
those he kept to the room.

A squaw was all right until she gave you a child.
Then he lay in front of you, ugly and he cried. What
could you do? Give him the best christian name
you could think of and let it go at that. Pedro,
Umberto, Blasco, Luis, — Archilde was a crazy name,
he didn't know where it came from, — these were the
names of his sons, much good it did him. For his squaw,
he heard no harsh words. She worked, not hard
and what she did was of little account, but she minded
her own business and never asked for anything. But
was she civilized? Was she a companion, friend,
an equal? Not for a thousand years yet.

Max had been talking with more and more heat.
There was a natural twist for sarcasm in his tongue
and after long disuse he was trying to get it
unlimbered today. The whiskey and hot stove
had flushed his face and he swung his
arms at times awkwardly, his eyes shone.

"I tell you we were born fools. Did we think we
could build a paradise here? Did we think the
Indians were lambs, free of sin and ready to
be made into christians? Look at them! They're
all diseased, many are born blind and crippled. The
rest are drinking themselves to death and gambling
away every penny, every shred of property that they
get their hands on. They'd sell their dogs. Nobody
knows who's the father of the papooses you

...are hanging on a squaw's back. Did we think they would make farmers? The government gave them land, wagons, horses, plows, harness, everything. But nobody works. They won't work. They sell or gamble away their government tools and then sit around the agency waiting for the government to make them a payment of twenty-five or fifty dollars. And the government does it, three or four times a year. Have we been fools?

"Now I'm an old man. In a few years I'll be dead. Who have I got to take my place? Nobody. I've worked thirty-five years in this valley building my ranch. I have money and lots of land. But none of my blood will use it when I am gone. I hoped it would be Archilde but he is in jail even now. How do I know what kind of a son he will be? Maybe he is innocent — but whats he doing in jail! White men have a way of staying out of jails when they live innocent lives.

"Father Grepilloux died of these savages but tomorrow morning they won't remember him. He had wisdom and the kindness of a saint. But he had just as well gone into the woods and baptised and preached to the trees. Friendship with an Indian is like the wind and you can't catch the wind in a sand.

"Aw, to hell with it! Isn't my car here yet?" Max poured another drink.

Moser was sitting in his chair with his feet perched up on an open drawer of his desk. He had a round little belly and his hands were clasped over it. He was half asleep.

"What? Oh no! Its been here for half an hour. That was a fine story Max. You make me feel very sad.

The Hungry Generations
by D'Arcy McNickle

Part One

Montana

Chapter One

Archilde had been away from home six months and when he returned and walked down to his mother's cabin she didn't notice him until he had stood beside her for several minutes. She was sitting on the ground and had to look up to see his face.

"So you have come back," she said.

"Yes, I am here."

"You don't look fat," were her next words.

Archilde stood and watched her.

"Sit down," she said and indicated a place on the ground by her side.

He didn't sit on the ground, however. He turned his suitcase over on its side and sat on it.

"Where have you been this time?" she asked.

"I went to the Pacific Coast," he said. "That's where the water is. They say you can ride on a boat for many days before you cross it."

His mother made a sound in her throat. Her bleary eyes were gazing toward the fringe of timber that lay a quarter of a mile away. There were some horses grazing down by the timber and some dark-skinned children were bathing in the creek.

"You have been gone a long time," his mother said.

"I had a good job. I played my fiddle with some white men."

She looked at him for the first time since he had sat down. Her glance was brief. He wore a blue suit and a white collar and his shoes were new and polished.

"Do they pay you for that?"

"Look!" he showed her a roll of money.

She barely glanced at the money, then turned her eyes to the timber again.

"Indian boys should stay home," she said with a slight sigh.

Archilde put his money away and didn't answer. They both sat silently for a long time.

The heat of the afternoon still lingered on and the horses in the pasture below the house were bothered by the flies. They had been in the timber across the creek since midday and had only come out a little while before. They moved along as they ate, stopping now and then to rub their muzzles on their forelegs or to kick themselves under the belly.

Archilde's eyes wandered from one sight to another; everything was as familiar and natural as the air he breathed. His mother squatted on the ground and looked no different than she had when he was a child. Her face was brown and wrinkled and her eyes were mere slits. She had a red cotton handkerchief tied around her head and her blue calico dress was long and full with a beaded belt holding it in about the waist. She wore elk skin moccasins on her feet. She had never looked any different.

The only unusual thing about sitting beside his mother that day was talking to her.

"The huckleberries are early this year. Next week we will go. We can load a horse in one day for the bushes are full," she told him.

He spread out his hand to signify his agreement.

"The stream is full of fish that are waiting for you. No one fishes when you are away. My bones are old and groan so loud when I walk that the fish stay under their rocks."

"How are my brothers?" Archilde asked.

His mother spat on the ground. "The priest himself told me that they will go to hell. Last spring I gave the priest two steers and it was all right then. But this summer they have broken into many white men's houses and the priest wants another steer."

Archilde rolled a cigarette and licked it with his tongue.

"The priests have more steers than you now," he said bluntly. His mother didn't answer that.

"Louis stole some horses last week. I think no one knows it yet. He crossed the mountains."

"He'll go to pen for that, if they find out," Archilde said and blew a cloud of smoke.

"He'll go to hell!" his mother said.

A small girl of about ten years of age came around the corner of the cabin. She wore shoes and stockings and her hair was braided with white strings tied at the end of each braid. She was bashful and kept her head down.

"Gran'pa wants to see you," she told Archilde when she was still a dozen paces away.

"Come and shake hands, Annie," he told her.

She looked at him but hugged the cabin wall.

Archilde got to his feet and stretched himself. He looked toward the mountains on the east and his eyes flashed. The sun was getting low. Down by the creek the two boys were standing uncertainly and watching the house. They had seen Archilde. Their shouts died away and they went behind the brush to put on their overalls. An Indian becomes a stranger soon in his family.

Archilde picked up his suitcase and walked toward his father's house.

His father had just awakened from his afternoon nap and was sitting on the front porch with his gray hair tousled and matted. Every afternoon when he awoke, he drank a whiskey eggnog and a half-empty glass sat on the table beside his chair. He stretched out his hand for Archilde.

Archilde felt a yielding, strengthless hand within his own. He looked down at it with some surprise. This was his father's hand.

"Sit down, my son. Agnes said you were here. Where have you been this time?"

"Out on the coast. Most of the time in Portland."

"They say it is a fair city, this Portland. And what did you do? I see you have good clothes."

"Yes, I made good money. I played in an orchestra."

"Really? What do you play—outside of the accordion and mouth harp?"

"The fiddle."

"Really? I've never heard you. You never play at home."

Archilde sat and looked at his Spanish father. He was of middle height and built of stocky limbs and trunk. His face was not clear but instead it sagged and had pouched and looked greasy through the stubble of gray whiskers. He had a high forehead and a long nose, otherwise he was quite commonplace. His eyes were dull and his mouth looked swollen. Archilde found it harder to talk to his father than to his mother, though he was as much of the one as of the other.

"Someday you must play for me," his father said.

"I have no fiddle now. I gave it to a friend."

"In a card game, perhaps?" his father asked with a slight smile.

"No. It was a present."

"But don't you play cards?"

"No."

"What kind of Indian are you, then?"

Archilde shrugged his shoulders.

"Perhaps your luck is bad," his father laughed.

"No, I've never tried it."

"At any rate, you are a good liar."

Archilde shrugged his shoulders again.

"You haven't many answers. But tell me this, have you any money left after working, as you say?"

"Yes. I have money." He took the money out of his pocket but kept it out of his father's reach.

"You better let me put it in the bank for you."

"No, I will keep it."

"So! You keep your own money and now you sit down and wait for me to die so you can have mine too!"

"No, you keep your money. Better you put it in your rotten grave with you. I do not want it."

"No, my boy, I will give it to you, to all of you. There is only one thing an Indian needs to send him to hell quick—that is money. I will give you boys my money and in my grave I will be laughing. For I will meet you again in hell."

Archilde shrugged his shoulders and stood up.

A horseman appeared in the lane and rode swiftly toward the gate in front of the house. A heavy cloud of dust hung in the air behind him. The rider was a white man.

"What is wrong now?" Max asked, and drank the last of his eggnog.

The rider, who was a rancher from farther down the valley, tied up his horse and walked to the house.

"Hello, Leon," the stranger said.

"You're riding fast on a hot day. Come up here in the shade."

The rancher looked from one side of the yard to the other and half paused in his hasty inspection before he went up the few steps to the porch.

"You have some fine grain down by the road," he said.

"Yes, it is a good field. I do not like grain."

"The land is better here near the mountains. Out on the flat we are burnt out."

"That is what I have heard. No doubt you are thirsty. Here, Agnes," Max called. "Bring some fresh water and a bottle."

Agnes was his eldest daughter. Her full-blood husband had his neck broken by a horse and now she kept house for Max with her three kids. She brought a pail of water out with a long-handled dipper and Max scowled.

"Where's the pitcher I bought you? You're not bringing water to an Indian!"

"I never drink out of a pitcher, this is all right," said the rancher.

Max motioned Agnes to get out of sight. He meant for the motion to include Archilde, but Archilde sat quietly looking out over the countryside and ignoring the two men.

"This is my son, Archilde," Max said to the rancher. "He has just returned from the coast."

Archilde got to his feet and shook hands.

54 | D'Arcy McNickle

"This is Arsheel, eh? How many boys have you got, Leon?"

"Four or five. I had seven; two are dead; I don't know where the third one is; dead too, I hope. Archilde tells me he plays the fiddle now."

"How long have you been out of the country, Arsheel?" the rancher asked.

"I left at the beginning of the spring. I returned this morning on NO. 4."

"Have you seen your brother Louis since you returned?" the rancher asked without turning to Max.

"No, I have only seen my mother and father."

"Are you looking for Luis?" Max asked. "God knows where he is. I know less about my family than you do, Pariseau."

"That's what I came to see you about."

Archilde got up. "Excuse me, I'm going in to see Agnes," he said. The rancher continued.

"There now, I was waiting for him to leave. You don't know where your son Louis is, eh?"

"No, I haven't seen him for two weeks."

The rancher looked shrewdly at Max.

"They say you always tell the truth, Leon."

Max sat forward. "No man has ever said otherwise," he looked fiercely at his guest.

"That's what I thought. What I came to tell you is that Louis has stolen some horses from me and my neighbor."

"What has that to do with me?" said Max.

"Nothing at all, Leon. I wondered if you'd seen Louis."

"I tell you I see none of these damn Indians, except when they come here for something to eat. And they never stay long."

"I didn't know how you felt. But I wanted to tell you that if we find him, this time it's gonna be hard for him. We've got the goods on him."

"So much the better then." Max sat back in his chair and appeared to relax. "So much the better."

"I guess you don't like your boys then?"

"No! Why should I? They have never worked. They do nothing but get me in trouble."

"Have you any notion which way Louis might go?"

The Hungry Generations | 55

"No. He has an aunt on the flat and cousins everywhere. Or he might be in the mountains. Don't ask me."

"Well, I'll go along. If you hear anything let me know. I guess you won't care if we send him up to pen?"

"I don't care where you send him. He is nothing to me."

"We used to be neighbors, you know, and I wanted to warn you."

"All right, Pariseau. I hope you get your horses."

The rancher rode away.

Max Leon sat motionless for several minutes, watching the rider disappear into a cloud of dust. His reflections seemed not to be peaceful. He got to his feet and looked around, then he left the porch. His legs were slightly bowed from many years in the saddle. He walked around the corner of the house and went toward his wife's cabin.

She was sitting as Archilde had left her an hour before. The shadow of the cabin had lengthened and fell across the ground several yards beyond her. Max stopped and looked down at his Indian wife for about a minute. She never raised her eyes, although she knew he was present.

"Where's Luis?" he asked.

"My sons never come home because of you—so how should I know!"

"Have you heard about him?"

"No. I hear nothing."

"He has stolen some horses."

"Was that the police who came here?"

"No. That was a friend come to warn me. He said the police were ready to hang him. So, if you know where he is, you'd better warn him."

"I know nothing."

"If you tell me I will send a rider at once."

"I don't know."

Leon's eyes bored into the back of her motionless head. He knew that she was lying.

"I will send him my fast car to get away in," he coaxed.

"I have said."

Max spat and walked away. He entered the back of his house through the kitchen. The kitchen was well furnished as in a white man's house. The stove had nickel trimmings and there was a blue linoleum carpet on the floor. A kitchen cabinet stood against the wall and the pantry was well stocked. Agnes sat on the floor by the window peeling potatoes. Max took a drink from the pail and asked:

"Where's Luis?"

"Perhaps in town. I don't know."

Max stood there for a moment ready to ask some more questions but changed his mind.

He found Archilde in the next room, which was the dining room, drinking coffee. Max motioned for him to follow him to the porch.

"Has your mother said anything about Luis to you?"

Archilde appeared to reflect.

"No, his name hasn't been mentioned. Did Pariseau want him?"

"Yes, he has been stealing horses and he will be hung if they catch him. Try to find out from the old lady where he is—she always knows. I want to save his damn neck."

Archilde started to walk away and Max called.

"Don't let her think that you know anything about it."

Archilde scowled when his back was turned and he walked down the field in the opposite direction from his mother's. Agnes had listened to the conversation between Max and the rancher, so Archilde knew that his father was lying when he said that he wanted to save Louis.

Archilde had been walking for some time when he suddenly became conscious of movement in a clump of willows by the creek alongside of him. He kept his eyes lowered as he walked along and took no notice. He waited until he had walked a little way past, then he suddenly whirled in his tracks.

He laughed as he caught his two small nephews unawares. They had been following him down the creek, too bashful to speak to him. They started to run, but he called to them.

"Hey there, Mike and Narcisse! Wait a minute. I've got a cigarette here."

They stopped and kept their heads lowered. He gave them each a cigarette and their eyes sparkled.

"Now tell me, why do you run like rabbits? Am I not your uncle?" he asked.

Neither of them answered at once, then the oldest, who was called Narcisse, said:

"Agnes says you got big money. Let's see your money." Archilde laughed.

"Sure I've got money. Look!"

Their eyes got big and they looked at their young uncle as though he were a god.

"Where you steal that?" asked the youngest.

"I didn't steal it, you Indian. I worked for it," said Archilde with a scowl. "Who tells you about stealing?"

"The old lady said maybe you steal it."

"She did, eh? You tell her to close her mouth when she talks about stealing," Archilde sat down in the grass and his nephews flopped down beside him. They weren't shy now.

"Listen, where's Louis?" he asked. They looked at one another and didn't answer.

"Don't look stupid like a calf. The old lady told me already. But don't tell Max, see? They want to put him in jail."

"That's what the old lady said," Narcisse remarked.

"How many horses did he steal?" Archilde asked.

"About fifty, I guess," Mike said proudly.

"Big liar!" Narcisse said and pushed him over in the grass. "The old lady said he stole six mares. He came here last week and got some dry meat. I guess he's up in the mountains."

"Last week I shot a grouse," Mike said to recover his composure.

"You shot him after he hit the ground. I shot him out of the tree," Narcisse remarked scornfully.

"But he wasn't dead and he was running away."

"Neither of you have caught any fish all summer, the old lady tells me," Archilde said.

"We have no hooks," Narcisse told him. "Agnes has a hook but she keeps it."

"Make a spear then."

"You talk crazy," said Mike who was only eight years old. "You got to have a hook to make a spear."

"That shows what an empty head you have," Archilde said. "All you need is a piece of wire. I will show you tomorrow."

"Buy us some hooks. That will be better," Narcisse said.

"Yes, I will buy you some hooks. Now tell what you have done. Did you stay in school as I said?"

"Sure," said Mike. "But the fathers don't know much."

"Is that so?" Archilde asked in mock surprise. "And how is that?" Mike wouldn't say. Narcisse spoke up.

"They called him Little Lord Jesus because he wouldn't cut off his hair like a white man."

"I guess anybody knows I don't look like Jesus," Mike said soberly. Archilde laughed.

"But they were fooling you. You must cut off your hair like mine and like Narcisse there."

"A white man's hair makes me sick," Mike said.

"He thinks he'll be a chief if he doesn't cut his hair," Narcisse said with some scorn.

"No, sir!" Mike said and kicked his brother and they both rolled over in the grass, Narcisse on top.

"Here! Are you like dogs to be fighting over such a matter. I will take Mike to the best barber in town and he will put some nice smell in your hair."

"Then I will smell like a skunk cabbage."

"No, like a horse's tail," Narcisse said and dodged behind Archilde.

"Stop your fighting or I'll crack your heads together. Let's go to the house. It's supper time."

Mike and Narcisse started a race across the field and Archilde loped easily behind them.

Chapter Two

After supper Archilde sat on the steps outside of the kitchen and talked with Agnes. Narcisse and Mike were playing in the yard and their sister, Annie, who came between the two, was trying to keep up with them. Most of their games made her the butt. She never complained.

"Maybe you will stay here now?" Agnes asked.

"When I left, I thought I would never come back. But here I am."

"A wolf knows his hole."

"But the world is big. I will be sick of it soon."

"What will you do with your land? The agent will give you a team and wagon if you ask."

"I want none of this land. I can make money."

"It is not the way of your people to go to those cities and live like a fat white man."

"Perhaps you would like me to be like Louis, or Pete or Umbert or Big Blase?"

"Max will die and somebody should keep this land and have cattle."

"Max will be old before he dies."

"Haven't you seen him? He is old already."

"But he is strong. His voice is full."

"A wet tree is often rotten."

"What is his talk about money?" Archilde asked suddenly. "He has no great money, has he?"

| 59

"He sold many cows and buffaloes this year. But I think he is loco. He showed us no money though he talks."

"You must keep the boys in school," he told her. "They have bad ideas."

"They get them from school, then. At home nobody bothers them."

"But the old lady talks about things that are not good for them to know."

"They are good boys. Narcisse made his First Communion."

"That's all right. Keep them in school."

"Perhaps they will be like you then, and go away all the time."

"Well—?"

"An Indian should stay with his people."

"You talk like the old lady."

"Is it a lie?"

"For me it is." He stood up and saw that evening had spread over the land. There were crickets in the damp grass and farm lights gleamed far away. Bats flew around their heads.

"How is my horse?" he asked.

"He is fat and mean. No one rides him."

"Tomorrow I will ride him."

"Max has a big blue auto."

"He can keep it," he said and walked away. He went toward the creek.

He sat on an old log by the side of the stream and listened to the water. It was the most peaceful sound he had heard for many months. Beyond the creek the forest loomed dark and silent. Two owls talked back and forth at long intervals. He still wore his city clothes and they hampered him. He was conscious of their tightness and pressure.

From the earliest memories of his childhood the creek had always been exactly as it was this evening. The sound had not changed in any way. The evening dampness was always as it was now. Something within himself responded to the sound and presence of the creek. His city clothes could not impede that. This, indeed, was his home.

He had caught many fish in the creek. From the time he was big enough to hold a willow pole and swing it over the water, he had been fishing. He had caught mink there too, in wintertime. His mother had

The Hungry Generations | 61

shown him how to build a trap with rocks and sticks. On the banks of the creek he had shot grouse and squirrels. The creek had been his nursery. He had gone high into the mountains and found the first waters bubbling from under a rock. He had walked miles across the flat and saw the swift, clear water throw itself against the sluggish green current of the "Big River." There was nothing about the creek that was unknown to him.

He heard the brush crackling on the other side of the stream and, involuntarily, he held his breath and searched the gloom. He heard a footstep and a heavy breath. A figure stepped out of the brush and paused. It was Louis.

Archilde stood up and whistled softly. Louis jerked his head in his direction, then he crossed the creek on a log.

Louis was a husky young buck with stern mouth and eyes like most savages. He looked at Archilde sharply.

"So, you are home again," he said.

"So, I am," Archilde said and grinned at his brother's stolidness.

Louis looked contemptuous and started to walk away, but Archilde called him:

"Wait, Louis. Max has not gone to bed yet and a white man came to see him today."

"Who was the white man?"

"Pariseau from out on the flat, I think."

Louis shrugged his shoulders. Archilde saw that his brother was carrying a rifle.

"I thought you were gonna be a white man," Louis said.

"Maybe, someday."

"You are chickenhearted."

Archilde grinned at him. "I am no fool."

"Come up in the mountains with me. My partner got scared and ran away. I have many horses. We will take them to the other side and sell them."

"They'll hang you by the neck first."

"Who?"

"The white men. They're looking for you."

"Pff. Let them catch me first!"

"Don't let Max see you, anyhow."

"Why? He can do nothing. He has clubbed me many times, but he never tries it anymore."

"But maybe he has made some promise to Pariseau."

"What do you mean?"

"I do not say it is true, but, maybe, he will try to catch you for the white men."

"He isn't such a fool! I will shoot him if he does that."

"Never mind shooting anybody. Horse stealing is enough."

"Come up in the mountains with me, then."

Archilde laughed at him. "Do I look like I was born yesterday? I want none of your horses."

"You're a coward."

"That doesn't bother me."

"You make me sick. Get out of here. I'm going to see the old lady and I don't want you with me."

"I've told you: don't let Max see you."

"Tell Max if he wants me he can come to the old lady's cabin. I'll be there with my gun."

"You talk like a bag of wind. Nobody's interested in seeing you hung. I'm going up in the pasture to see my horse."

"What horse?"

"My Nigger."

Louis grinned. "So that is your horse? Well, I am riding him now."

"Are you lying? Agnes said he was in the pasture."

"Agnes never goes to the pasture. I have had him for a month. But he is no good; you can have him back after a while."

"You Indian bastard!" Archilde stood there and called him a string of names. "When you get through with a horse, no one else will ever ride him. You break his wind and cripple his legs. That horse cost me a hundred dollars and you will pay me someday."

Louis scowled and wanted to call for a fight, but Archilde walked past him, almost brushing him to one side.

Up at the cabin Louis found his mother getting ready for bed. She had taken off her dress and several petticoats and was sitting in the doorway, braiding her hair. She made a guttural sound that indicated displeasure when her son appeared.

The Hungry Generations | 63

"When did that fool Archilde come?" he asked.

"Today."

"What does he want here? He's no good to you. He will make trouble, you see."

"He will not make trouble like you. He is a man."

"He is a chicken. Just now I asked him to fight and he ran away."

"Don't talk like a windbag. Whom did you ever fight? What man has ever been afraid of you?"

"Listen," Louis said, changing the subject. "My partner, Steve, ran away. You must get Archilde to come with me."

"Go your own way and don't take others with you. Archilde will be a better man than any of you and you must not lead him away. All of you have been too wise to listen to me—and where are they all? Big Blase is in jail, maybe they have hanged him. Umbert had to run away to Canada. Pete lives with his squaw over the mountains and will not come home. And you must steal horses and the white men will put you in jail, too. I have told each one of you to live peacefully and I have given many steers to the fathers to make prayers for you. But you never listen. Now, when I am old, I see only black days and my sons running away like dogs. I have one good son and you want to take him away. But talk to him yourself. You will see that he is wise."

"I didn't come for your preaching. I must have some meat."

"The mountains are full of meat and fish. Are you too lazy to live, then?"

"Tomorrow I am going across the mountains. I have no time to hunt."

"Stay where you are! If you cross the mountains, they will catch you. You took all my dry meat last week. I have none."

"That is not true. You had two big sacks left."

"What will I eat then when it is winter? You think it is all right if I starve, eh? Go back to the mountains and turn those horses loose, they will find their way home. Then you can come back and live in peace."

"Give me some meat and save your words for Archilde who is such a good fellow."

"I have no meat."

"Then I will take some."

"If you can find it. I am no fool."

Louis scowled and held his tongue for a while. He knew that it would be wise to change his tactics. After he had considered for a moment he said:

"I will do as you say. I will turn the horses loose. I will even drive them back to the flat. In a week I will be home again and the white man will have nothing to say."

"Good. Only do it."

"I have said I would. Let me have a little meat now. I have not eaten today."

The old lady turned her bleary eyes on his dim outline. In her heart she knew that he was lying, but she had no defense. She got to her feet with infinite labor and waddled into the darkness of her low cabin. In a moment she returned with a small bundle.

"This is the last time you will get anything, unless you do as you say," she gave him the sack. "If you are hungry, I have some supper."

"No, I will eat some of this. Tell Archilde that, the next time I see him, I shall kick his behind." He got to his feet and walked away.

"Dear Jesus," she said, "save him from hell!" She rocked back and forth on her haunches in the dark.

Chapter Three

Archilde was drawing pictures on the new hat he had just bought. In front he had drawn a lean buffalo bull feeding on a hillside. On the left side he made a picture of an old cow and her calf standing with their butts turned to a blizzard. On the right side a mare was running with her colt and biting at it to keep it away from her front feet. The back of the hat was still unadorned and Mike and Narcisse were advising him on a fit subject.

"You gotta have a bucking horse," Mike said.

"I have said no three times already," Archilde said. "I want no buckaroos on my hat."

"A bucking steer, then," Mike persisted.

"He doesn't want no kind of bucking," Narcisse said. "Make a grizzly bear."

"That's no good," said Mike. "Make a coyote stealing a chicken."

"You always think about stealing," Archilde told him. "How about geese flying in spring?"

"How can you make it look like spring?" Narcisse asked.

"Make a mountain lion catching a deer."

"I know. I'll make an elk by a big tree."

"That's no good!" Mike protested. "Make a fence post, that's the best you can do."

"Good!" Archilde cried. "I'll make a fence post with an old chicken hawk sitting on it."

| 65

"An' I'll come along and shoot it," Narcisse said.

"Ho! You couldn't shoot a haystack!" Mike said with scorn.

"Ah, you liar!" Narcisse shouted and pushed him off the kitchen porch.

Archilde set to his drawing. He had an indelible pencil and he spat on the end of it before each stroke. His fingers had lightning in their tips, just a few lines here and there and another spit and the picture was finished. There was a chicken hawk coming to rest on a barbwire fence with his wings still spread and his tail dipped. He had a mouse in his beak.

Mike looked at the picture and made a face. "Who wants to look at a hawk," he said.

"Then don't look," Archilde said.

"Now you've got to give us our hooks and come fishing. There are some big ones, you will see."

Archilde no longer wore his city clothes. He had on a pair of waist length overalls with a broad bucking belt studded with nickel spots. For shoes he wore half-length riding boots with high heels and he had leather cuffs on his arms. With his big Stetson hat he looked like any other breed. He walked with a swagger and felt in an excellent mood.

Max had his car backed out of the garage and was polishing it with a rag. It was a sky blue color with nickel trimmings that flashed in the sun.

Archilde and the two boys passed on their way to the creek. Max called out:

"So you've joined the tribe again, eh?"

"I'm going fishing," Archilde said.

"Yeh, next week you'll be wearin' your blanket."

"Well, what about it?"

"You'll make a good Indian yet," Max said with a scowl.

Archilde shrugged his shoulders and walked on. Max looked angry when he jumped in the seat and started the engine. It answered the throttle with a roar. He left it running while he went in the house to get his hat. When he saw Agnes he said:

"I'll be back tonight and I want a good supper."

Max was driving to town to hire men to cut his grain. All the work on the ranch was done by hired hands as there was no one at home to do it. And Max was in a bad temper every time he went for help.

He went into the store and looked around. Some breeds were sitting around the tobacco counter, which was near the front, but Max hardly looked at them. He went through to the back of the store and entered the office.

The storekeeper was fat and of medium height and he always appeared to be in good humor. He wore his glasses pinched on his nose and was fond of holding them in his hand and looking for specks of lint on them as he talked. He had been talking to one of his clerks, and when Max came in, he smiled and invited him to a chair.

"You are in town early today," he said.

"I want four harvest hands. Do you know of any?"

"Some of those fellows in front of the store are looking for work. Did you notice them?"

"Yes, I did."

"You don't want 'em?"

"No, I have some just like 'em!"

The storekeeper laughed loudly, but Max didn't change expression.

"I see," the storekeeper said turning serious all at once. "I think I can fix you up. Will you be in town all day?"

"Yes, if you can find the men, I'll take 'em back with me."

"Good, I'll see what I can do. Come in my office a minute, won't you?" He had a private room at one side of the office and they entered it. The storekeeper gave Max a drink and drew a chair up for him.

"I hear that Louis is up to something again."

Max didn't answer but merely stared at the storekeeper.

"Well, let's talk about this thing. There's no good staring a hole in me. If they catch your boy, it'll go pretty hard with him. He's been up to so many tricks, you know. There was a meeting last night. The banker and postmaster and that new lawyer and a few others. I was there too since they asked me. And it was arranged to put up a reward for him, one thousand dollars. Think of it! They'll scratch this country over with a hay rake until they find him."

"Well, what do you expect me to do—put up another thousand?" Max asked.

68 | D'Arcy McNickle

"No. I wanted to tell you. If you know where he is—perhaps you can get word to him to lay low. I know how you feel. He's your boy, but he's in a pretty bad scrape this time. Boys all have too much of the devil in them, I know from my own case. It's too bad that Louis wasn't a little more even tempered."

Max sat without offering a word. His hands lay palms upward in his lap and he seemed singularly listless. Whatever was going on inside his head didn't portray itself on his face.

"I understand that your youngest boy is home," the storekeeper said in an attempt to get a word from Max. "He's a pretty promising youngster, don't you think?"

"Yes, if you don't expect too much."

"I don't know. He strikes me as being a bright fellow."

"Then why isn't he working? I've got four sections of land out there. I've had to sell my stock because I couldn't handle 'em. Now I'm in town looking for help and what's he doin'? Goin' fishin' with my daughter's little boys!"

"Well, give him a little talk. Many a young fellow's been set straight by a word from the old man. I understand he's becoming quite a musician."

"What's a musician? He's a fiddler!"

"Tell you what I'm going to do, Max. I'm going to talk to him myself. As for selling your stock, that was the wisest thing you could have done. You got the best price that we've had in five years. What's more, this country isn't a stock country anymore. Next year all the open range on the Big River where you've been running your cattle will be thrown open to homestead. That means no more stock. But you, you're ahead of the game. The money's in your pocket and you've got nothing to worry about. You should spend the rest of your days in peace. You see, I'm talking as an old friend. It's too bad that your family, your children I mean, have been so wild. But in—what's his name, Archilde?—you have a good son. How about another drink? I don't keep much of this here, just a drop for a friend now and then."

Max stood up to take the drink, then walked to the door.

"Well," he said. "Find me four harvest hands. I'll be back this afternoon. As for Archilde—he is what he is. I have nothing to say to him."

The storekeeper followed him into the store, feeling that the conversation had not ended well.

People in the store greeted Max, and after he had passed, they continued to watch his square-set, belligerent figure.

It was true that the years had worn an angry furrow between Max's eyes. Everything made him angry. A slow rage had burned in him for years and he never knew relief.

He left his car by the store and walked toward the Jesuit mission. He opened a white gate in a thorn hedge and a large iron weight tied with a rope shut the gate behind him. He walked down a lane of tall poplar trees and many birds made drowsy sounds in the noon heat. On either side of the poplar trees gardens stretched and several brothers were at work in the immaculate rows of vegetables and berry bushes. The air was sweet with damp loam and vegetable growth. The buildings were old and painted rather bizarrely in yellow and red with green roofs. He walked through a cobbled yard to the front entrance and rang a bell that sounded very rusty.

Father Grepilloux was an old man, fond of a cigar and a quiet story. His room had a great window, but because of the big trees outside not much light entered. All the walls were hidden by bookshelves and the two tables that stood in the center of the room were heavily burdened. The table before which he sat had a small space cleared so that he could work. For many years now, he had been writing the history of his labors and trials in founding "his most holy Mission." Father Grepilloux had been a man of great energy. He had brought life to a little world in the wilderness.

"Ah, it is you, Leon!" he said and took off his silver spectacles. "You are a fine visitor for you always come just as I am thinking of you and wishing to see you. Are you well?"

"Yes, Father. And how are you?"

"Always the same, Leon. Always the same. But my memory is bad. This little book should have been finished long ago, but I find some days that I cannot remember the most important details. Indeed, it will only be with the kind indulgence of my friends that it will ever get finished, for they are called on to assist me more and more. Now there are some things that I want to ask you about—but later on. First I want to hear about you. I understand that your youngest boy has just returned."

"Yes, he came yesterday—or I believe it was the day before."

"I suppose he is glad to be back. The youngsters like to roam but in the end home is the best."

"It was that way with me and with my family—but with these boys, I do not know, Father. It is not easy to understand them."

"Perhaps you judge too quickly, Leon. Boys are simple at heart and you must appeal to them simply. We teach many boys here each year. Your Archilde, when he was with us, was very honest and faithful, I thought."

Max was silent for a while and then his thoughts began to resolve themselves into words and, gradually, he found himself talking.

"It is about my boys that I have come to see you. No doubt you have heard that Luis has stolen some horses and they are hunting him. For my older boys, Blasco and Pedro and Umberto, I do not care a straw. It is a long time since they have been in my house, and even before that, I had ceased to call them my sons. Luis, I thought, would make a good man. When he was young, he used to ride with me and he knew how to run stock and be useful to me. But for five years now he has been drinking and going with bad Indians. Now he is as bad as any. Archilde, as you say, has always been an honest boy, but he will be no better than the others. At home my fields are standing with ripe grain—I have not much, enough for flour and to have a little in the granary. But he goes fishing and does not even see the fields. He tells me that he makes his living as a fiddler. Indeed he had money when he came home, but I think he did not get it honestly. No one is paid money to play the fiddle."

Father Grepilloux was silent now. Many times before he had heard Leon's story of his sons and it was a mounting tragedy. There was no way to take hold of the problem and give it a solution. He nodded his gray head back and forth.

"My dear Leon, you must not give way to despair. Someday you will still be happy. I am sure of it. The ways of Our Savior are inscrutable—but they are just. Your sorrow has been great, but your joy will be as much. Is there not some way to attract Archilde's attention? Some device?"

"Only by draining his Indian blood from his system. I have tried it with the others."

"You must not say that for your own blood may be as much at fault, though I am sorry to say it."

The Hungry Generations | 71

"Maybe you're right. I have thought of that. Today the storekeeper told me that a reward had been offered for Luis, and he hinted that I should warn him if I didn't want to see him caught. I say truthfully to you, I do not care if he is caught. But the storekeeper thought, 'He is your son, your blood, even if he is an outlaw!' He is not my son! I will have nothing to do with him!" Max went on rumbling his protests for some time. Father Grepilloux was the only soul to whom he talked and the priest had grown accustomed to his blasphemies against his sons for which he afterward absolved him. Today Max was particularly bitter and resentful. He could not always find the words for which he sought, and it was with great presence of mind that he kept from swearing and disturbing the peace of his friend's study.

"They pity me and I cannot stand that. If I didn't have a little money, I would be no better than any other squaw-man. They feel sorry for me and want to talk to my sons for me. The storekeeper today said he would talk to Archilde. What am I to do, Father? I am going to be an old man soon and do I have to be a mouse and hide from everybody?"

"Leon, you make me very sad. You are a strong man and your life has been successful in material things. At heart you are good for I know. Yet, this one thing is overmastering you. Who would have thought that it would turn out this way! When I married you thirty years ago, you were looking forward to happiness and well-being. But here you sit in my old room and your spirit seems defeated. Isn't it strange?"

Max held his silence. His broad, thick shoulders hid the back of his chair and his head was bent forward. His grizzled hair caught the faint light from the high window and glowed dully. Father Grepilloux tried to lead his thoughts out farther for he knew that he had not said everything that was on his mind.

"I did not know Archilde played the violin. When did he learn?"

"I don't know."

"I have been trying to build up a choir, but I have had no good instruments to accompany it, perhaps I can get him to play for me. Do you think?"

The question didn't interest Max. "He is a fiddler," he said. "He plays for dances."

"But we will make him a musician. You shall see." The pink face of Father Grepilloux had begun to glow.

"Everybody makes it too simple," Max said with some irritation. "Everybody thinks he can take those boys and make them into men. As for myself, I wash my hands."

"You should not be resentful toward your friends."

"Excuse me. I did not mean to include you. For you are truly my friend. But what can the storekeeper do? He is too much like a woman. If I didn't have money, he wouldn't know me on the street. Don't shake your head. Did he ever speak to me until a few years ago when my herds had grown really large and I began to sell stock? Now he wants to keep his fingers on my boys in case I leave my money to them."

Father Grepilloux continued to shake his head.

"Sometimes your thoughts are black and sinful. Remember you are an old man now and you should be winning peace. It is true the storekeeper is greedy for land and money and it wouldn't be good to trust his advice to your sons. But a wise man softens his tongue, isn't it true?"

"He makes me mad."

Father Grepilloux smiled and blessed his friend with his fingers.

"You are a big bear, Leon, but you have never bitten anyone yet. I hope you will learn to love peace as I do.

"Come now, to this history! You must tell me the years of your arrival in this valley and how it seemed to you then. What were the Indians like? How long were you here before I came the first time with my little band?"

Max leaned back in his chair and let his legs stretch out before. He did not speak at once.

"Your head is very fuddled if you have forgotten what it was like! I shall never forget.

"We came over from Bannock on horseback. We had been riding a week. We were planning to strike the Clearwater and follow it to the Columbia for we had been told that the heaviest trapping was down there. But when we climbed this hill from the Jacko River, just to see what it would be like, we knelt and made a prayer to the good God. It was most beautiful. The mountains had snow halfway down and the valley was a bed of green. We never found the Columbia."

"But what year was that?" the father reminded him.

"Oh, the year? I have forgotten."

"How am I to write my history then? I must have dates."

"Write it without dates. What are dates? Say it was beautiful, with the snow on the mountains and the grass in the valley."

"That is very true but I must have dates. Now try to remember—when were you born?"

"That I don't know. It was a long time ago. I came from Spain when I was a small boy and I don't remember the town in which I was born. If I hadn't married a squaw, no doubt I should have been happy."

"You strike a sour note. Tell me now, how long were you here before I married you? I know what year that was."

This questioning continued for a long time, but on the whole the good father didn't write much history. Max had too many tracks to follow.

Chapter Four

At the dinner table the storekeeper said to his wife:
"We must have Leon here to dinner soon."

She looked up without speaking.

"He is a good man, but no one seems to realize it. I want to get ahold of that young son, Archilde. Where did they find that name? People say he plays the violin, so you must ask him to play for us."

She made no comment but continued to stare at her food.

"Perhaps in another year there will be more money in the country."

"Will we ever leave?" she asked.

"What? I thought you had gotten over that. Of course we'll leave, but we've got to get some money out of here before we do. We can't take mortgaged land with us."

"You've said that for so many years."

"Well, you watch and see! We'll get out of here all right. Leon is the man to go after. Have a good dinner when he comes. I'll ask him next week. He's got over a hundred thousand. How would a hundred thousand suit you? It'll be a shame if we don't get it. Somebody will."

*

They were cutting the grain on Max Leon's ranch. He only had a quarter of a section in grain. His hay fields were much larger, but he had only put up a small part of the hay since he no longer had stock to feed. His land stretched from the foothills at the base of the mountains far out upon the flat. Several streams flowed through the land and clumps of tall pines and cottonwoods followed the courses of the water. Hay sheds could be seen near and far, but this year they were not filled with hay. The cattle were gone.

Max put on his riding boots and followed the men with their two binders into the field. He rode a white mare with a well-shaped head. The binders were oiled and given a last tightening up, then they set to work. The white arms began to revolve and to toss the tall grain stalks onto the moving aprons. A bundle collected at the side and was tied with twine and kicked into the carriage. A second one followed and a third. The wheat was heavy and the bundles came through quickly. The second binder started into motion.

Max got off his horse and walked into the midst of the grain, checking wheat heads between his hands and blowing away the chaff to count the berries.

"Will there be twenty-five bushels?" he asked one of the men who was waiting until another swath or two had been cut, so he could begin bunching the sheaves.

"There ought to be thirty. This is a fine stand, hey Bill?"

The other man agreed that it was a fine stand. "But it won't go thirty," he said.

"Bah, wheat is a hell of a thing to raise!" Max said.

"Well, it's a mighty fine crop when you raise it right. Now this land here I'd say had been worked proper. You won't find many stands as good as this around here," the first man said.

Max walked away without any more talk. He watched the binders moving along. He got on his horse again and trotted up with the binders. Then he rode alongside for a while watching the machinery work. Just as they started the second round, the first binder stopped with a banging noise.

"Just as I thought!" Max growled. "I've never seen one of these damn machines yet that would run without breaking down! What's the matter?"

A chain was broken.

"That's all right, Max," the driver said calmly. "I've got some extra links here and it'll be fixed in two jerks."

"In a few more days that grain'll be too ripe, so you've got to keep those machines running," he said. Then he got on his horse and rode back to the house. He rode up to the kitchen door and called Agnes.

"Send your boys out to the field with a jug of water. Tell 'em to stay there until the water's drunk up and then fetch more. They've got to tend to that as long as the men are working or I'll give 'em my whip."

Agnes looked around the yard. "But they're not here," she said. "I think they're up the creek fishing. I don't know."

"Well, you'd better find them. Somebody's got to bring water to those men."

Max scowled and looked toward the creek. Then he turned his horse and started up the creek himself. He turned to look back and Agnes had already gone into the house without making any effort to find the boys.

Up in the timber everything was quiet. Max stopped and let his horse drink at the creek, and then he got off and drank lying on his belly. He followed a trail through the brush along the creek.

He rode for about an hour before he found the boys. They were lying quietly on a pile of driftwood in the center of the stream, waiting for an opportunity to put a spear into the water without driving the fish away. Archilde was with them and it was he that handled the spear. They were too engrossed in their business to notice anything else.

Max rode up closely and then shouted. The small boys were on their feet in a second and ready to run, but Max told them to stand still.

"Why don't you stay at home!" he said. "You've got to carry water to the men in the field."

"Aw, let Agnes do it. We want to fish," said Mike.

"You fish and run in the woods every day in the year. Now you must come and work like men for once. It will not hurt you."

The boys stood looking at one another. Max had not spoken to Archilde. "Come on, now. You can get behind me on my horse."

"That old horse will buck us off," Narcisse said.

"No, she doesn't buck."

"We don't want to go back," Mike said. "Archilde's got to come too, then," he added.

"Archilde can stay and be a buck Indian," Max said. "Come on, get up behind me, you two."

The Hungry Generations | 77

It was such an unusual offer that the two young fellows were quite flattered. In spite of their strong inclination to dive into the brush, they stood there debating. Then Archilde spoke.

"Yes, you two. Go on and help Max. The fish will stay in the creek. Maybe I'll come too." He did not look up, but Max gave him a sharp look. Mike and Narcisse crawled up behind their grandfather and the white mare switched her tail a few times and tried to walk sideways, but in the end she went all right.

"Make her run," Mike said and kicked her with his heels. The mare turned back her ears and started down the trail at a gallop.

"You little devils, keep your feet still, now!" Max said.

Archilde got to his feet and started slowly after them. His hands were tucked into his belt and he carried his spear under his arm.

That afternoon one of the binders broke down again and Max had to drive to town for repairs. He was in a bad temper.

"Pshaw, that's all right," the storekeeper said. "You always have a few stops when you first start your harvesting. From now on everything will run smooth, you'll see. Have you got enough oil? How's the twine?"

"They must make this farm machinery out of paper. When you're raising cattle, all you need is a horse and there's nothing to break."

"By the way," the storekeeper said suddenly. "Why don't you come down and have dinner with us some night as soon as your grain is cut? Bring Archilde with you if you wish."

"Sure, I'll come and eat with you, but I'll be damned if I'll bring him!"

"Just as you wish. But do that, won't you?" the storekeeper had a big smile.

"Yeh. Now, I've got to get back and start those men working again. As soon as I turn around, they stop and fill their pipes."

The storekeeper walked out with him to his car. "That's certainly a beautiful machine you've got there. The more I see it the better I like it. I've been thinking of getting one like it myself."

Max started the engine with a roar. "It's a nice car all right. See you later."

The second binder was making its monotonous round of the field. Sometimes, as it started up a slight rise in the ground, the whirring sound of its sickle could be heard plainly and then, as it dipped down, the sound faded away. Max stopped his car at the roadside and walked across the field with his repair parts. He glanced shrewdly at the width of the cut land and estimated how long the second binder had been idle.

"Say, you're sure lucky the store had the spare part on hand. We was layin' five to one they'd have to tellygraph for it."

The afternoon was slipping away and the heat was no longer intense. Over against the timber the shadows lay long and cool. The binder was repaired and started off once more.

The men who were bunching the sheaves had made the circle of the field and now they were approaching Max as he stood watching the flying arms of the reaper. He turned toward the men and saw that Archilde was working with them. A strange look appeared on his face.

He walked over and watched Archilde pick up the bundles under his arms and place them on end leaning against each other for support. When he had completed a bunch, Max said:

"Why didn't you tell me you would help? Now I have an extra man."

"You didn't ask me."

"You've got eyes. You saw this field ready to be cut."

"I didn't think of it, I guess."

"Where'd you learn to shock wheat?" was the next question.

"I just watched 'em doing it."

"Well, I'll let the other man go then. Where's those two kids? Have they been carrying water?"

"Yeh, they went for a fresh jug."

Archilde went on working and the conversation stopped. Max went over to his car where he could watch the men working. He sat there for some time and, finally, drove to the house.

"Have you got a good supper?" he asked Agnes. "Those men are good workers and you must feed them well." He went into the kitchen and looked into her pots. "You must keep it clean around here," he said.

Agnes walked about noiselessly on her moccasined feet and paid no attention to Max. Her little girl sat in the doorway nursing a stick of wood wrapped in an old shawl.

Max walked down to the creek. There was a fall of three or four feet over a large boulder and Max had often thought of building a dam and putting in a waterwheel for a small mill. The plan recurred to him and he surveyed the spot with considerable attention. The place seemed a very good one. A considerable volume of water flowed in the stream throughout most of the year. Every farmer in the countryside bought flour from the store, though many of them had facilities for doing their own grinding. With his own mill he could grind flour and feed for himself and a few neighbors for considerably less than the storekeeper, who had it shipped in by railroad from a town a hundred miles away. Slothfulness was the great disease of every farmer in the country. They were all in debt to the storekeeper and made no effort to get out of debt.

Heretofore Max had been raising cattle and hadn't bothered much with economics. Things had always been different in the older days at any rate. Living had been cheap, wages were low, and one's needs were simple. A change was coming over the world now and new management was necessary. Perhaps Max had a mental picture of a strong young man going about and changing things according to the new order. New ideas and fresh strength were necessary. It was too bad that thousands of acres lay idle.

When Max returned to the house, the men were coming in from the field.

They had separated the four horses from each binder and each man rode a horse. Even Narcisse and Mike had a horse apiece. The tug chains jingled softly and someone was whistling a tune.

The sun had set and brilliant colors began to form in the sky.

Chapter Five

The threshing machine was a long time getting to Max Leon's ranch. It rained steadily throughout one week and there were the usual breakdowns and delays. The wheat shocks in the field were no longer the brilliant golden color they had been when first bunched. They had been bleached out and now they looked dirty and gray. Max feared that the wheat heads would be beaten out by the rains and wind, as indeed had happened somewhat. But the thresher, drawn by its belching steam engine, finally squared off in the middle of the field and the last stage of the harvesting began.

The crew of twelve or fifteen men stayed at the ranch two nights and they were quartered in the barn, granary, and bunkhouse.

Max had a feeling of great relief when everything was over. The unusual problems and worries of this new kind of farming had tired him. He sat in the shade of his wide porch and enjoyed his nap and eggnog with greater relish than he had in some time.

The season had changed considerably with the passing weeks. The sun was always seen through a mist. There were many forest fires lingering in the surrounding mountains and some days when the wind was right, the world seemed to be wandering all at sea in a warm fog. The nights sparkled with frost and mist rose from the earth until the middle of the forenoon. Sounds hung in the air with a reluctance to die. Sometimes men talking in a distant field sounded near at hand. The world had become enchanted.

The tamarack forests had turned and sometimes when the sky cleared and the sun shone brilliantly against a mountainside the whole thing seemed to be bursting into flame.

Max had two men plowing and at many other ranches the brown stubble was being broken up once more into black loam. October was halfway along and the frosts would soon seal up the earth's pores. Archilde had helped straight through the harvesting and Max had told him not to do any plowing, so Archilde was getting ready for a hunting trip into the mountains.

Max had been sitting on the porch since his midday meal. He had aches in his bones and ascribed them to the approaching frosts. As a matter of fact, he was feeling his age. His face showed it. The broad, heavy features looked thinner and the lines had deepened. His shoulders were more hunched than they had been the year before. He mumbled words to himself and watched the men in the field through a pair of binoculars.

A dust cloud appeared at the end of the lane where the road dipped downward to cross a dried creek bed. Presently, an automobile appeared through the dust and Max swung his binoculars to examine it. It was the storekeeper.

Ever genial and smiling broadly, the storekeeper left his car at the front gate and walked up the path to the house. His broad, freckled face gave an impression of honesty and good fellowship. There were people who distrusted that appearance, but there it was.

"Well, Max, how did the crop turn out?" he called out as he opened the screen door of the porch.

"Very good, they tell me. Have a chair."

"I've driven all over the valley, been going since early this morning. Everybody's having a good year. They're all happy. How much did your wheat average?"

"Why, I guess it was over thirty bushels."

"No, you don't say! That's the best I've heard. You must be a fine farmer."

"It's the land. Cattle have run on all this land for the last twenty-five years; it ought to be good, eh? This is my second year as a wheat farmer; I know a little bit but not much."

82 | D'Arcy McNickle

"I've been watching for you to come to town the last few days."

"I've been home taking a rest. I'm not going anywhere for another week."

"I see. When are you going to haul your grain? I've got lots of room in my elevator, so I can take care of it any time you start hauling."

"You will have more room four or five months from now—and the price will be much better," Max said with a smile.

"No. Don't be too sure, now. It is over a dollar, the best price we've had in years. It'll begin to go down from now on."

"I will take the chance," Max said still smiling. "I think it will go up again. If I am not mistaken, I think you will hold your elevator full too. So you can come and ask for my grain when you get ready to sell, but not now."

"All right, old fox! That's a bargain! But here's what I came out to see you about. I told you when you had dinner with me last month that I'd have a proposition for you. Do you remember?"

"Yes. I guess you did say that."

"Well, it wasn't hot air, though maybe you thought so. I'll tell you what it is; we want to make you a director in our bank. You're our largest depositor at the present time and you're getting just the usual 3 percent. But as a director we can earn you a minimum of 7 percent for the amount you invest."

"You mean, I'll buy stock in the bank?"

"Yes. At the present time there are four of us in the bank. We held a meeting last week and it was the agreement that I should speak to you and see how you felt about it—if you are willing to join, then we'll vote in the usual way. I think we'll be able to let you have about 20 percent of the stock. If you want more than that, I suppose you can get it. I'll tell you, privately of course, the bank has been making big profits ever since we chartered it."

"That's very fine of you," Max looked intensely satisfied. "Look we haven't had anything to drink and you must be quite dry after riding all day. Agnes! You must excuse me, I am getting very forgetful." Agnes appeared and he ordered her to bring glasses and whiskey.

"I want to tell you, Leon, that this country owes a great deal to you. You were, I believe, the first white man in here and you are by far the most successful. It is my opinion that the bank should never have been organized without you but, of course, I wasn't in on organizing it. What we want is new heads and you're the very man for it. That's exactly what I told them the other night."

"Well, that was putting it a bit strong. I know a thing or two about cattle but banking—that's not in my line."

"I guess you know the difference between a nickel and a [?]. The very man we want is one who knows cattle and farming. The book-keeper does the banking."

"Well, now, come down to the creek and I'll show you a proposition I've had in mind," Max said after the storekeeper had drunk a toast to the future bank director.

"I'll show you something down here that ought to set you thinking. I pay too damn much for flour and you do too. Besides your flour's no good or else my daughter's a bad cook—which is no lie maybe. But take a look down here and tell me what you think."

Max took him down to the creek and showed him the proposed mill site and explained at length how he proposed to build it. At first the storekeeper appeared skeptical, but presently, he became as inspired with the idea as though it had been his own. He took out a pencil and piece of paper and began to figure costs and estimate the amount of materials needed.

"You're a true genius, Leon. Why haven't you done this before?"

"Well, the Jesuits have a small mill you know and I always expected that they would enlarge it, but they haven't and I asked Father Grepilloux not long ago if they ever would. He said they wouldn't and encouraged me to go ahead. It's too bad that the people have to pay the freight on their own wheat to Missoula and back again. I think we should do something."

The storekeeper stayed to supper after some persuasion for he had promised his wife that he would return.

"She will think I have gone off with a woman," he said in his genial way.

"So much the better."

No one but Max and an occasional friend ever ate in the dining room. It was a large room with a tall sideboard filled with many odd-shaped glasses. On the walls were hung two buffalo bull heads, an elk head, and a long-horned steer head. The floor was covered with a thick carpet and in one corner there was a tall heating stove with shining nickel parts. Agnes kept things fairly clean, although Max was always grumbling on that score.

All through the meal they talked alternately of the bank and the proposed mill.

"But I am getting old, Moser," Leon said in sudden remembrance. "It may be that I will not see these changes come about. Do you know that I am over sixty?"

"Pshaw! What a way to talk! You look younger than me—and what am I?—just past forty. You're good for twenty years, Leon."

"Did I tell you that Archilde helped me harvest? He worked every day."

"Didn't I tell you! You're going to have a fine boy there. Where is he tonight?"

"He went to town this afternoon to buy a horse. He wants to take a hunting trip. I am hungry for a venison steak myself. But I don't think his mind is here, Moser. I shouldn't have let him wander around so much. When a boy gets a taste of the world, it's hard telling where he'll land."

"You worry too much. Tell you what you do, Leon. When he gets back from his hunting trip, tell him about this mill proposition. Get him interested, see. Then tell him to go ahead and build it. Let it be his own job. Let him think it's his own plan and everything. You'll get him to stay, all right."

Max brightened. "That is a fine idea! That's capital!" He thumped the table with his fist and poured out a drink of brandy to finish the meal on.

The storekeeper drove away with a feeling of personal well-being. The night was soft and cool and his motor purred easily. The warm fumes of brandy went through his head and made his thoughts slow.

When he got home, his wife was sitting in the dark front room crying.

"My God! You have been gone all day and not a word from you!" she sobbed.

He fumbled for the light switch and tried to cheer her up.

The Hungry Generations | 85

"What's the matter, Sara? You don't want to get worried when I don't get back."

"Don't turn on the light! Your dinner's on the table. It's all cold."

"That's all right. I just had a light lunch with Max Leon. I've been there most of the afternoon. What's the matter?" He found her chair in the dark.

She hid her face in her hands and hunched her shoulders together as if he couldn't touch her there.

"I want to leave this filthy town at once! I won't stay any longer! You've been promising for five years to go away, but I know you don't mean it. Maybe you enjoy associating with Indians all day long—but, I tell you, I *don't*. We simply have got to leave!"

"All our money's invested. We can't leave at once."

"You certainly have enough money to buy me a railroad ticket. I tell you I want to go!"

The storekeeper sat down and stared through the darkness to his wife's blurred form. He didn't speak for a moment. Her demand was childish and only a word was necessary to silence her and show her how unreasonable she was. But he couldn't find the word. He made several sounds in his throat as if a word had started out, but it remained unspoken.

"That's no way to talk. You don't give me a chance." Her sobs broke out anew.

"It isn't enough to be forced to live in this desolate place, but you must spend your whole day away without even telling me where you are or what you are doing. When you come home to lunch, you hardly speak. When you're here at night, you sit and read or do anything but notice that I'm alive. Then you say I don't give you a chance. I wish you'd only give me a chance!"

Moser took a deep breath and began to talk with great patience and restraint.

"But you see, Sara, everything is difficult and complicated and we can't get exactly what we want when we want it. Now there's only one man in this valley can help us and that's Max Leon. He's the only man's got money enough to buy our interests, but he's got to be handled carefully. I can't just go to him all at once and ask him to buy me out—he'd say no, thank you. But I'm getting around him just the same. I've arranged to make him a part owner of the bank; he doesn't know it yet, but I'm selling him part of my stock. That'll give us about ten or twelve thousand dollars. But, if I can't sell him my store, then all this is wasted effort. I've got to sell him the store and that's what I'm leading up to. But it can't be done all at once. Surely you must see that!

"Furthermore, we wouldn't have found ourselves in such a tight place if things had gone right. But how was I to know that everybody was going to get as poor as they are at present? I own lots of mortgages and, as soon's things pick up, they'll be worth money. You've got to consider all these things."

"Well, I can't stand it, that's all! If we're not out of here by next spring, I'll go mad."

There was another silence. The clock ticked with measured, deliberate strokes in the dark room. The room seemed to be completely empty—nothing seemed to have a connection. His wife had stopped crying but shudders ran through her.

"Aw, hell! You get my goat!" Moser said. "I don't know how to please you. I've told you I'm doing my best and explained why it can't be different. The way I look at it is this: we're here on the earth to make the best of what we got. If we don't like the way things are why, I guess they'll be different later on. But when that comes around, we'll be wanting something else. So why not be satisfied with what you got! This talk about going mad is all humbug. Take things as they come is the way I look at it, and it's never hurt me any."

"That's because you don't know," she stopped to blow her nose. "You don't know that there are other places in the world besides this and other people more like—ourselves. Or else you've forgotten. I don't mind putting up with things if I have my friends—and the things I'm used to. There's something more to life than just living for the sake of being alive."

Gradually she grew calmer and the tension between them slackened. Moser talked for a long time and before long he was feeling good himself. They left the room without turning on the light and went to bed.

Outside a strong wind had risen and began to sweep the loose dirt and dust from the roads and fields. It was baring the earth's surface to the chilling winds that were to follow. There was no moon and the sky was pitch black; the only light that could be seen at all came from an occasional star that shone through the rapidly moving clouds.

One by one the lights over the countryside blinked out as farmers went to bed. The town was too small and poor to support streetlamps and even it became totally dark in time, the pool halls and restaurants holding out until the last.

So the town finally gave over to the night and became one with it. The wind whipped back and forth through the empty streets and over the prairie and shadows drifted in quiet succession across the land. The mountains stood by, ponderous and dark.

Chapter Six

Max went to town in the forenoon to have a talk with Father Grepilloux. It would be pleasant news for his friend to hear that he was a bank director now.

In the yard before the church and surrounding the mission buildings the tall poplar trees were quickly becoming bare of their brittle leaves. Every flurry of wind sent a handful streaming through the air. School had started again and many voices were heard in the playground behind the high board fence, but in the buildings themselves the quiet was undisturbed.

The door was opened by Brother Menenger who was telling his beads and looking unusually solemn.

"Whom do you wish to see?" he asked. It was unusual to ask Max what he wished.

"Father Grepilloux if he is around."

"The holy father is very ill. He must not be disturbed."

"Sick, you say? Then tell him I am here. Since when has he been sick?"

"Then you weren't at Mass Sunday? Father Cyrile announced it from the pulpit and asked that prayers be said. Since then he has turned worse. You should have been at Mass."

"Ask Father Grepilloux if he will see me."

The good brother who was quite stupid took to solemn airs with alacrity. He turned and walked down the hall as if he were the emissary

88 |

of death himself. His throaty cough and rustling beads echoed with a dull sound.

On the wall of the little waiting room there was a large painting of Grepilloux meeting the Indians when he first came to the valley. There wasn't much light in the room and the artist, who had once been a brother at the mission, had performed a subtle trick of making the priest stand out of the dim background in radiance. Max stood watching the face.

"The holy father will see you," the brother said and went on with his beads.

The bedroom was small and stuffy. The shades had been drawn against the light and several large candles burned near the bed. In the chapel at the end of the hall a group of nuns were praying.

"My good friend, you will die soon at this rate!" Max said.

The priest smiled feebly and motioned Leon to a chair at his head. The attendants had gone into the hall.

"No," he said. "Prayers do not frighten me. They are soothing. It was my wish that they should leave the door open."

"But you have no air in here—and no light. These candles make the air thick."

"You spend your life out-of-doors. I am used to it. That's the difference. I am quite happy. And how are you?"

"Happy? When you are sick?"

"Yes. I have no pain and soon I will be called away. Then I shall pray for happiness to come to you too."

Leon suddenly lost his tongue. He sat and stared at his friend with wondering eyes. He was aware that their beliefs were far apart. He had never believed simply and implicitly that dying was going away where you could still pray for your friends as this man did.

"Is death as easy as that, then?" he asked and his ears could scarcely believe that he had asked such a thing.

"Yes, it is easy."

"But you will live many years yet, you see. How's the history? You haven't even finished that yet."

"I was never meant to be a historian. Much better that I have been a simple priest."

"We'd have had no church or no school otherwise! That is true. But you will be well again. Now look at me, am I a young man? No, but I have just been made a director in the bank. So you mustn't forget that history."

"You are a director in the bank now? That is fine. It does not surprise me for you are very rich. You mustn't forget the church. Our school needs many things. My part in those things has been of little importance. I have merely been a witness at the building of the temple of God that is in every man. Even the Indians knew what I meant when I explained it to them first. So it was very simple. I found my materials inexhaustible. But I cannot write a history of it. I confuse the vision and the act; it must be left to abler hands. How is your son Archilde?"

"I have news about him. He has been helping me through the harvest. He worked every day. Now he has gone on a hunting trip."

The priest brightened. "That is very good news. I am quite happy."

"When he comes back, I have a plan to get him started in his own way. Moser, the storekeeper, got the idea."

"You are with Moser a lot, aren't you?"

"He comes to see me or else calls me into his store."

"He was never that way before, Leon. When you have money you will have many advisers. You should be careful. Moser has dealt badly with many of my people."

Max nodded in agreement. "At heart he is a good man. We shouldn't blame him if he tries to get as much as he can. We all do it."

"Not rightfully, Leon. Better to have much less and help others to get more when they have little. But you are a worldling and will not listen to me, eh?" he said with a bright smile.

"I always listen and you are right. But I haven't even been able to give much to my sons for they will not use it. They throw everything away. So how am I to do it? Isn't it better that Moser should get money and power when he knows what it is worth and can use it than my son Luis, say, who would only drink it and waste it?"

The priest meditated for a moment. "Neither should have it, but of the two Moser has less claim. Now I will say why: because Moser understands money and knows how it is regarded in the world, yet he will deliberately make his gains at the expense even of people much weaker and more in need. He will take what does not belong to him except by right of his greater cunning. Your son Louis, now, will bring the greatest unhappiness on himself—and his father it is true. But he is a child who commits sin unknowingly."

"Maybe you are right but I shall never give Luis a cent. Sometimes I have had wild dreams of giving my money to those worthless sons to let them have a better chance to kill themselves. They would all be dead from drinking in a short time. But it is better to forget them.

"Well now it is getting late, so I'd better leave. You must get better soon and finish the history. If you don't write it, who will?"

"There will be able hands, Leon. We are only the first men. Many more will come after us and many of them will be better."

"You are the first man and you will always be. Don't forget it. Now I'll go and see my two grandsons. I hear they are blockheads."

"Come again soon." Father Grepilloux made the sign of the cross in blessing. "They cannot make the little one, Mike, cut off his hair. But they are bright boys. We will make fine men of them, you see."

Out in the playground there was bedlam. Max stood by the high entrance gate and looked for Mike and Narcisse. When he found them, their first words were:

"Are you gonna take us home?"

"What's the matter? You've only been here two or three weeks."

"The food gives me a bellyache," Mike said. "Why doesn't Archilde come to see us?"

"Archilde is working hard every day."

"No, sir. I'll bet he's gone hunting."

"What do you learn in school? You, Mike, why don't you let them cut your hair?"

"Everybody wants to cut my hair. Isn't it all right?" Strangely enough he seemed ready to cry. He turned his back. "I don't want to stay here. I'm gonna run away."

"Has Archilde gone hunting?" Narcisse asked.

"No, I guess not. He's just taking a trip in the mountains for a couple days."

"That's what I want to do!" Mike said. "This school's no good. Every day I get a bellyache."

"Listen here," Max said sternly. "When you get through school, you'll be a white man. Cut out this talk about bellyaches and running away and let them cut your hair or I'll do something worse than that."

"It's true that he gets sick every day," Narcisse said. "I think he swallows soap when he washes his face."

"No, sir, I don't swallow soap! It's because it smells rotten. Just the smell makes me sick."

"Well, you boys behave yourselves and I will tell Archilde to come see you next week. Here's a quarter apiece for you to buy candy or whatever you like." He put his hand on their shoulders for a moment and he could feel them writhe. They looked happier with money in their hands and the promise of a visit from Archilde.

When Max was going to the gate, he met the prefect.

"Mike tells me he gets sick. Is there anything to it or is he ornery?" The prefect was a young Irishman with a severe stare and heavy jaws.

"Many of the boys have minor complaints when they arrive each year. It is the change in food and water."

"That's what I thought." Max turned and surveyed the yard full of lusty youngsters and shook his head.

"How do you get 'em to do what you want? Those two grandsons of mine will do nothing without a bribe. It is the wrong way to handle 'em, I know, but what can you do!"

The prefect smiled. "It takes patience but in the end it is easy enough. We will get some fine boys out of that group."

Max studied the prefect for a moment. He looked like an animal trainer.

"You are too hopeful. Father Grepilloux tells me the same thing—but you can't fool me. Maybe you can teach them a few tricks now, but as soon as they leave they forget."

Max was sure of what he said and when he walked away he felt depressed. His boys had all attended the Jesuit school and they had turned into scoundrels. Every time his mind confronted an Indian boy he felt baffled. He could not see into the enigma. They were not animals for they could think—but their ideas were always of no value; their actions borne of their thinking were always contrary and childish.

He could not think of that yard full of energetic youngsters without a shudder. In his mind's eye he saw them as they would be in ten or fifteen years. He saw the misery they would bring to themselves and such of their relatives as had any sense. They would all be a drain upon the community, for there would be but few who would earn their livings honestly. The community was at their mercy; it could never develop under such a handicap. Yet, it was a rich and beautiful valley in which they lived.

He was responsible for some part of the condition. In the enthusiasm of conquest he had turned squaw-man and now he could walk along the road and reflect on its consequences. Never had he seen a white man who was happy with his Indian wife and family. Many didn't care and weren't much better themselves, but mostly they kept out of sight and avoided their fellow men; they took to wearing moccasins and shuffling along with averted faces like any full-blood; when they were addressed, they kept their eyes on the ground and escaped as soon as possible.

Not that Max had ever done anything of the sort. His gray eyes were as proud and challenging as any and he said bluntly what he meant. But it had required effort. Any man resents gaining with effort what other men arrive at naturally. It was something to be a bank director at last.

When he got back to his car, which was standing beside the store, he saw that Pariseau was standing near, evidently waiting for him. He waved his hand in greeting but made no other effort to meet the man. He got into his car and started the engine, then he saw that Pariseau had followed and was standing near. He let his engine slow down.

"Hello," Max said. "Is your threshing finished?"

"Yeh, I had a good year. They say you got over thirty bushels."

"That's what they tell me."

"I say," Pariseau began with some embarrassment. "My horses showed up a week or two after I saw you and they was all right. I don't know where the hell they came from, but I found them in my lane. You haven't seen Louis, I guess?"

"If I had seen Luis, you know where he would be now."

"I dunno. Maybe we was wrong about him. If that's the case, I want to tell you I'm darn sorry for talking about him."

"Forget it. Keep an eye on your horses after this."

Max drove away. He had no inclination to discuss his sons with his neighbors.

94 | D'Arcy McNickle

After supper that night he went into the kitchen to talk with Agnes. He had a mild affection for her, though he rarely stopped to give her as much as a word. She kept his house in order, not too carefully, and never asked for anything. Outside of her marriage she had never done anything that was either clever or stupid. Max had hated her for marrying a full-blood, but after her husband got killed, he ceased to speak harshly to her. Now he began to appreciate her stolid loyalty and his attitude gradually softened.

"I saw Mike and Narcisse today. They look fine," he told her. She looked up and flushed slightly.

"Are they lonesome?" she asked in a low voice. She was setting yeast for a batch of bread.

"Yes, boys are always lonesome when they first go away. But they have lots of friends and they'll get along all right. Mike won't let them cut his hair."

"I guess Mike is pretty tough."

"Well, he isn't afraid to say what he wants. He will make a good boy if he will learn a few things now. He's not afraid of people like most Indian boys. You must go and see them soon and tell them to listen to the teachers. Tell me when you want to go and I'll drive you in my car."

"I'd rather go in the buggy," she said without raising her head.

"Sure, go in the buggy then. But tell them to stay in school. Bring something for them to eat or a jackknife maybe. I don't want them to take a notion to run away, so we'll have to keep them happy. Archilde must go to see them too. Did he leave yesterday?"

"Yes, he and the old lady went last night."

"What, she went too?"

"Yes."

"She's too old to go in the mountains. Didn't you tell her?"

"No."

"When will they come back?"

"When they get some deer, I guess."

"Listen. Have you heard Archilde talk? Will he stay here this time or will he go away soon? What does he say?"

"He is very quiet. He doesn't talk."

"But he must say something! Do you think he is happy here?"

The Hungry Generations | 95

"He doesn't want to be Indian. So I don't think he likes it here."

"Do you think he would like to run my ranch?"

"I think he will go away again. He is not like other boys."

"Maybe so. Did you know he played the fiddle before he went away?"

"He plays for dances many times. When he was a small boy he could play at dances."

"I've never heard that before. Has he got a fiddle with him?"

"No."

"Well, don't tell him I said so, but let him know that this ranch is his if he wants to run it. I'll give him a good start. Don't say that we talked this way, see? Let him think you figured it out for yourself. And now keep your children happy at school. They must grow up and be good people."

He walked out into the darkness. A wind was tossing the tall pines in great sweeps back and forth across the sky. He walked through the barnyard from one building to another. His horse barn was large and had a great mow overhead, but now it gave shelter to only two or three horses. He went to the cowshed, which was never used. He had tried to keep a few milk cows on several occasions but no one would milk them, so now he had none at all. He bought butter and condensed milk at the store. He went to the wagon shed and looked at his binders, mowing machines, plows, seeders, wagons, and cultivators one by one. Nothing was used. He went to the pig shed and his two sows grunted and moved in their sleep. He had shelter and troughs for a couple dozen pigs if someone would take an interest and keep them fed. He had tried many ways of improving his farm but nothing lasted. He himself could do none of the work as he didn't have a hand for it. Few could equal him at handling cattle, but outside of the saddle he was no good.

He went from place to place in the yard making plans. He saw how many things a young man could do in the way of improvements and developments. Success had come to him as a cattle rancher; now that the new day was coming and new methods becoming necessary he foresaw the success that should come again in the new era. Before his eyes he saw a great house with tall poplar trees in full leaf. Back from the house stood two broad barns painted white; in one, cattle stood at the stanchions feeding while they were being milked; he had heard that milking machines were being used now and that was what he would have. In the other barn big, round, muscled horses stood in their mangers and whinnied for their oats after a day in the field. Over at one side were chicken houses; a line of hog houses stood facing each other like a street in a town. In the fields alfalfa and grain stood heavy and pleasant in smell. And, yes, down beside the creek stood the tall flour mill with a farmer waiting outside to get a load of flour and feed in exchange for the wheat he had just handed in. All this passed before his eyes. Back of it all he saw Archilde walking around easily and giving instructions about one thing and another.

The new day was coming and Max looked ahead with a pleasant smile.

Chapter Seven

Game was scarce that fall. Archilde and his mother rode for two days into the hills without finding any signs. He rode ahead with a pack strapped behind his saddle; his mother followed a hundred yards behind. She was not too old to ride a horse by any means. Her mare walked along with head close to the ground and never once slipped or stumbled on the steep trails. Twice they had forded deep streams and the old lady threw her legs up on the horse's back without any effort. All day long she rode with her eyes on the swaying back of her son.

They passed from sun to shade. Sometimes they were in a dark canyon and then again they followed a high ridge or hogback. Now and again they skirted a blue lake, and frequently, they came to banks of crusted snow that they carefully avoided. On the third day they pitched their short teepee in the middle of the afternoon. If they rode for another day, they would be across the mountains and out of the game country. Archilde wanted to look around on foot.

"The flies have driven them way back in the woods," he said.

His mother nodded her head. He took his rifle and went off leaving her to make camp.

They had stopped at the edge of a park or open place in the midst of high mountains. A swift stream flowed nearby and there was an abundance of rich feed for the horses. Giant yellow pines skirted the park and high above them several rocky peaks loomed. The sky was clear, but there wasn't much warmth in the sun's rays. Snow had already fallen on the heights.

The old lady went to the creek to catch some fish for their evening meal.

Archilde found many deer tracks. About a mile above the camp there was a slough and the deer came there in the early morning, he thought. The place was cut through in every direction with their trails. During the day they went farther back into the timber. He would go up before dawn.

"They will be there tonight," his mother said.

"No, I think not. They come at dawn and stay all morning while it is cool. In the afternoon the sun hits it sharp and drives them out. You will see." They made a meal out of fish.

Just before dark came the horses threw up their heads and gazed down through the timber. The old lady's mare whinnied and another horse answered. Archilde and his mother sat stolidly with their eyes watching the trail where it disappeared beyond the creek. A rider was approaching. It was Louis.

"I saw you coming up this way yesterday," he told them.

"Is that so?" Archilde said. "You didn't say anything."

Louis didn't answer but proceeded to pull the saddle and bridle off his horse and picket him on his lariat.

"What you got to eat?" he asked coming to the fire. The old lady grumbled and set about cooking a large fish that she had been saving for breakfast.

"When his belly is empty he comes!" she said.

"What have you been doing?" Archilde asked.

"Taking it easy."

"Still got some horses?"

Louis cursed. "They got away. I couldn't hold 'em alone. I told you to help me and now we'd have some money."

"Eat your fish and stop this talk about horses."

"Louis doesn't want to get hung alone. He likes company," Archilde laughed.

"Shut your mouth!"

"Be quiet! In the morning you will go with Archilde and help him get a deer. He has found where they feed in the morning."

"O-ho! I will, eh? I like to sleep in the morning."

"I will go alone," Archilde said. "Louis is no hunter. His feet get tangled in the brush."

Louis glared threateningly, but Archilde only laughed. He did not look like an Indian when he laughed; his teeth gleamed and his eyes showed merriment.

Archilde and his mother slept in the teepee, but Louis refused to sleep with them though they offered to make a bed. He rolled up in a blanket by the fire.

The sky was full of stars and the grass blades were tipped with bright frost. Archilde lay by the half-closed opening and he could hear the horses breathing and moaning in their sleep; they had lain down in a group close together. Owls were calling to each other, some at a great distance. Everything was familiar and friendly. The house in which he had been born and raised was no more his home than a mountain night. He had lain down in the company of friends. Sleep came upon him and found him smiling pleasantly.

In the morning he was up before the first light of dawn had appeared. The frost was heavy on the grass and a thin sheet of ice had formed along the edges of the stream. He dashed the chill water on his face and felt his cheeks burn; then he ate a piece of baking powder bread and started up the creek with his rifle tucked under his arm. He left Louis sleeping.

The light was just breaking over the mountaintops as he selected a hiding place and lay down to wait for the deer to approach. A damp fern slapped his face and made him shiver. From his position he could see the main watering hole in full view and the trail that led down to it. He was wearing a sheepskin coat and the soft wool around his neck was pleasant.

The trees stood out against the gray sky on the high ridge before him. They looked as though they were marching up and down the rising and falling skyline. A flicker of sunlight picked out a high brown rock and like an electric signal everything seemed to come to life. Birds moved and rustled their feathers, then began to emit sounds from their throats. A full song broke forth. At the same moment the first squirrel started to chatter in a pine tree.

Just then a tall buck appeared at the head of the trail and with erect head surveyed the scene before him. His nose was in the air with the nostrils dilated. Several other heads appeared just behind and waited for his signal to advance.

Archilde had his rifle trained dead to the buck's breast. Peering through the sights, he could see a ball of white fur. But his finger hesitated on the trigger. He lifted his head from the sighting and watched the buck with deep satisfaction. He had never beheld such pride and confidence. He decided to wait and shoot a younger buck.

One by one the deer filed down the steep trail and stood knee-deep in the water. When they lifted their heads from drinking, a stream of water dripped from their black muzzles.

Archilde aimed his rifle first at one and then another, but they kept moving just enough to make a dead shot improbable. The one he wanted never came into full view. He didn't want to shoot any of them. Already he could hear the shattering explosion of his rifle in the perfect quiet of the dawn and he hesitated.

He became aware of how intensely excited he was when he found perspiration on his forehead. He was breathing quickly and his chest felt hot. Once more he brought his gun to his shoulder and deliberately took aim, but his hands were quivering. He couldn't hold the gun steady. He had never experienced such a thing before and he couldn't understand it. He closed his eyes and pulled the trigger. When he looked up again not a deer was in sight and he could still hear the shot echoing against the mountainside. The water was muddy and the bank of the creek was wet where the deer had splashed ashore.

Never had such a thing happened to him and as he started back to camp he felt silly. He had only gone part of the way when he met his mother. She had a short knife in her hand and was coming to skin the deer.

"Did you pick a fat one?" she asked.

"I didn't get one," he said and couldn't think of anything else to say. He walked past and continued toward camp.

He took a long time to drink his cup of coffee. The old lady gave him some bread with bacon grease smeared on it.

"The fish aren't biting yet," she said.

He laid back with his head on his saddle and watched a few thin clouds drifting through the pale sky. The sun had completely risen.

"Something scared them just as they came down to the water," he said absently. "I was waiting for them to get close, but they jumped. When I shot, there was nothing but air."

"A young man always waits for a better shot and he hits nothing," the old lady remarked. "An old man makes the best of it and gets his meat."

"When the smoke clears away the old women are always jabbering," Archilde said and got to his feet.

"Where's Louis?" he asked.

"I don't know. He took his gun and went off," she waved her hand in a general direction. "He can skin his own game."

At that moment a rifle cracked and the sound seemed to fly though the air above their heads.

"I guess he's shooting squirrels," Archilde said and poured another cup of coffee. He drank it standing up and with his eyes scanning the mountainside. The tamaracks were shedding heavily and where they stood the mountain had turned to a light purple. Clouds were coming up quickly and already the sky was growing overcast. The early breeze turned sharper and Archilde inclined his head and took in a deep breath.

"I can smell snow," he said.

The old lady grunted. "Have you been asleep? It was in the wind last night. By dark it will be here."

He led the horses to the creek for water and then drove the stakes down in fresh grass. The horses weren't shod and he foresaw a difficult trip home on a slippery trail. When he came back to the camp, he unrolled his fish line and tied it to a fresh willow pole he had just cut.

"I will get some fish before it clouds up," he said.

Louis came out of the brush at that moment with a small deer across his shoulder.

"Here, old lady, get busy before the hide is cold. Where is your deer, you windbag?"

Archilde grinned. "Why didn't you pick a newborn calf? Was that the smallest one you could find? That won't make a mouthful for a man like you. As for its hide, you will never stretch it to make new soles for your moccasins even."

"You lie! That is a yearling doe. I picked it because it would be tender. Show me yours now. I suppose you shot a fifteen-year-old buck like a goddamned white man!"

"What do you care what he shot," the old lady grumbled. "You pick a quarrel with everybody. Come and help me with the skinning before the hide sets."

"Let the young squaw help you. I want some breakfast."

"Help yourself," Archilde said. "I drank the coffee and ate the bread. But here's water for more coffee and fish in the creek too. Here, old lady, take a leg. We'll rip it off. If you want to see my deer, it's up the creek by those willows, hanging until it cools." He pointed to a group of willows about half a mile away. Louis turned and was on the point of starting off to see for himself when a stranger suddenly appeared before them.

He had approached, on horseback, entirely unobserved from the down trail. He wore a pair of waist overalls and a flannel shirt. His feet were enclosed in hobnailed boots and a broad hat sat on his head. On his vest, which hung loosely and unbuttoned, he wore a game warden's badge. He had a lean face with sharp, shrewd eyes. He sat looking over the camp for some time before he spoke.

"I thought I heard some shootin' and I was wonderin' who was up this way. I see you got something there."

Archilde rose to his feet. "Yeh, we just shot a small deer," he said.

"I shot it," Louis interrupted.

"Oh, you did, eh?" The game warden dismounted and walked nearer to the slain animal with his bridle reins in his hand. "Well, you know it's against the law to shoot a doe, don't you?"

Louis turned pale. The mention of the law was a sinister threat at any time.

"Since when?" Archilde asked.

"For a long time, my friend. It's darn serious to go shootin' female deer, I want to tell you."

"You realize we're Indians, don't you? And that we have been exempted from the game laws?" Archilde asked.

"Well, I guess I wouldn't mistake your breed," he said, "but it happens that you're not exempt on this score. You can shoot deer anytime of the year but that don't give you permission to shoot a doe."

"I think you're wrong there. The Indians are exempt from all game laws by special treaty."

"I've been a game warden for twenty-five years, young fellow, and

I know what the law is. I say you've violated the law or the other fellow has since he admits doin' the shootin'. How many more did you get?"

"This is all."

"No, sir. There's another one up the creek," Louis said, hoping to divide the blame.

"Oh there is! Supposin' you go up after it," he said to Archilde. "No monkey business, see! I'll have to bring you all out."

"There's nothing up the creek," the old lady said. "Get the horses and we will go." .

"No, by God! We're going to see what's up the creek!"

"The old lady is right. I was joking my brother a while ago and I told him I had shot a deer and left it up by those willows. I give you my word, there's nothing there."

"I take an Indian's word like I'd take strychnine. Go and bring in the deer!"

"Go and see for yourself, then. We will wait here," Archilde said with a shrug.

The game warden jumped on his horse. "You're all under arrest. Now get busy and bust up this camp. I'll take you all up there. Tell the old squaw to clean out the deer but, if she cuts the rump away, I'll make it tough for all of you!"

Louis and the old lady were carrying on a heated conversation in their guttural tongue which Archilde could not follow. It was evident that Louis was scared and wanted to make a dash, but the old lady called him a fool and a coward.

"Wipe your nose and get ready!" she said finally. Louis was black in the face with rage. He thought Archilde was lying about the deer he had killed in order to avoid blame. His rifle was leaning against a tree and he walked quickly toward it. He looked fiercely at Archilde.

He had barely touched his rifle when a shattering explosion broke the stillness.

"Damn you!" the game warden screamed. "Stand still, all of you! One more move like that and I'll finish everyone!" His horse was rearing and prancing, but he kept it under control.

Archilde looked stupefied. Louis had sunk to the ground with blood flowing from his mouth.

The old lady covered her face with her shawl and cried with piercing shrieks.

"You fool! You've killed him!" Archilde said in a quiet voice.

"Well, what was he going to do to me? I got him first. What's wrong with that?"

"No, you're all wrong. There's a mistake. The old lady told us to get ready and he reached for his gun without thinking. That was all he had."

The game warden dismounted again. "Stand off to one side," he said, "and keep your hands still." He stooped down to examine Louis.

There was no accounting for what happened next. Archilde saw only a flash of action. In a movement that seemed quicker than sight the old lady had acted. The game warden had stooped over to examine Louis and in the next moment he was sinking to his knees with a pale face. The old lady had hit him in the head with the hatchet.

Archilde fainted. At least he grew nauseated and leaned against a tree with no strength to move or speak.

He recovered in a moment and stood looking at his mother. A feeling of intense revulsion and hatred came to life in his breast, and he had an impulse to drive her away. He was ashamed of being an Indian and part of her. Perhaps what sickened and enraged him was that he saw in a flash the difficulties that would follow her action. She had placed him in jeopardy.

The game warden was quite dead. The old lady was sitting down beside Louis, rocking back and forth and moaning.

Archilde couldn't think of anything to do. He had an intense fear of someone else appearing on the scene, although they were twenty miles from any habitation. He took hold of the game warden and half carried, half dragged him behind a tree. He picked up the hatchet and threw it into the brush. Then he scuffed up the ground with his foot to obliterate the blood stains. He looked at the sky wondering if it would snow.

"Look here! Get up! We've got to dig a hole."

"Not for Louis!" she said.

"Yes—for both! Think I want to get hung for him? No, sir! How can we prove we didn't shoot him?"

He couldn't find anything to dig with, so he went to find the hatchet he had thrown away.

The old lady wouldn't let him bury Louis. She threatened to tell everything when they got back. He used threats too, but she wouldn't give in.

"It will be three days before we get back. We can't carry him all the way."

"I will walk and put him on my horse. We will travel night and day and tomorrow night we will be there."

Archilde had moments of nausea. Many times he had an impulse to jump on his horse and cross the mountains to the other side and there disappear. But everything seemed difficult, in fact hopeless. Some deep instinct told him that he must go back and clear himself. This became more clear when he realized that it would have been Louis's trick to run away. From then on he began to act with a clearer judgment.

He buried the game warden without compunction. He had determined to swear that he had found Louis already shot. He would say nothing about the game warden. Let him be found first. His mind was clear on every detail and he saw how everything should be done.

He cut down two long and slender lodge-pole pines and made a travois out of the canvas from the teepee. He wrapped Louis in this and tied him securely. Then he fastened the poles to his saddle. He saddled Louis's horse and broke the bridle reins off short at the bit so that the horse would not get hung up and also to have it appear that the horse had broken them off himself. He gave the horse a blow with his quirt and saw him disappear into the timber. He took Louis's gun with him.

The old lady no longer spoke or appeared to know what was being done. She covered her head with her shawl leaving only a small opening to see through. It was late afternoon before they started, and out of the leaden sky the snow began to fall suddenly. In a moment a twilight had fallen over the world.

The night that followed was too strange for words. Archilde felt his horse moving under his legs and felt him slip and slide on the steep trail that was quickly being covered with snow. As soon as darkness came, it was impossible to see farther than a foot or two on each side. A small mound of snow had collected on his horse's head, and he kept his eyes fastened on that as though it were a beacon light.

Never for a moment did he cease to hear the slipping sound of the poles behind him on which his dead brother was strapped. Sometimes he heard his mother's horse blowing.

At midnight they stopped and made coffee. His mother said nothing all the time. He gave the horses a feed of oats from a small bag he had brought.

They rode on again. Toward morning he began to doze and sway in the saddle. Never for a moment did he lose the motion of his horse or the sounds around him, but his mind was numb and lost in cloudy dreams.

No longer did he feel that these mountains were his home. They had become alien and forbidding. He was dreaming of the great cities beyond the mountains.

Suddenly he had a longing to be far away such as he had never known before. Hitherto he had gone away out of curiosity and restlessness. But now he wanted to go away forever. He wanted to go farther than he had ever gone.

Chapter Eight

They stopped again sometime during the morning.
The snow had turned to a fine dry powder, but it still fell without a letup. Under the trees there was not a single sound.

Archilde gave the horses the last feed of oats in the sack and let them stand under a huge fir tree where the snow had scarcely penetrated. He built a fire under the same tree and the old lady cooked a meal. They rested for several hours, more for the sake of the horses than for themselves, although Archilde dozed off momentarily from time to time. They expected to reach home sometime during the coming night if they rode continually.

Archilde began to think more clearly. He became impressed with the event in all its significance, and where before he had acted positively out of impulse, he now began to have doubts.

At the moment he was strongly impelled to return for the game warden. He was struck with the inhumanness of his act. Immediately, however, he was assailed by many difficulties. He could not answer them.

In the first place, he could not present a case to clear himself. He would undoubtedly be convicted for the man's murder. To tell the story as it had actually happened seemed to him more cowardly than his present action. Moreover, he could probably convince no one that his story was truthful.

He shrewdly estimated that there would not be an intensive investigation regarding Louis's death. The charge of horse stealing was still hanging over his head though the search had been dropped. Many people would sigh relief, and even the police officers would be willing to believe the story of finding him shot. He had enemies enough.

The seriousness of the case would develop as soon as the game warden was missed. Questions would be asked, a search party might be sent out. There was no possibility of finding the body, however, until spring. The snow would conceal everything, and all he had to do was to declare that he had been hunting in another section of the country. They would never get a word out of the old lady.

The matter was clear enough, but he could not let it rest there. He turned it over ceaselessly looking for loopholes, knowing that they existed somewhere but unable to locate them. He shared somewhat his mother's primitive concept of the Law—confusing it with deity and divine might—something omniscient and equipped with the power to pierce through the subterfuges of the ordinary mortal. Yet, his saner mind told him that this was not so. He need only stick to his story and he would be safe.

What made him feel most helpless and disheartened was the thought that a single incident, happening so quickly and with such little reason, could become a serious obstacle to his life, even a threat. Every thought that entered his head became wrecked on that one inescapable boulder of a fact.

The daylight gradually faded and merged with night and they were still riding. The horses were playing out rapidly. Archilde had changed the travois to his mother's horse and back to his own several times. When they forded a stream, he carried the body across his shoulders.

At midnight they emerged from the mountains and were met by a chill wind that blew across the prairie. The snow had gradually ceased, but the wind carried it along in heavy stinging gusts. Archilde got off and walked beside his horse to keep his feet from freezing. He shouted back to the old lady several times but received no answer. She sat atop her horse like a great bundle of rags. Perhaps she was reciting the catastrophe over and over in her mind too. She hadn't uttered a word since they had started their journey.

When they reached home, everyone had been in bed for hours. Max was the first to awaken. He put on his great fur-lined moccasins and a heavy coat and came out, lantern in hand.

The Hungry Generations | 109

Archilde was so stiff with frost that he had difficulty getting off his horse. He could not speak. The old lady fell into a heap in the snow.

Max held his lantern over the travois and tried to discover what was under the frozen canvas.

"Meat?" he asked Archilde in a genial tone. He held the lantern higher to light up his son's face and was surprised at the look he saw.

"No. It is Louis." Agnes had come out.

"Take the old lady in," Max directed. "Then put the horses up." He turned to Archilde.

"The horses are ready to drop. You must have done some traveling. What did you say was in here?" He brought the lantern around to the travois again.

Archilde didn't answer but set to undoing the frozen mass. His hands were too stiff to obey his command, so he merely pointed and said:

"That's Louis. We found him yesterday—or I guess it was the day before. Shot."

Max understood at last and drew back. "Go in the house," he said. "I'll undo this."

An hour later everyone was in bed. The wind increased its fury and piled the snow on the window ledges, only to blow it off again as it changed to a different quarter. The heavy fall that had settled in the pine tops now was shaken loose and it went streaming through the air. Winter had descended in all its vigor. Life had retreated.

Chapter Nine

Father Grepilloux was dead. Mass was being said and the church was filled to overflowing. Max, however, was hardly conscious of anyone. In fact, he paid but little attention to the services. His feeling was dulled and his thoughts were confused.

Light poured through the small round windows in the vaulted ceiling and the air was heavy with a resinous incense. The choir filled the remotest corners of the church with its swelling and ebbing flood of music. The singing had a tone of unusual melancholy and devotion.

Many women were in tears, and in the Indian section at the back of the church there was an undertone of wailing that occasionally rose into a high, sharp crescendo and drowned out all other sounds and produced a dismal, eerie sensation. Many heads were bowed forward until they touched the back of the bench. Tapers were placed around the coffin and the flame of each one wavered from time to time.

Max remained aloof. Sometimes he lifted his head and gazed at the fresco that covered the wall back of the altar. The picture meant nothing, however. He saw only a confusion of color and figures. At other times he turned slightly to the right and saw the coffin through the tail of his eye. He was to be one of the pallbearers and his seat was opposite the coffin. He tried to form a picture in his mind of what his friend looked like but found that he could not do it. This was most surprising for he had been at his bedside only a few days ago. He recalled the unfinished history and wondered vaguely if it would ever be written. He

The Hungry Generations | 111

thought that people should know about Father Grepilloux, the patient friend of many unknown men, the saintly hero who had worked in his day like a peasant to make a garden in this wilderness. He had seen him chopping trees and carrying stone to build his first church. He had [heartened?] many of the early settlers to perform tasks that were not as heavy as his own. Few of his early friends ever thought of him as a churchman. He took no liberties because of his robes, and when he gave counsel or advice to a man, he spoke outright and did not have a feeling of remoteness in his speech. His friends were indifferently Catholic and Protestant alike. In the early days when he was the only religious in the community, he had helped to bury and minister to the sick of all sects alike. He had caught the imagination of the Indians from the very first and attached himself in their loyalty. It was significant that while in almost every other section of the country settlement and cultivation were only carried on at the expense of bloodshed and flagrant injustice, there was never an uprising in the section where Grepilloux held his influence. He had been the forerunner. Throughout the sixty-mile valley banks, stores, and farmhouses flourished; the railroad had pushed through in time and every day its trains rushed along, carrying the produce of many laborers; children were born and studied in the schools; old men passed their last days and were laid to rest with the same peace and security that attended any province in the Old World: and for all of this Grepilloux was the trailblazer. It was as though he had opened his hands in a simple gesture of benediction—and a new world had unrolled at his feet. Max was not inclined to put much importance on the part he had played as a trailblazer and pioneer. His efforts had been self-interested, he realized, and he hardly thought them worth mentioning—certainly not in the same breath as Grepilloux's. At any rate, it took a priest or doctor, or, at least, a lawyer to make things go.

To the banks of the stream where this great church now stood the priest had wandered. Here he met the Indians and in simple words told them of his plans. They did not understand, to be sure, but they trusted his words. Now the ancient world had pressed its way along the faint path that the father had left behind and life and industry had flowed in to fill the valley from mountain to mountain. Thus he had welded the old and the new.

Scores of thoughts of this nature passed through Max's brain, yet he knelt there and could not recall his friend's face.

Max was not a pious man and he had often wondered how it was that he and Grepilloux had grown so friendly. Of course, their acquaintance had been fostered in the days when hardship and toil beat down the wall between many men; more than that, Grepilloux had a simplicity and warmth that drew friends easily. But that was not enough to account for it. Their friendship was greater than priest or man. Grepilloux assumed no spiritual guidance over Max and that in itself was extraordinary. Max wasn't looking for a confessor and had he found one in Grepilloux, he wouldn't have had the friend. It was an unusual relationship and Max was aware of it. Often he had amused himself by appearing blunt and profane. He wanted to see the priest come to the front. But Grepilloux would smile indulgently.

"You need more sugar in your liver today. Or as we used to say when we were children, you got up on the wrong side of the bed. You don't look like a bear."

Moreover, he could judge a cigar better than Max could.

The singing was over. A melancholy more pronounced than ever entered the church as everyone sat back waiting for the priests to appear from the chancel and start the procession. Grepilloux was to leave his mortal friends at last.

When Max took his place at the casket, he began to flush and burn. He felt as if he alone were carrying his friend and the weight was unendurable.

Outside a flurry of snow was blowing and it was cold. They slipped the casket into the horse-drawn funeral coach, and someone appeared and gave Max his fur coat. The procession formed and started for the cemetery.

The thoughts that came to Max were sharper but more confused than ever. His spirit grew weaker with each step toward the cemetery. It was difficult walking as he had to follow in the narrow rut made by the horses and wagon. The snow kept falling in a slow and methodical way. Everyone in the village and for miles around had turned out for the funeral. The procession was half a mile long, and it proceeded solemnly up the white road. Village dogs came out to bark at the strange sight, but everyone moved so deliberately and with such indifference that the dogs ceased their clamor and sat down in the snow to watch. Finally, they went away one by one to find the warm corner they had left.

Max was still trying to recollect his friend's face, and as he failed repeatedly, a kind of despair took possession of his soul.

He had won respect for himself at last and today it was for more than his money. People had been anxious enough to shake his hand after the rumor spread that he had become associated with the bank. Already they had started coming to ask if their mortgages couldn't be extended and the interest deferred for a year. But today he had risen to even greater importance. He had borne the casket of his friend and before him walked the district judge and in back of him a state senator. Today he had risen among the mighty—to help carry his friend to the cemetery. He was more than a squaw-man with a batch of evil sons.

An unpleasant reflection caused his brow to wrinkle. Archilde was not witnessing the funeral. It would have been pleasant to have had his *one* son present upon this occasion. Archilde was in jail, however.

The snow stopped as though by a signal just as the open grave was reached. Pieces of canvas covered the opening and the pile of earth that had been thrown out. There was also a rough sort of pavilion over the heads of those immediately at the grave. The snow was yellow and soiled where gravel had been spilled over it.

The canvas was removed from the grave and the coffin placed immediately over it until the time when it should be lowered. The pallbearers had performed their last earthly duty for the priest and they drew back. A stupor began to come over Max and to numb his senses. His head had been uncovered for a long time now, and at times, he seemed to feel the chill stinging his brain.

A funeral address was given and Max caught only the words: "We had a saint with us, but he is gone from our house!" The words stuck in his mind and kept repeating themselves over and over. What made them seem most real was the fact that they recalled to him how the priest had looked just before he died. His hair had turned pure white during his illness, and his skin had taken on a strange transparency that gave the illusion of a light burning within. Max couldn't forget that.

The address came to an end and the last prayers were recited.

Whimpering and low cries began and long wailing sounds came from the group of Indians. Everybody seemed utterly downcast and over-whelmed by the spectacle of the grave. The nuns in their black gowns seemed to be standing with bowed heads waiting to be struck down.

Eastward the mountains appeared out of the departing storm clouds, and as a bit of sunlight struck them, they shone with blinding splendor. The unbroken whiteness gave them a molded quality and made them appear twice their ordinary size. They rose to astonishing heights.

The coffin began to sink and in a moment it was out of sight. The priest threw on the first shovel of dirt. It was frozen solid and sounded like a rock when it hit the lid of the box. The sound emphasized the chill and hardness of the ground.

Max remembered nothing else clearly. He had said his farewell.

When he passed the cemetery gate, he turned and started aimlessly away. Someone reached his side and took his arm. It was the storekeeper.

"My God, man! Where's your hat? You'll catch pneumonia!"

Max turned and stared but gave no indication that he had heard.

"Then turn your coat collar up. You are the greatest man in our town today and you can't afford to be reckless. Didn't we all see you up there in front with the bishops and judges and all the rest? Come in the store and get thawed out. I'll send someone to the garage for your car."

Moser could just as well have brought Max through the back door that led directly into his office, but he preferred not to. He took him around to the front where crowds of people had already entered. He walked the whole length of the store, greeting people right and left and making way for Max. It was a triumphal entry, but Max was uncon-scious of it all.

There was a hot fire in the office stove and Moser gave his guest some whiskey. Max had had nothing to eat and in a moment his head was spinning.

Moser was filled with an insatiable desire for talk as usual. He had not seen Max for over a week, and he wanted to know everything that had happened in that time. He asked every conceivable question but he could get nothing more than a blank look or a toss of the head from Leon.

"I never saw such a funeral in my life. Everybody and his brother was there. And there was Max up in the very front with the bishop! I

The Hungry Generations | 115

don't suppose you saw me, did you? No, I guess you didn't. I made a motion to you when you passed, but you weren't looking.

"I never realized before that there were so many people in this neck of the woods. It's a shame they don't come to town more often. The store is full of people now, but they're only standing around absorbing the free heat before they start for home. Just the same, I'm glad to have 'em and I hope they come oftener. Nothing helps business better than to have lots of people around. We need more civic activities. Do you know, I've had it in my head for a long time now to put on a sort of fair. Have exhibits of wheat and oats and livestock and let the women bring butter and cheese. In most places now they have calf and pig clubs among the boys and girls, and every year they bring these to the fair and the judges choose the best and give a prize. That's what I'd like to do. I've been thinking about it for a long time. I think we ought to make up a committee and get some money together for prizes and things. How does it seem to you? Do you think we could make it?"

Max looked at the storekeeper for almost half a minute before he awakened.

"Excuse me," he said. "I was thinking of how frosty the ground is."

"I guess I shouldn't talk so much. I know you're thinking of other things." Moser was like a boy, always ready to apologize. But he had too much to say; he couldn't keep his tongue quiet.

"Death is a mighty strange thing. We all know we've got to die, but we never get used to it. You might think we would. Personally, I don't know whether I'm afraid of it or not. If you asked me bluntly right at this moment, I'd say no, but you never can tell. I suppose I'd be a little more uncertain if I knew it was actually going to happen. But I feel that there are lots of other things just as bad. For instance, I haven't any children, but supposing I had two or three children just old enough to understand things and know what kind of daddy they had. Say I was working in a large bank, I was the cashier, say, and thousands of dollars passed through my hands every day. I'd be living in a city where everybody knew me. My wife would travel in the best circles and her house would be full of friends. I would belong to many clubs and would be a member of several boards of directors. Then supposing something happened. Supposing I should be found short in some of my accounts.

I wouldn't know how it happened, but there the facts would stand before me. I would be accused of embezzlement. I would be tried and convicted. Everything would crash. My wife would be sneered at and turned away. My children would look at me and ask what was the matter. They would learn to despise me.

"That, Max, would be hell! That would be worse than death! Why, man, sometimes I wake up still dreaming that such a thing has happened and I tell you that sweat pours off my body!"

Max regarded him steadfastly for a moment and then asked:

"Do you believe in saints?"

"What do you mean, ghosts?"

"No, saints. If a man appeared in your doorway there with a face so kind that you knew at once that a better man had never lived and if a kind of warm light seemed to surround the man—would you believe him a saint?"

"Why, yes. I guess there used to be lots of 'em in the old days."

"All right. Would you like to have one for a friend?"

"Well, I don't know. I'm not much that way myself and I suppose I'd feel out of place most of the time."

"No, you don't understand. A real saint never makes you feel that way. He even lets you feel superior."

Max didn't pursue his thought any farther. Indeed, he seemed to forget it entirely and for the first time he began to show interest in his surroundings. He'd already had several drinks of whiskey and now he took another. Moser poured out one for himself.

"Max," the storekeeper said. "I've got a mighty fine proposition for you. I'm coming up to see you in a few days and talk it over."

"You're a great man for ideas and propositions. Always got something new. Let's hear it. We'll talk it over now."

"No, I want to give it another turn or two in my mind. I'll have all the details for you when I come up."

"All right, suit yourself. But there's no time like the present. That's fine whiskey. Guess I'll have another drink."

"You'll be drunk."

"I'm drunk now. Where's my car?"

"It'll be here any minute. I sent around for it. Sit down."

The Hungry Generations | 117

"No, I'm damned if I'll sit down! I want my car."

"All right, I'll send somebody else over to see what's wrong." Moser got up and left the office. He was gone for about two minutes, and when he returned, Max was sitting forward with his head between his hands. He began to talk and the words came forth in a torrent.

"Moser, I don't think life is worth a damn!" That was his first remark, but he said much more. He went to the beginnings and told of his arrival in the country and the hardships of the first few years, the blizzards and heavy snows. He told how he had invested every cent he had in a hundred head of cattle, and during the winter of the third year all but an even ten were frozen or starved to death. He hadn't been able to cut enough hay. There wasn't another settlement within twenty-five miles. Father Grepilloux had just arrived in the country and was going about preaching peace and brotherliness to the Indians and doing a fine job of it.

Those were makeshift days; everything you used was a makeshift for the real article. Thus a hole in the roof served for a stovepipe or brick chimney, with an ax you chopped a tree, drove a spike, or stirred your shirts in a can of boiling water; you used your hat to cover your head, to sleep on at night, or to drink out of during the day; in winter you stuck your extra shirt or pants in the hole that you had used as a window in summer; Father Grepilloux had used a clean white shirt as an altar piece.

Wives were makeshift too. A white man married a squaw in the same way that he put dirt on the roof of his cabin in place of shingles. That was how he married a squaw. Father Grepilloux praised him for it. In his opinion, it was better than the preachings of the missionaries; it was simpler but more, much more, effective. There could be no misunderstanding such an action. Possibly Grepilloux had even thought of putting aside the robe and living what he thought was more powerful than the word. His wisdom was that he kept to the robe.

A squaw was all right until she gave you a child. There he lay in front of you, ugly and black. What could you do? Give him the best Christian name you could think of and let it go at that. Thus, Pedro, Umberto, Blasco, Luis—Archilde was a crazy name, he didn't know where it came from—these were the names of his sons, much good it did him. For his squaw, he had no harsh words. She worked, not hard and what she did was of little account, but she minded her own business and never asked for anything. But was she civilized? Was she a companion, friend, an equal? Could she sit at the head of his table? Not for a thousand years yet.

Max had been talking with more and more heat. There was a natural twist for sarcasm in his tongue, and after long disuse, he was trying to get it unlimbered today. The whiskey and hot stove had flushed his face and he swung his arms at times awkwardly. His eyes shone.

"I tell you we've been fools. Did we think we could build a paradise here? Did we think the Indians were lambs, free of sin and ready to be made into Christians? Look at them! They're all diseased, many are born blind and crippled. The rest are drinking themselves to death and gambling away every penny, every shred of property that they get their hands on. They breed like dogs. Nobody knows who's the father of the papooses you see hanging on a squaw's back. Did we think they would make farmers? The government gave them land, wagons, houses, plows, harnesses, everything. But nobody works. They won't work. They sell or gamble away their horses and tools and then sit around the agency waiting for the government to make them a payment of twenty-five or fifty dollars. And the government does it, three or four times a year. Have we been fools?

"Now I'm an old man. In a few years I'll be dead. Who've I got to take my place? Nobody. I've worked thirty-five years in this valley building my ranch. I have money and lots of land. But none of my blood will use it when I am gone. I hoped it would be Archilde but he is in jail even now. How do I know what kind of a son he will be? Maybe he is innocent—but what's he doing in jail! White men have a way of staying out of jails when they live innocent lives.

"Father Grepilloux died working with these savages, but tomorrow morning they won't remember him. He had wisdom and the kindness of a saint, but he could just as well have gone into the woods and baptized and preached to the trees. Friendship with an Indian is like the wind and you can't catch the wind in a sack.

"Aw, to hell with it! Isn't my car here yet?" Max poured another drink.

The Hungry Generations | 119

Moser was sitting in his chair with his feet perched up on an open drawer of his desk. He had a round little belly and his hands were clasped over it. He was half asleep.

"What? Your car? It's been here for half an hour. That was a fine story, Max. You make me feel very sad.

"So you think that's the truth, do you? Won't they ever work? But look here, I've mortgages on many Indian ranches. Won't they ever pay it off? That's too bad. That puts me in a very tight place.

"But look here, you're wrong about Archilde. You've got a good son there, Max. If he was my son, I wouldn't hesitate at all to turn over my entire estate to him. You mark my words, he's gonna be all right. He's in a tight place just now, but we all know he's innocent. You mustn't take these questionings and grand jury sittings too seriously. We all know what kind of a fellow Archilde is and he'll be out of jail in no time. If it was a serious matter, do you think they'd have him at the agency still? Not at all. He'd have been turned over to the state before this." The last thing Moser said was:

"Remember that I have a very important proposition for you. I'll see you in a few days."

Max drove away with scarcely another word. He had talked until he had no thoughts, no feelings left. As he drove swiftly out of town a sharp wind tugged at the curtains of his car and blew powdered snow across the road. Night was approaching rapidly and the air was sharp and cold.

Images of the funeral kept returning to his mind and for the first time he felt the melancholy of the occasion. Before he had resented his friend's death. A good man should never die. But now, as night came on, he was facing emptiness. He would not go to the mission anymore. In the back of his brain he still heard the Indians wailing in that dismal tone and he wondered if, after all, they did have human feelings and if their weeping was genuine. He didn't pretend to understand them.

When he reached home he was cold and tired. He had a touch of fever in his blood and his bones ached as if he had been laboring strenuously.

Chapter Ten

Archilde was sitting in the anteroom waiting to see the agent. An Indian policeman stood near him with his thumbs tucked into his belt and carried on a slow, guttural conversation with a tall buck who wore a red blanket and had long hair. The room was half filled with Indians who sat around as patiently as though waiting for the end of time. The odor of smoked buckskin was predominant, although there were actually dozens of odors blended into one. The room was stifling.

The furnishings were the most barren and uninviting imaginable. The pale, cheap varnish on the benches and chairs was blackened where people sat on them and scratched and scarred where they had rested their feet. The floor hadn't been varnished for several years. There was a single radiator in the room and it gave forth a continuous hammering sound. On the walls hung a series of cross sections of native trees, with varnished surfaces. Each cross section was labeled with its Latin name and a short explanatory note mentioning the altitude at which it flourished.

On another wall there were two flags hung with their staffs crossing each other. At the end of the room there was a low railing and beyond that was the general office where clerks sat writing in huge ledgers or punching the keys of an adding machine. The agency was situated in a desolate section among low sand hills and stunted trees. Through the window Archilde could see the snow blowing from hillock to hillock unceasingly. It was a dismal morning.

The Hungry Generations | 121

He was aware that the Indians were discussing him. He could only understand a few phrases in the language, but even though they never looked up and though their voices were almost inaudible, he knew that they were talking about him. He felt as if he were being vivisected, analyzed, and judged by the lowest stratum of society in the world. He gazed steadfastly at the blank wall before him and looked at no one.

The door near his chair opened and the agent appeared, ushering out an old squaw who was bundled in rags until she appeared of prodigious size. With her was her young son who had returned from Chemawa the year before, and he wore a blue suit with a handkerchief tied around his neck and a big Stetson hat on his head. There was some intelligence in his face, but it was hidden behind a stolid, immobile expression.

"Tell your mother that I am doing everything I can for her," the agent said. "But things must wait their turns. As soon as I hear something definite I will let her know. She needn't come to see me until then. Tell her."

That was the same story he gave everybody. Archilde had heard it before; everybody had heard it. But no one believed him or maybe they expected to hear a different story the next time. They kept coming in an endless string to see "the agent" about the pasture they had rented or the timber they had sold to a white man. Sometimes they sold a bit of land or some water right for cash outright, and after they had received the money and spent it, they kept returning for more; they couldn't comprehend that once a thing was sold it was gone forever and they no longer had a claim to it. The yard before the agency was littered with rickety buggies and crow-bait horses. They would stand there all day fighting flies and making piles of dung while their guttural-toned masters waited in the shade or the steam-heated anteroom to see "the agent." Indian horses were no less stolid and resigned than their owners. They knew how to wait.

The agent was a tall, thin man with gray temples. He was dressed in leather puttees, khaki riding breeches, a dark coat, and a white shirt and collar with a black tie. He dismissed the squaw and her son and then looked from one group to another. He called to several and asked what they wanted of him. He couldn't get a satisfactory answer. They wouldn't tell their business before others, although they had probably been discussing it for hours.

Finally the agent saw Archilde and his face cleared.

"So, you are here! Come in." Before he closed his door he announced that he would see no one else until the afternoon. Unless their business was urgent, they had better wait until another day. Nobody moved.

He motioned Archilde to a chair and busied himself with some papers on his desk for several minutes. Finally, he pushed these aside and looked up.

"Well, Archilde, you've caused me a lot of worry. I don't know what to do with you. The prosecuting attorney wants me to turn you over to the county court, but I'm not sure I want to. If you went before a civilian court, I have no doubt they would make it hot for you. But I believe you are innocent and I don't think it would do any good to drag this out any longer. If it were one of your—well, almost any of the boys on the reservation—my hands would be tied. You'd have been in the county attorney's hands before this. But you have a good record, Archilde. I think you are one of our best boys and I hate to see a good boy get a bad start. You understand, don't you, that if you went to trial over this matter, the people would never forget it?"

He didn't wait for Archilde to reply. "I've kept you in jail for your own good," he continued. "I know that jail isn't pleasant, but you have behaved like a gentleman and I want to assure you that it was for your own good. If I hadn't held you here, the county authorities would have made things hot for me. Once more, I want to ask you, did you or did you not see the game warden at any time during your hunting trip?"

Archilde didn't hesitate or change expression. "No, sir. I have shown you on the map exactly where we traveled and told you what trails we followed going and coming. We saw no one until we found Louis, as I have explained."

"All right, Archilde. I'm going to let you go. You'll be on probation, understand, and if this thing comes up again, I want you to come forward like a man and tell exactly what you know. I'll see that your rights are protected in every way. That's my job. Do you agree?"

Archilde felt his heart grow warm. Indians generally distrust their agent and even Archilde had looked upon this man with doubt and scorn; he had always appeared cold and officious. The cheap furniture in the anteroom and the Latin names for the familiar trees had appeared

The Hungry Generations | 123

to be one with him. But here he was offering his hand and speaking in a voice that could not be mistaken. He was aware too that he had won this man's confidence by a trick and a lie, but his heart told him that it could not be otherwise.

He took the hand that was offered him and gave his promise.

"What do you intend to do?" the agent asked at the door. "Are you going to help your father on the ranch?"

"For the time being, yes. I don't know much about farming yet."

"There's lots to know. The country needs good men and I hope that you will be one of them. The Indians must succeed by their own merits like anyone else, understand?"

Archilde signified that he did. He was in a daze. He had grasped something that had been unknown to him before. It was vague but, yet, it was something. Mountains and skies were pushed aside and he saw beyond to a new horizon.

The Indian policeman was to drive Archilde home. He was waiting in front with the noisy Ford car. The side curtains were only fastened in a few places and the loose ends flapped in the strong wind.

"Tell your father that I will drop in to see him sometime. Give him my regards," were the agent's last words.

Archilde had not spent a pleasant time in jail.

His actions were fearful to him. He was not in a position of safety and he could manufacture no argument that would put him on firmer ground. Whether it was this latter fact or because he knew that his words were false and his actions guilty that made him afraid he himself did not know. Day after day he had spent in jail analyzing and weighing his predicament, but in all that time he had discovered nothing new. In every case he had fallen back to his original position, which was a sort of negative attitude. It was the easiest and probably the first line of defense that anyone would have resorted to. A kind of inner voice kept prodding him on with the illusion that a more vigorous and intelligent person would have struck upon a simpler and more logical defense. What he really wanted was an explanation that would prove satisfactory to both the police authorities and his own feelings. He hadn't found any such explanation, and therefore, his repeated denials of ever having seen the game warden were doubly disagreeable.

He hadn't seen his mother during the month that he had been held in jail, and although he had relented somewhat in his attitude toward her, he was still angry; resentment was too mild a word. The more powerless he felt the angrier he got. If he had been outright guilty, it would have been easier to come out and admit his guilt—even easier to lie about it. Under his present circumstances there was nothing for him to do but drown in uncertainty. But already he was putting it behind him. The car had no sooner started down the road than his mind began closing itself to the impressions so lately occupying his whole attention.

As the car rolled along the road these thoughts and emotions began to slip away. The chill breeze that tore through the flapping side curtains was too uncomfortable to allow any feeling to exist.

Jim, the Indian policeman, had nothing to say. He had a lean face with the usual broad cheekbones. His expression was particularly pleasant, and he did not look at all like an officer of the law. He wore a big hat and a gray plaid shirt with a heavy mackinaw over it. On his feet he had heavy boots and gray woolen socks like a lumberjack. He drove the car as if it were a cow pony; he was hunched forward over the wheel and his steering was quick and erratic. He turned the wheel only to avoid running out of the road—not to miss rough spots or to keep the car under control. He drove at a furious speed.

Archilde had been in school with this Jim. Years before at Chemawa. Jim was older and lived with the big boys while he stayed in the Small Boys' Home. Yet, Archilde searched vainly in his mind for something to say.

It seemed to him that Jim must have changed a lot. They had been more than two boys from the same town in the same school; they were even more intimate than that. Jim had taken the position of an older brother, and Archilde would always go to him for protection when he got into difficulties with the other boys. Jim used to win marbles and give them to him, and many a night he brought Archilde to his room to share a feast that he had bought with a few dollars from home.

He remembered in particular one warm summer afternoon when he and Jim were lying on the lawn before the music school. He recalled the scene the more vividly because it was in such contrast to the winter day with the sharp wind blowing snow against the car and through the insecure storm curtains. He could see the tall walnut trees with the sun shining through the irregular breaks in the foliage. The nuts were just beginning to ripen, and the green husks on the ones that had fallen were gradually turning black. Someone in the music school was playing a violin, and the sound was particularly sweet and peaceful. Jim and Archilde lay on their backs a few feet apart in a kind of lazy ecstasy. The violin played on for hours. In all these years Archilde hadn't forgotten it.

Toward Jim, however, he had an unfamiliar and awkward feeling. It didn't seem possible that this was the same person. A hundred topics came to his mind, any one of which might have started a conversation; they all seemed inappropriate. He couldn't imagine Jim being interested or having anything to say about any of them. So it struck him that Jim had changed into quite a different person. It didn't occur to him that the change had taken place in himself. A world had intervened and Archilde could feel no common ground between them.

Sometime later he heard Jim say, "It's going to snow." Archilde agreed.

The car sped forward going uphill and down. The road was not too well traveled, and at times, they skidded badly into the deep snow at the side. This was dangerous for they were traveling through a narrow river canyon and often the road was on a high grade above the riverbed. Jim appeared totally indifferent. Once, as they went along, they caught sight of a herd of buffalo standing in the lee of a great shoulder of a hill. These buffalo had come from his father's herd, and they were now in a government park.

After a while, the road crossed the river over a shaky bridge and began to climb the left bank over a long, steep grade. The afternoon faded gradually and the skies darkened. They reached the top of the climb just in time to catch a fading glimpse of the high mountains that formed a great unbroken wall against the eastern sky. Their snow-covered ridges and sharp peaks looked like mounds of flour created by a boy playing a game. Then the snow began to fall softly, and the mountains and the valley below them faded out of sight.

"This is a hell of a day!" Jim said.

Unconsciously Archilde drew a little nearer to Jim who appeared not to notice the cold at all. He suddenly felt considerable friendliness for his companion whom he hadn't even thought of for years and before whom he was totally dumb. Archilde was glad that Jim hadn't tried to get him to tell about the hunting trip. He had shown no curiosity or interest in the affair whatever. A white man, he was sure, would have been prying into it, trying to get at the personal details.

For the first time Archilde became aware of a tangible distinction between the two races. Likewise he was aware, for the first time, of consciously comparing the two.

As they approached the village Archilde wanted to stop for the night. It was still snowing and it had become pitch dark. They could stay at the hotel. Jim, however, thought it would be better to drive to the ranch that night as it was only three miles farther, and now that they were down in the valley the wind had stopped and it was much warmer.

They drove through town without stopping and headed the car eastward to the mountains.

The car stopped before the front gate. Archilde got out and stretched his cramped and chilled limbs and told Jim he would go ahead and open the garage door.

"No," Jim said. "I will go back to town."

"Not at all. You must stay here tonight. Agnes will get supper for us."

While they were standing talking, the front door opened and Max appeared with a shawl around his head and neck.

"Hello!" he called out. "Who's there?"

"It's Archilde!"

"The hell you say! Come on in and bring whoever you've got with you."

Max stood holding the door open. He had a heavy robe on and had been lying down on the lounge near the stove. As he stood waiting for his son to appear, the muscles in his face kept twitching.

Archilde came in and paused, half blinded by the gasoline lamp. Max looked at him steadily and then took his hand from the door and placed it on Archilde's shoulder.

"I'm damn glad to see you, my boy!" he said and turned away. He called to Agnes and ordered her to get something on the table quick.

He shook hands with Jim and poured whiskey for everybody. He had Agnes in to shake up the fire and take the coats and hats away.

The Hungry Generations | 127

"You fellows must be damn near frozen!" he kept saying every minute. "Sit down here and put your feet up to the fire."

He moved about the room, picking up things and putting them down again. He made several trips to the dining room to see that Agnes wasn't delaying things. His eyes rested on Archilde almost continually. No matter in what part of the room he happened to be he looked across at his son.

"We've got lots of room here, Jim, and you'd better spend the night with us."

Chapter Eleven

Archilde and his father sat together before the stove.
Everyone else had gone to bed and the house was darkened. They sat there a few feet apart and for the first fifteen minutes they said nothing. The longer they sat the harder it became to find a natural beginning.

"You must have had a tough trip," Max said.

"Yeh, there was a stiff wind on top of the hill."

"Did you get stuck anywhere?"

"I had to push him out of a snowdrift twice. Jim drives like a house-a-fire."

"You're not looking very good."

"I feel fine. You look bad yourself."

"No, it's nothing. I've had a touch of grippe for the last couple days."

"I heard about Father Grepilloux dying," Archilde said after another pause.

"That was mighty sad. He was buried last Tuesday. I've been home ever since. I was going to get you today, but the doctor said I had to stay home."

Archilde looked surprised. "You knew I was coming then?"

"Oh yes. I talked with the agent over the phone a couple days ago."

Max let the silence continue for several minutes, then he looked up suddenly and asked:

128 |

The Hungry Generations | 129

"Well, what are your plans. Will you go away?"

Archilde didn't have a ready answer, although he knew that some such question would be asked.

"Yes, I guess so," he finally said.

It was Max's turn to be silent.

Thus they continued for several hours and for a long time neither could find out what he wanted to know. They dodged behind words and unfinished sentences and did their best to elude each other in spite of a natural desire for an understanding.

Max tried to get Archilde to say that he didn't want to go away. He wanted to know whether or not the boy had any desire to try his hand at the ranch. When Archilde was away, Max wasn't inclined to think much of him. He was tempted to classify him as one with his other sons and the rest of the boys on the reservation. It was his habit to speak contemptuously of those other boys without making an exception of his youngest son. However, when he talked with Archilde and sat face to face with him, his fears seemed to vanish. He was aware of a person of some quality and understanding, and immediately, he tried to be friendly. He realized to his chagrin that they were strangers. He had never thought to win the boy's confidence when he was younger. That, of course, was because he hadn't expected him to amount to anything. Now he needed a son badly, and it was no small job reclaiming one that he had discarded.

As for Archilde, he had not forgotten the sarcastic speeches of his father on many past occasions. He was always surprised at any show of friendliness for he had grown accustomed to abuse, which was sometimes outright and only occasionally veiled. He didn't think his father had any lively interest in his present affairs. He expected to find Max simulating concern and grief over the shooting in the mountains and the suspicion that was cast on him when the game warden was found missing, but he was prepared to doubt any unnecessary emotion on the matter.

He had no real desire to go away. Rather he didn't know exactly what his feeling was on the subject. He was pretty sure where his father's interest lay; he wanted someone to take over the ranch, he was certain of that. But did his father expect it merely as a sort of family obligation or did he actually think enough of him to want to bestow it on him as a token of respect and confidence? Before the agent had spoken with him he was fairly burning with impatience to be out of jail and to go as far as possible. But the agent had pierced him with his few words, and now he had an impulse to stay and make himself known and respected. At the moment he was undecided. The right word or argument would have sent him headlong to a fresh conclusion and understanding of himself. But he sat beside his father, teetering back and forth, and the right word wasn't said.

It looked indeed as if nothing satisfactory would come of the meeting. The long silences were ominous, and after a while, they began to feel uneasy when the quiet lasted for any length of time. They began to yawn and move in their chairs.

From where Archilde sat he could see through the window, and when he looked out, he was surprised to find that the snow had stopped and the sky cleared. A full moon was shining and the world had suddenly turned bright and clear. At the same moment his own thoughts seemed to reveal themselves in sharp outlines. He had become decided. He turned to his father and began to talk in a loud, emphatic voice.

"I'll tell you why I want to leave. I'll tell you exactly what happened on the hunting trip and then you will understand.

"We didn't find Louis already shot and dead. That was a lie. It is not true that we never saw the game warden. I made a lie about that too. Here is what happened.

"Louis came to our camp one night and slept with us. The next morning I went to a marsh to shoot a deer. I had seen their tracks the day before. The deer came as I expected, but I missed my shot. When I got back to camp, Louis was gone; the old lady said he went after a deer too. I ate breakfast and then we heard a shot. Louis came back with a deer on his back; it was a yearling doe.

"We were sitting there talking about the deer when the game warden came along. He saw the doe and told Louis that it was against the law to shoot a doe and, therefore, he was under arrest. I didn't think he was right because Indians are exempt from game laws. He got angry and ordered us to break camp as we were all arrested.

"Louis had his gun standing against a tree, and when he reached for it, the game warden got scared and shot him. Louis only meant to pick up his gun and start for home. The game warden got off his horse and went to look at Louis. While he was bending over, the old lady picked up the axe and hit the game warden on the head. They were both dead. We buried the game warden and brought Louis home.

"You can see now why I can't stay. If it was myself, I wouldn't care so much. I wouldn't have lied about anything. But, if I stay, sometime I might let a word slip out. If I go away, people will forget and the old lady will die. Then I can come back and tell what I know. That is the story."

Max looked up with a stupefied expression and it was only slowly that the words sank into his brain. When he got the full meaning, he lowered his gaze again and stared at the carpet.

At first Archilde thought to wait until his father made some reply, but a new thought occurred to him and caused him to ask:

"Maybe you think I'm wrong? Would it be better to stay and tell the truth?"

Max began to talk then, and as his words warmed up, he began to feel an affection for his son such as he had never expected to experience. Never before had he been allowed to look into the mind of any of his children and he was surprised and suddenly happy.

"I didn't know you could be honest, Archilde," were his words. "I didn't think anybody born and raised in this country could be. I don't know how you found out about it. Now I wish Grepilloux were alive to hear this!

"Archilde, I will be truthful too. I thought you were a—fool. I saw your brothers grow up, the first one especially, Pedro. Do you know that, when he was your age, he was already serving a term in penitentiary for robbing and half killing an old woman? The next one, Blasco, shot the Indian agent because he was caught with a bottle of whiskey. As for Umberto, I think he was an imbecile. He married a squaw much older than himself who already had two children, one was a girl about fourteen years old. He fixed the girl up, and when she had a child, his wife went crazy and almost cut his head off with a hatchet. He picked up a disease either from his wife or some other squaw, and he is blind and an idiot today. Luis followed in their tracks. They all drank and gambled, and when they were drunk, they were devils. Before you were four years old, I had my stomach fall. I didn't want to know you or even see you.

132 | D'Arcy McNickle

If you had been born a few years later, I probably would have strangled you at birth. That is the truth.

"But you had one friend, that was Grepilloux. I think you served Mass for him, didn't you? I thought so. For many years now he has talked about you. He wanted me to take you in hand. It was he that arranged for you to go away to school. He said you were smart. I didn't believe him.

"But it is too late now.

"Look, Archilde," Max swung his arm outward with a sweeping gesture. "This is my hand. I have not been a good farmer and many things are left undone—yet, I have money and a few things of my own. I want a son to stand in my tracks. On this place we should have the biggest and wealthiest ranch in the state. Our name should become respected and honored. That was why I bought this land. I have more than anyone in the valley; I knew what I wanted. Five years ago I gave up and began selling my stock; today I have none left. I saw nothing in the future but a dismal grave. Perhaps my heart had broken.

"Today, Archilde, I claim you back; you are my son and I was the fool. But it is too late.

"You have told me your story and at last I understand you. I know now that you are a different breed entirely; you belong to my father's family. I can't understand it. This is the first time we have ever talked and my head is full of thoughts and my heart is choking me.

"You ask me if you are wrong in this matter. Perhaps you are. According to the law, which we make to protect ourselves, you are responsible for the truth of what you know. But I will take that responsibility myself, Archilde. Haven't I the first claim to you? No, let me finish. I am calm now.

"I think it is best for you to go away. Sometimes we must take things into our own hands. Who knows, perhaps they will never find the game warden. He made a mistake when he shot—what can be done!

"I dreamed that we should make a great name for ourselves, but I don't care anymore so long as I am seeing you. When your day comes, you will prosper. I see it clearly. You will go away now and learn a few things and don't stop for anything but the best. From now on I have a new dream. I am getting old, you see, and I must have something to turn over in my mind as I wait for my grave clothes.

"Archilde, you are my son and you must forgive me. I have been a fool."

As Max talked on, Archilde's face grew bright with wonder. Never had he heard such remarkable words. All his life he had lived in a world where speech was not used to portray a man. He had lived objectively and by inference. Now he saw a man step forward and lay the materials from his mind before his eyes. That this man was his father made it even stranger. From his cradle he had been given to understand that his father was a distant god—or perhaps devil. He had never attempted to approach the man, and around his own person he had kept a protecting shield that he might never become visible. Now they stood eye to eye and understood each other. Almost for the first time he became conscious of himself as an individual, and he felt a slow but burning excitement entering his blood and filling his body. He seemed to grow in stature and in understanding. Life began to move before his eyes in a meaningful sequence. He heard tramping feet and, as it were, the voices of people. He had burst the bonds of one world and was standing on the threshold of another. What was yet to come before his eyes he could not say, he had no way of knowing. But a certain knowledge came to him like a familiar scent upon the wind. He threw his head back like an aboriginal man and began to take his bearings from his senses and instincts.

The conversation did not continue long after that. Max had grown exhausted, and the room had turned so cold that he was shivering violently. Archilde took his arm and helped him upstairs to his bedroom. At the doorway Max stopped a moment and they shook hands. They said good night and were both smiling, though tears stood in Max's eyes.

Max did not sleep that night. A raging fever entered his veins and by morning he was delirious. That was their first and only conversation.

Chapter Twelve

It was spring and Archilde was going away.
His trunk was packed, and he stood out in the yard looking at the green that had started to appear on the brown hill in front of the house. The cottonwoods by the creek were bursting their sticky, pungent buds while the gooseberry bushes growing at their feet had already shot themselves into showers of green spray.

Archilde had not put on his city clothes yet; he still wore overalls and riding boots with the nickel-studded bucking belt around his waist. The drawings on his hat had become faded and all but obliterated. He stuck his hands into his pockets and strolled toward the barn and sheds to give things a last calm examination. He stopped unintentionally and stood watching a group of chickens that were scratching in the yard. They had only been turned loose after their winter's confinement the previous week, and they appeared to find the damp earth a real novelty. One could sense from the energetic manner with which they set about searching for food, the quickness of their movements, and the pronounced excitement with which the old rooster collected his hens together when he made a rich find in an old pile of horse dung that it was spring. Archilde found himself smiling at their air of stupid contentment and walked away. Down in the pasture a meadowlark was calling at regular intervals. Birds were flying in and out of the haymow with bits of straw for their nests. In the cottonwoods along the creek, which was about fifty yards beyond the barn, a group of magpies were jabbering in

134

The Hungry Generations | 135

their loudest and sauciest tones. A flock of crows kept continually flying back and forth between a thornbush thicket half a mile below the house and a point of timber that extended into the pasture above the house; as they flew they emitted their cries of *caw—caw—caw* and their shadows flew with them across the fields.

The air was light and exhilarating, and Archilde felt half intoxicated as he walked around. His mother's cabin stood off by itself. The door was closed and there was no sign of life around it, except for the thin trickle of smoke that floated out of the chimney and was immediately lost against the hazy sky. She had scarcely been outside her door throughout the entire winter. Sometime during the day he would have to go and talk with her, but he put it off for the present. He knew that she would be squatting on the floor sewing moccasins in the dim light or else merely sitting there with her shawl drawn around her shoulders.

He walked on to the horse barn and peered into its dusky interior. The strong odor struck pleasantly on his nostrils and brought a multitude of recollections to his mind from his earliest childhood. In former times the loft was filled to the roof with hay, and he and the neighbor boys dug tunnels to follow the crossbeams that were buried in the middle of the hay. In summer he always slept up there, and on rainy nights the great roof fairly roared under the battering water drops. Today, when he looked in the barn, there were only three horses standing in the mangers. One horse Agnes used to drive to town every other day. The second was his and the third had belonged to his father. When Archilde turned away from the barn, the day had become less exhilarating.

He walked down to the creek and stood on the bank and stared absently at the water. The snow had not yet started to melt in the hills and the creek sounded weak and passive. There were large chunks of ice still attached to the bank where the shade was heavy, and the water had a yellowish color. The underbrush was beaten down and black ooze lay at the bottom of the hollows. He walked back to the house with slow steps and his eye on the ground.

He had been on the porch five minutes when Moser, the storekeeper, drove up. Archilde did not remember hearing the car and he was greatly surprised when he saw the short, round figure close the gate and walk up the beaten path.

"Hello, Mr. Moser," he said and opened the screen door of the porch. "How are the roads—still muddy?"

"Yes, I have seen them drier. When are you leaving? Or have you changed your mind?"

"No. I'm planning to go away all right. In fact, I'm all ready."

"Say, there's nothing slow about *you*, is there! Will you go next week?"

"Tomorrow."

"No! Really?"

Archilde smiled and nodded. Moser did not appear as affable as was his habit. He looked a bit worn and crumpled.

"Which way are you heading?" he asked.

"I have a ticket for New York—but I don't know exactly what I'll do. If I can get into a university out there, I'll probably try that and see how it goes."

Moser looked up and studied him momentarily and then dropped his eyes. He drummed his fingers on the small, round table by his chair and was silent. Whether he had heard Archilde's words or not wasn't apparent; at any rate he made no comment. When he finally spoke, it was on quite a different subject.

"Your father and me were discussing a proposition some time ago—it was late last fall, to be exact, but as things got pretty lively just about that time we never did get to thresh it out and I'm wonderin' if he ever talked it over with you. I'll tell you what it was. I'm not bragging about myself, but I just want to say, as a sort of preliminary, that I've helped your father along from time to time and we all know, of course, that there was no man in the country as appreciative as Max when you did him a good turn. I appointed him director in the bank, for example." He paused and glanced at Archilde.

"Oh, is that so?" Archilde asked.

"Yes. Well, that's just an example. As I say, Max was quick to appreciate any favor done him and so, when I came to him with a proposition of mine last fall, he was interested right away. Other things came up as you know and we never got back to the subject. I'm going to tell you about it, privately, of course, just as it was with him.

"I don't know whether you're aware or not, but Max was, that I own some property back east in Pennsylvania. My wife has considerable interests out there too. We were born and raised in the same town in fact, near Pittsburgh. You'll pass through it if you take the Pennsylvania!"

"I think my ticket's on the New York Central."

"Is it? Well, never mind. What I want to bring out is that it is becoming more and more imperative as the days go by that I go back there and take care of my interests. Not that they're very large, mind you, in a sense they're not as interesting and promising as what I've got on my hands out here. It's mostly a kind of sentimental reason. It's property, you see, that has been in my family's name for several generations now, and as I understand, everything is becoming run down. I could sell it or have an agent sell it for me and frankly I wouldn't profit from it one way or another. It's not a healthy little business such as I have here, I mean. That would be the sensible thing I realize. A man with a greater interest in business would have let it go long before this. But I'm not that way, and frankly, I'm glad of it.

"No, I'm going to do something that I realize is not entirely sensible or businesslike—I'm going to sell my interests here. I mean the store first of all, that's the principal thing. My wife thinks I'm foolish. Even Max tried to talk me out of it. But I'm determined.

"I made an offer to Max—guess how much—a ridiculous price, seventy-five thousand dollars! Why, I've got over forty thousand in farm machinery alone and my grain elevator cost twenty thousand! Now I'll tell you, Archilde, if you're interested, I'll make you an even better price. What do you say? Let's get right down and thresh this out. Understand now, I'm not saying that your father made any promises whatever, or if he did, we'll simply put that aside. I don't want to make you feel obligated in any way. This is between ourselves entirely. How about it? By the way, have you got a drink? I'm a bit dry."

"Excuse me," Archilde said awkwardly, "I'm kind of a bad host." He went inside the door and spoke to Agnes. When he came out again, Moser was wearing his broadest smile.

"You're all right, my boy. After a few years back east we'll never know you."

Archilde was evidently finding it difficult to make an answer. He frowned slightly and studied the floor. His hands were tucked into his

138 | D'Arcy McNickle

belt and he tilted his chair against the wall. When Agnes came with a pitcher of water and a bottle of whiskey and glasses, he paid no attention and did not offer to pour out the drinks. Moser reached out and filled the glasses.

"Do you want water in yours?" he asked. Archilde shook his head.

"I realize that it's a big idea to take in all at once," Moser continued. "Let me show it to you in another way." He paused momentarily.

"Supposing you go to school back east and take a degree. You may stay around out there for several years, get a job you know and find things interesting. Supposing you do that for ten years to come. I don't care how long you stay away or what you do—eventually, you will want to come back. More than that, you will want to go into a business of your own. Every man does after he works for someone else for a while. And it's only when you have your own business that you will really begin to make money and live properly.

"Now old George Eagan has been with me for over ten years, and he knows the store from cellar to office. He has always been my cashier; you could leave him to manage the store for you and I'll guarantee you that he will keep it running first-rate. Think what a pleasure it will be to return after a few years knocking around and step right into a fully developed business!

"I tell you truthfully, Archilde, it's an opportunity you should never miss. In one stroke you can combine the two biggest undertakings in this valley—your father's ranch and my various interests."

"No," Archilde said and got up from his chair to walk to the door of the porch. His eyes wandered for a moment to the hill that stood a half mile away. Green shades were appearing, as if by magic, upon the dead brown slopes. He took a deep breath and turned to face his guest.

"No, when I go away, I want to make a complete break. I don't want nothing holding me back. I want to say good-bye, good luck, and forget everything for two, five, ten years—maybe forever. I don't know what I'll find out there, but I know it'll be different and I think I will like it. Max told me to do it, in fact. That's why I don't understand why he didn't tell me about your store. He told me to learn as much as I could and to forget everything else for a while. I think he's right.

"I've already put the money away in a Missoula bank. I've fixed it

The Hungry Generations | 139

so that Agnes and the old lady will always have something to live on, and the only reason I'm keeping the ranch is so they can have somewhere to live. I don't know whether I'll ever come back to it or not. Max wanted me to, but he wouldn't tell me that I should. He said to go away first and see how I felt afterward.

"So you can see my position. I'd like to do it if it would help you, as I know you thought a lot of Max and helped him many times. But I don't know my own plans well enough to decide such a thing at present."

"Well, I don't think your ideas are very sensible. I can understand how Max would talk that way because he was sick and his mind wasn't very rational. But you should know better, Archilde. If I was trying to sell you something worthless, there might be a reason for your holding back; I tell you honestly that I'm not only offering you a sound, healthy business, but I'm practically offering it to you as a gift!"

"No," Archilde said and sat down again. He had made up his mind firmly by now and it was plain that he had no intentions of being persuaded otherwise. "I know that I may not sound sensible, but I'm going to do it just the same. I want to get away—completely. Do you understand what it means to me to go away? I've lived here too long—I want to forget it. That's all I can tell you."

"Listen to me." Moser leaned forward and emphasized his words by thumping the edge of the table with his finger. "Your father was on the point of throwing you out of the house on several occasions last summer. I told him he was wrong, I stood up for you time and again. Do you realize that he would have disinherited you? I talked to him for hours at a time and risked my own friendship trying to calm him down. I knew you had good stuff in you and I wanted to see you get a chance. But you assume a distant attitude now and you have closed your ears to all reasoning. I never once thought you would be that kind of fellow."

Archilde was unmoved. "I have told you my position and I can't add anything to it. I am acting according to my father's wishes two days before he died. And he was perfectly rational."

Moser's face had flushed more and more during Archilde's last speech. He no longer made an attempt to conceal his feelings or to speak in friendly tones. He was enraged.

"Then you turn me down flat, eh? That's to be my thanks, is it?

Your language is certainly plain enough, I compliment you on that. There's no possibility of mistaking your intention; you're careful not to show me any gratitude or thanks. I've done many a good turn for your family—I naturally thought that, if the day ever came, I could expect as much from you. But, evidently, you don't believe in that kind of friendship. You want whatever you can get out of your friends, but when they come to you—oh no, that's a different story. Well, there's no mistaking where that characteristic comes from. Your father warned me against it. I daresay he had felt it all right. *It's the Indian in you!*" He shouted and saliva dripped from his mouth as he spoke the words.

Archilde turned pale. Inwardly he was hot with rage, and he imagined that he had his hands around the storekeeper's throat and was shaking the breath out of his mouth. He pictured himself rubbing his face in the dirt and bumping his head up and down.

But actually he didn't stir. He stood perfectly straight and still and felt paralyzed. His voice was steady when he spoke.

"At any rate," he said, "you'll get no satisfaction by blustering. I might have given you some kind of promise if you'd continued to talk reasonably. But I don't want your damn store and that's the end of it. Now get out!"

"You're a damn Indian and you'll never be anything else!" Moser shouted and left the porch in one jump when Archilde took a step forward. All the way to the front gate he uttered blasphemy and threats, turning around continually to see if he was followed. As he jumped in his car and drove away, he shook his pudgy fist.

Archilde sat down on the steps of the porch and broke a stick slowly and methodically between his hands. The breath hissed in his nose and he felt hot and cold by turns. Suddenly he jumped up and started to walk straight across the field, and he stumbled and swayed as he walked for tears were blinding his eyes.

A picture had come into his mind and he couldn't shake it off.

Years before, when he was in school at Chemawa, he got into a fight with a fellow who was a couple years older than himself and had the reputation of being tough and fearless. The fight took place on a warm day behind a large white building. There were half a dozen other boys there, all friends of the other boy, Georgie. How the fight started,

Archilde couldn't remember. Georgie slapped him in the face all of a sudden, and the next moment they were on their feet eying each other and circling around. Time and again they grappled and struck at each other, pounding and tearing away at anything that came within the reach of their fists. Several times they were on the ground rolling and biting. The other boys stood around cheering Georgie.

But Archilde got the best of the fight. Someone came and tore them apart, and when they took stock of each other, it became evident that Georgie was badly used. His nose was bleeding and one eye was blackened. Archilde didn't have a mark outside of his tousled clothes. They were brought before the matron who was very fond of Archilde. He felt proud and righteous as he started for her room. He hadn't started the fight, but he had won it. He was sure that the matron would praise him.

The matron was sitting at her sewing machine when they entered. Sunlight poured through her white curtains, and a cat was sleeping on a pillow in the broad windowsill. She was a kindhearted woman who could wrap Archilde around her finger with a single word. He had never known anyone like her before.

As he came into the room, he was walking very erect and confidently. She turned from her machine and uttered a cry.

"Why, boys!" she said, looking from one to the other in a bewildered way.

Archilde started to speak, but instead he burst into tears. Georgie, the culprit and the vanquished, remained calm and stalwart.

When the others had gone, Archilde remained with his head in the matron's lap and the tears wouldn't stop. He was too ashamed to lift his head.

Chapter Thirteen

Archilde sat on the hill and gazed calmly over the countryside. Immediately below the hill was the ranch house and his father's land extended on every side far out into the prairie. As he looked northward, he could see farm after farm in the bright noon sun. Streams crossed the valley floor at intervals and their courses were marked by lines of dark pine and barren cottonwoods. He could see several small ponds, and far off on the very horizon, he could discern another small town. He could hear nothing besides the faint sound of crows and magpies calling. The sun had a pleasant warmth and mist was rising from the earth. He looked from time to time for the traces of green grass that he had seen from below, but the most he could find was an occasional single blade or tiny wad just appearing through the moist earth. Up here everything seemed dead and bleached by the winter snows.

He was thinking of the times long ago when he used to come to this hill with his mother to pick strawberries. It was positively the finest place in the world, as he recalled it. From no other place was it possible to see so much and to feel the wind so strong and warm. There were more different kinds of birds and plants on the hill than he had ever seen around the house or creek. Indeed, everything was different. But what had given him the greatest sensation was to look at the house and particularly the horse barn. Down on the ground it was a mountain in itself, but from the hillside even the barn looked like a toadstool. Recollections of these fancies haunted his mind and caused him to smile.

The Hungry Generations | 143

He began to think of his relations with his mother then and a frown appeared. In those early days, he was about seven years old, his mother was as much to him as the sun. His day started and ended with her. They went everywhere together. If she went on horseback to gather chokecherries on Dry Creek, she put him behind her saddle and tied him to her with a shawl so that he wouldn't tumble off. When they came up the hill for strawberries at the end of June, she did all the picking and allowed him to run hither and thither and tramp the berries into the ground. Sometimes she called him a name, but usually she went on with her business and acted as if he didn't exist.

When he was tired, he came and laid down with his head against her and after that she wouldn't move. She would take her shawl and cover his shoulders and then, with her hand before her mouth, sing a wordless song that was pitched in such a voice that it sounded as if it were coming from a great distance. He remembered the pleasant odor on her clothes and around her person. He often slept until evening had started on its way, and when he awoke, she would push him away and grumble at his laziness. He would sit up and start eating the berries out of her bucket until she banged his head. But if she didn't have many, she would let him eat all of them.

In those days he asked no questions whatever. He followed her as faithfully as a newly foaled colt and she fulfilled every requirement.

But here he sat, ready to start on a journey that would take him he knew not where; nor did he know how long he would be gone. In his heart he promised himself that it would be forever. In his mind, however, he kept the thought uppermost that he would be back in a few years. And at this moment he felt utterly detached from his mother. He felt no love, no hatred, no friendliness, nothing in particular at the thought of her. He told himself that this was wrong. He said over and over: "She is my mother!" But the words could stir nothing. He wondered if he was unnatural, if it was true that he was not capable of gratitude. Everyone loved his mother as a matter of course. But he couldn't even feel affection on principle. She was totally foreign and unappealing. He did not like the odor of smoked buckskin, in spite of the fact that that peculiar odor was tied up with all of his childhood memories, most of which were pleasant.

144 | D'Arcy McNickle

He said to himself, "She is changed. She doesn't like me since I have been to school and have learned to talk and dress like a white man. She thinks I look down on her and despise her. She thinks I put on airs and try to be above her. But it is God's truth that I don't. I try to be as natural and straightforward as possible, but that makes me uncomfortable. No, the truth is that I have changed. Not that I meant to or tried in any particular way. I wasn't ashamed of my blood to begin with because I never even thought about it. I didn't think about anything. It is only now that I have grown ashamed of it, now that I have seen things, as it were, for the first time. Now I do want to be somebody else. But not before her. She can't help it—"

So he continued. It was only recently that he had ever held consultations with himself. For almost the first time in his life he peered into his thoughts and feelings and attempted to discover just what he did think and feel. It was a novel process, but it did not make him any more sure of himself. He never knew when he was looking at the real thing and when at something imaginary and fleeting.

After a while he left the warm hill and started back to the house. Agnes had killed two chickens that morning and they were probably cooked. Mike and Narcisse were coming home, and he wanted to be there to meet them.

"Mike, I give you my horse," Archilde said after the chickens were cleared away and they sat eating some pie. A silence fell around the table. Mike had a napkin tied around his neck and his mouth was full of pie. Archilde continued.

"You, Narcisse, shall have your grandfather's big white mare."

"Jesus," Mike said softly. "I can have your horse for good? And your saddle and bridle too?"

"Yes, everything that goes with the horses you two can have. To Annie I give a horse and buggy. I bought them yesterday and the man at the livery stable will drive it out this afternoon.

"Now, listen!" he had to shout as loud as he could for pandemonium had broken loose with everybody talking and laughing at once. When he managed to silence them, he went on.

The Hungry Generations | 145

"You are to live in the big house here, and Agnes, you must get the old lady to move in. She's already got rheumatism sitting in her cabin, and she's apt to get something worse. So you must get her to move in. I leave the house in your charge, and I want you to keep it as clean as if Max were still living in it. This spring you will want to have it painted. I have already spoken to the agent and he will pay for it. Anytime you want anything for the house you are to go to him and every month he will send you money. It is arranged. This is your house as long as you live and you should take good care of it."

He turned once more to the boys.

"In the fall the agent will send you to Chemawa, to the same school I went to. You will be happy there for it is a fine place and there are many boys. You will live like soldiers and learn to farm and drive horses. Someday I will come back, and if you have taken care of yourselves and learned something, then I will take you back east with me and show you what a big world we live in and all the fine cities. Now what is it you want to say?"

"What does a soldier live like?" Narcisse asked.

"He lives like anybody else, but he learns to walk straight, and he gets up every morning for breakfast."

"That's the way we live at the fathers' and it makes me sick," Mike said.

"They showed you how to eat with a napkin, didn't they?"

Mike tore the napkin off his neck scornfully and threw it on the floor.

"Wait a minute," Archilde cautioned him. "How about that horse? You want him, don't you? Then you better pick up the napkin."

Mike had no objection to offer. He got down and put the napkin around his neck again, all the time wearing a sheepish grin.

"We stayed in school, didn't we?" he asked, though that had nothing to do with the matter.

"Yes, you did. That's why I'm giving you each a horse. Every year, after this, the agent will write and tell me what sort of fellows you have been, and if he is able to tell me something good each time, I'll see that you get a present that is worth something. That's my promise to you— do you agree that it is good?"

"What do we have to do?" they asked in unison.

"Nothing unusual. Stay in school, make good marks for yourselves. Never steal or get drunk. Understand?"

"And what will we get?" Mike inquired further.

"Ah, maybe a threshing machine or else a big railroad engine."

"You're making fun. You won't get us anything."

"No, I mean it. I don't mean the threshing machine, that was a joke. But I'll get you a good present. How about a silver-mounted saddle next year?"

"Gosh, that will be fine. Do you promise that?"

"If you live up to your share of the agreement, yes. I'll get you saddles with silver dollars tied all over them."

"Now you're lying again," Mike said suspiciously.

"No, by [?]. I'll stick the dollars on myself if I have to."

"All right, that's a go. Now can we go look at the horses? Are they in the barn?"

"Go ahead, but there's one thing more. Don't ever use spurs or a whip on that white mare or she'll throw you into the middle of next week."

They disappeared from the room with a rush. For a moment they could be heard shouting through the yard, and then they reached the barn.

Archilde felt the time drawing near, and he began to burn slowly with excitement. He got up from the table and went to his room upstairs. Everything was ready. His small trunk was locked and lying in the middle of the room. His suitcase was on top of the bed. His blue suit had been pressed at the tailor's and it was spread out over a chair. He paced the floor for a time as if he were studying something, but as a matter of fact, his mind was blank. He looked through the open window and was shocked to find everything so quiet and still. Tiny clouds were coming up from the south and melting into the general haze. The earth had dried considerably since morning.

As he entered the hall again to go downstairs, he paused unintentionally before his father's closed door. For a moment he felt as if someone were in there and a strange, hot sensation passed through his body from head to foot. But, when he opened the door, the curtains were blown back from the open window and the room was completely barren of life. The white bedspread was clean and unwrinkled.

In the kitchen Agnes and little Annie were washing dishes. Archilde made a pretense of drinking water from the dipper, but he was watching his sister and wondering what she was thinking about.

"Where did you learn to keep things clean?" he asked her.

"Is it clean?"

"Yes, cleaner than most houses."

"Max said it was dirty."

"No, it is clean."

He went outside and walked aimlessly with his hands in his pockets. Presently he came to his mother's cabin and stopped. He started to turn away and stopped again. When he went around to the door, he found her sitting on the step, looking down toward the creek. Perhaps she had understood that something was going on. He stood in front of her and waited for her to say something.

Her hair had turned white and her face was thin. Her skin was completely filled with wrinkles and her eyes appeared sightless.

"Spring is early," she said.

He squatted on his heels and rolled a cigarette.

"The hay will be heavy," he said, "and there will be many berries on Dry Creek."

"I can smell green grass."

"Yes, it is already coming through the wet ground. Next week they will be plowing."

"Is the snow deep on the mountains yet?"

"Yes."

"I can't see in this strong light. Maybe in two or three days I can see more."

"Yes. The light is strong." He looked at her eyes and knew that she would soon be blind.

"I heard Mike and Narcisse talking."

"Yes, they are home today."

Nothing more was said for some time. A woodpecker was pounding against a dead tree. Archilde smoked his cigarette until it burned his fingers and then tossed it aside.

Mike and Narcisse had saddled their horses, and they were racing in the pasture.

Archilde sat with his mother until evening came. He watched the sun dip out of sight and realized that it was the last sun he would see at home. The sky was aflame with color and in the warm glow shadows were long and cool. The chickens had gone to roost, and they made subdued clucking sounds to each other as they settled down.

"You will live with Agnes in the big house," he said to her. "It will be warmer there."

She didn't answer.

"Well, good-bye," he said and took her hand.

"Good-bye," she answered and her hand dropped into her lap when he let go of it.

In the dawn he drove away. His trunk was tied to the running board of his father's car and his suitcase was near his feet. The air was frosty.

As he drove along, excitement and exhilaration began to pump his blood faster and faster. He could scarcely believe that here he was at last, starting his journey.

The ruts in the road had frozen stiff, and he found it necessary every few minutes to cut the speed of the car to keep from flying out of his seat entirely. It was hard to drive slowly. When he came to a stretch of smooth road he shot ahead like an impatient hound.

Familiar spots caught his eye as he passed and he smiled to them as to a person. Over and over he was saying, "good-bye, good-bye!"

When he entered town, a figure stepped out from a pool hall as if by previous appointment. It was Jim, the Indian policeman.

They greeted each other and Jim got into the car. They had reached the stage road now, and Archilde sped like the wind toward the south and the railroad station. They climbed up the same road that they had come over during the winter from the agency. As they came to the top of the hill, the sun appeared and flooded them with its first shafts. Archilde turned and saw one edge over a high mountain ridge. The mountains looked blue and cold. The car started down the other side of the hill and once more they were in shadow.

Jim and Archilde said nothing until they were almost to the depot.
"The agent said, 'Good-bye and find out about something.'"
"Find out what?"
"I don't know. He means go to school, I guess."
"All right. Watch Mike and Narcisse. Don't let them drink."
At the station they stopped and got out. Jim put the trunk on his
shoulder and carried it up the steps. Archilde took his suitcase and went
to get the trunk checked. He came back to where Jim was standing. They
shook hands and Archilde pointed to the automobile.
"It is yours now. Good luck."
Jim grinned.
"Good luck yourself."
The train whistled, and in another moment the huge wheels of the
engine roared past Archilde and shook the platform. It screeched to a
stop, and Archilde disappeared into a Pullman coach. The train rolled
slowly down the tracks, and the engine whistled shrilly as it disappeared
into the narrow canyon ahead.
The sun had just appeared above the hills and the morning was
fresh and cool.

Part Two

Paris

Chapter One

Archilde had been in Paris for four months, and he knew no one besides the girl at his hotel and a young Dane whom he sometimes met at the Café d'Harcourt.

He was sitting in the café one day, hoping that the Dane would appear. It was still wintertime, and although it was only a little after four o'clock, a twilight was already settling over the houses. People began coming into the café in increasing numbers and the orchestra members entered the small pit at one side of the room and began to tune up their instruments and sort out their music.

Archilde had been walking through a drizzling rain throughout most of the afternoon and his feet were damp. He sat in a corner where he could watch the front door and paid but little attention to those around him. At the next table to him sat a group of girls who appeared to be enjoying themselves considerably at his expense. One after another they tried to draw his attention by various tricks but he remained, on the surface at least, indifferent. He was helped in this respect by the fact that he couldn't follow their conversation and was only guessing at most of what they said. He was aware, however, that they considered him a stick.

The garçon who was serving him was also amused. He went so far as to suggest that Archilde might very well have an entertaining friend on such a clammy night. Archilde did not know exactly what sort of answer to make, so dismissed him with a smile and a shake of the head.

He felt uncomfortable sitting there and when his friend didn't appear after a time, he paid for his two drinks and went out. Down the street farther he came to a small café with some tables under an awning. He sat down there and ordered beer. It was almost dark.

He drank two beers and then went up the Boulevard Saint-Michel again to his restaurant. The place was already crowded, but the fat proprietress in a faded brown sweater scurried around and found him a seat. She said something about him looking very hungry, but he didn't hear it clearly. He smiled and said it was very wet.

"Indeed!" she replied. "You should have a good wine!" and brought him the wine tariff with the bill of fare. Every night she found him a seat and brought the wine tariff.

The room was in a basement and it was brilliantly lit. The walls were paneled with mirrors, and on the four sides of the square pillars in the center of the room there were mirrors also. The walls were white with gilt decorations. Everything served to increase the brightness until the room was fairly dazzling.

The people talked and laughed incessantly, and the waitresses in their black dresses were kept on the run. Dishes clattered, and every time the doors were swung open, an argument could be heard in the kitchen.

His eyes glanced from face to face as if searching for someone who might be friendly. Most of the faces were totally foreign, they weren't even French. He had acquired the habit of looking at people and wondering what they were like. He had never before studied faces, and now he found most of them inscrutable. Occasionally, he saw someone who attracted his attention immediately, but he did not know how to approach. Somehow people struck up acquaintances and made friends but he could not imagine how to go about it. He was bewildered and lonely.

The only chance acquaintance he had was the Dane, but as neither of them spoke French very well and the Dane knew but little English, they did not get on satisfactorily. They had met in a small, stuffy cinema where Archilde had gone to escape the rain. During the intermission he lit a cigarette and was surprised when his neighbor asked him for a light. Archilde turned and saw a young blond giant sitting beside him and smiling. After that, they left the theater together and had a drink. The Dane was also alone and eager to talk to someone.

He knew no one else, except the girl clerk at his hotel who could say in English, "You have no letter today, monsieur." She was anxious enough to talk but her speech was explosive and he could not follow half of it. Sometimes she tried hard and talked in a slow, even tone, and then they had a better time. He had taken her to a theater once, but she laughed loud enough to attract everyone's attention, so he hadn't tried it again.

For some months he had done nothing but walk from place to place and eat regularly. He was getting fat and more and more depressed. Never yet had he seen the sun and a blue sky and that alone was disturbing.

He finished his meal and smoked a cigarette. The fat proprietress came and pulled the table away so that he could get out between it and the neighboring table. She smiled and hoped that he had eaten well. He thanked her, but he did not feel thankful or cheered by her attention. He was revolted at the sight of her and many times he had gone to other restaurants, but he always came back. Something attracted him. Perhaps, after all, it was her smile when he entered and her even larger smile when he paid his bill and her good-night greeting. But on the face of it, she was disagreeable, and he always left the restaurant feeling acutely depressed.

The rain had cleared at last and he decided to walk home. As he went through the black Rue de Vangirard, he could hear raindrops falling from the eaves and splashing the pavement. He passed tobacco shops and a bakery where people were standing and gossiping. The clouds began to break overhead and he could pick out one or two stars.

When he reached his hotel, his dinner felt heavy in his stomach and he continued to walk. In front of the Gare Montparnasse some laborers were welding the streetcar tracks with an electric arc, and intense blue and purple flames flickered over the faces of the dark buildings. The cafés were full and everyone seemed to be talking English. At the Avenue de l'Observatoire he turned and retraced his steps. He felt stuffed and he knew that walking could not help much. He spent most of his days walking and it did not suffice. His body craved violent physical action, but he did not know how to get it. He was wearing heavy woolen clothes to keep the cold and damp out, and they were uncomfortable. He did not feel healthy; he had taken on too much fat.

When he reached his hotel again he thought, "Well, another day is past. But it is a shame to go to bed. Nothing has been accomplished."

Chapter Two

In the morning he drank his chocolate in bed and then went out for an hour until his room should be put in order.

He was in the happiest possible frame of mind for the clouds were still broken in the sky, and at intervals the sun shone through and dried the water and mud in the streets. A warm breeze blew continually. He walked to the Luxembourg gardens and watched some children sailing boats on the circular lake. He stood and looked absently at the Medici fountain, and then it began to cloud up again. In a few minutes the day had grown dark and somber. He walked back to his hotel quickly, but he was glad that he had seen the sun for even five minutes. Just as he got inside the door, a slow drizzle began to fall and a heavy mist had descended into the streets.

For the rest of the morning he stayed in his room and practiced on his violin. He felt like an aristocrat every time he picked up his fiddle and began to practice, first finger exercises then bowing, then the same tune over and over.

There was an old woman who had a little shop in the Rue de Seine. In her window she had scarves of colored silks and Archilde could never pass without stopping to look. Several times he had gone inside and the elderly madame was extremely nice. He went to see her on that afternoon. That is, he had passed her shop and had stopped to look in the usual way. He did not quite have nerve enough to go in, though it was a strictly business affair and all he needed to do was ask to see a scarf. He had already bought half a dozen in the same way. As he stood hesitating, she saw him through the window and nodded in such a friendly way that his fears vanished.

She had a little porcelain stove in her one-room shop, and it gave forth a mild, pleasant heat.

"It is damp today," she said. "Perhaps you would like to see some batiks that my daughter has just finished?"

"Oh, you have some new ones? That is fine. Do you ever have sunshine in this town?" he asked haltingly.

"Certainly, certainly. Wait but a few weeks now and you will see." She knew that he did not have a good command of the language, and she always spoke slowly and with clear enunciation, all the while smiling and making him feel quite at home.

"Look now, here is a piece—but no, I do not like that.

"Tell me, is it for your young lady that you are buying these scarves?"

Archilde colored slightly, from confusion, not embarrassment. "Yes—but I should also like something for my mother," he added hastily.

"For your mother, is it so? Good. I have the very thing." She went behind a screen and brought out some silken shawls with small, intricate designs and pale colors. She spread them before his eyes and her face fairly glowed.

"Your mother will be delighted with one of these. When I go to see my oldest daughter in the Rue Saint-Dominique, I wear one myself. Look!" she threw one across her shoulders to show the effect.

Archilde became absentminded and made no sign that he had been pleased. He stared vacantly.

"Perhaps you have been away from home a long time?" she asked.

"Yes. It is almost three years, now."

"So long! Aren't you lonesome then?"

"No," he said, but when he saw her look of surprise, he knew that it was the wrong thing to say. "She will think me cold and unnatural," he thought.

"I get lonesome for my mother, but for home, no," he explained and felt relieved when she smiled again.

"Yes, it is that way with all of us. The old house will not hold us as soon as we can move around by ourselves. And America is so far away!"

"That is true and my home is on the other side of America. At New York I am just halfway home."

"Is that so? But isn't it all a big desert on the other side?"

"No, it is mountains and valleys and swift creeks that are full of fish."

"And what do you do? Are there any people?"

"Yes, there are people."

"What does your father do? Does he own a farm?"

"Yes, a very large farm."

"Excuse me for asking, but it seems so strange."

Archilde didn't object to her questions at all. He felt comfortable in the warm shop and it was a satisfying experience to sit there and talk about his home in an objective way—although he realized from his vague, inconclusive answers that he was really telling her nothing. But even if he had answered with painstaking care and truthfulness, she wouldn't understand much better. He noticed that she didn't listen attentively to his answers. Perhaps she made up her own answers to her questions as quickly as she asked them. For instance, when she asked if America wasn't a great desert, her manner seemed to say that she was certain that it was and she took little notice of his words. What else could she do! Perhaps that picture of a desert had been in her mind for twenty-five or thirty years. A word couldn't erase it. She merely smiled and nodded and asked another question.

But, nevertheless, Archilde enjoyed talking to Madame Ernest. They continued their conversation for almost two hours along the same lines. In the end they felt an even more friendly regard for each other and drank a cup of tea together. And when he went away, he carried a shawl and a handsome scarf to add to the collection in his room.

He sat in the little lounge on the first floor of his hotel and waited for dinnertime. He was too weary to go and sit in a café, although he had sensed that everyone did it just before dinner. He sat and read a book of history and found it, as he found all history, too annoying for words. He was inclined to pass it all off as fairy tales, but finally it stuck in his head that he was learning of actual happenings in the past. He read a book of history as most people would read a novel—with breathless excitement and complete absorption.

One question he always asked himself after reading a history of one of the French kings or of a certain episode in the life of a nation: why did they make so many mistakes? Or the same ones over and over? And if the man who wrote the history is smart enough to pick out their errors one by one and explain how they could have been avoided—why couldn't the king do the same? Often he ended up by chucking the book away. It didn't seem reasonable that a historian should be smarter than all the men before his time.

As he sat there reading, a young American came up from the street and stopped in the lounge to read a New York paper. He was a striking young man, and Archilde had watched him secretly but with the greatest interest for several weeks. He had a long, narrow face with a high forehead and full, round crown with short-cropped hair. His room was on the next floor above, and he spent almost the entire day playing the piano. Archilde marveled that anyone could keep at it so long. At some time or other he had heard genius discussed, and he was certain that this young fellow was a genius if there ever was one.

Sometimes—almost every day in fact, a young, dark, vivacious girl came to see him and they went into his room and after that the piano would thump continually for several hours, and then he would come out with his overcoat on and they would go for tea. This girl was just as attractive—perhaps even more—although she had none of the oddities of a genius. The interesting thing about her was her unbounded energy and spirit.

Archilde never saw this young man without thinking at once of the girl. They seemed to be very close friends and this in itself made him feel warm toward them. He enjoyed their friendship as if he shared it with them.

As he sat there pretending to read, he watched the young fellow through the corner of his eyes and noted each detail of his dress and actions. He appeared nervous and impressionable, and as he read his paper, his brow was continually frowning and clearing again.

Archilde longed to go forward and start a conversation. There were any of a dozen ways in which he might do it; he might ask for the time and pretend that his watch had stopped, or he might inquire when a certain boat would dock—but all these plans, simple as they were, seemed fantastic and rude. He buried himself in his book and put the thought out of his head.

In a few minutes the young man jumped up and went to his room, throwing the paper on the table as he left. He had left the door to his room open and he could be heard whistling. All at once a massive, voluminous sound poured from his piano, but it lasted for only a second and ended in a crash. A moment later the young man was dashing downstairs with a raincoat over his arm.

Archilde picked up the discarded newspaper and much to his surprise found the young man's picture on the music page. Beneath the picture was a short notice stating that the promising young American pianist, Mitchell Feure, would make his debut in the spring at the Salle Gaveau. Archilde felt excited and was more certain than ever that anybody with such a long head must be a genius.

As he walked to his restaurant, his thoughts were taken up entirely with the young pianist. There were dozens of things that he was curious about, and he knew without any doubt that here, at last, was a friend. Somehow he must meet him. He imagined the conversations they would have and the things they would do together. He needed a friend for he realized that he was living on the outermost border of things. He was seeing or doing nothing and inside he felt completely blank and barren.

He himself was aware that this was an unusual condition. Never at any time in his life had he felt the need of cultivating friendships. He had never been curious about his associates, and he either spoke or refrained from speaking to them according to his desire at the moment. But something of a change had come over him, and he felt unaccountably dependent and uncertain. He did not always understand what he saw going on around him, and he wanted to ask somebody in order to have his confidence restored. He felt in the full sense of the word that he was a stranger.

His head was full of these thoughts and reflections as he walked through the dark Rue de Vangirard. The Rue de Vangirard is a rather narrow and twisting little street and after sundown it becomes quiet and deserted. From the boulevards a short distance away there came the faint sound of the rush of traffic with its bleating of horns and roaring of motors. In his preoccupation he heard nothing except at intervals.

There was no rain, but the air itself was laden with damp vapor. When he looked against a streetlamp, he could see a blur of mist. It was not particularly cold but yet the air was disagreeable. The pavement was sloppy.

He had just passed the Odeon and was walking down the short hill toward Saint-Michel when a dark, slender figure stepped out of a corner and stopped immediately in front of him. Simultaneously he felt a hand grip his arm tightly.

For the first moment or two he felt a thrill of fear and a burning sensation seized his chest. He had often considered the possibility of being held up and robbed in this dark street. Just then the figure looked up in such a way that a glimmer of light fell upon the face, and Archilde saw that it was a girl.

"I am hungry," she said.

In the faint light her face looked pale and thin. Her eyes were lost in shadows and her cheeks appeared hollow.

"Really?" Archilde exclaimed and for a moment said nothing more. Her hand tightened slightly on his arm as if she were again telling him of her hunger. It was an intimate, appealing gesture.

"Here, I have a ten-franc note. Is that enough?"

"Let me go eat with monsieur! I would like that better. I have not eaten today."

"Well, all right." At first he was uncertain and hesitant but that passed and a vague excitement began to stir his blood. Here, at last, he thought, was that chance acquaintance, that unexpected meeting that would give him the friend he wanted. Not for a moment did he consider the significance of her approach. He was only excited and pleased to think that at last someone had stepped forward as he had wished but had been too timid to do. He wanted to see her face and figure in the light. It did not once occur to him that she would be anything but attractive. It could not be otherwise.

"You say you have not eaten today?" he asked.

"Nothing at all." She went on to say something about the injustice of everything and how miserable she was, but her speech was so explosive and run together that Archilde could not follow and he merely said, "Yes, yes. That is true."

He did not go to his customary eating place; for once he would escape the fat madame in her faded brown sweater. Tonight he could laugh at her and feel that she did not exist! They walked down the boulevard farther and came to a place that was not so noisy and not so rushed. The food was not of the best, he had learned, but it would suffice.

They entered, and as he stood holding the door open for her, he looked at her for the first time.

Once she had been young—but no longer. Once she may have had a certain beauty—but that was gone. As Archilde looked, he could feel himself turn pale; he was stupefied. He let the door go and it almost slammed against her.

The thought occurred to him to press money into her hands and leave her, but it seemed to be too late. She had walked farther into the room and he could not reach her without being noticed. Moreover, his body seemed to be out of control of his mind; he was thinking continually, but his legs carried him forward unwittingly. In another moment they were seated at a table and she was talking rapidly and smiling. He couldn't understand a word.

People looked and laughed, comments ran from table to table—or so it seemed to Archilde. He was sure everybody was looking. He looked at the bill of fare and the words jumped up and down. His companion was not unknown, and she nodded once or twice to other tables and kept turning around to see or be seen by anyone else she knew.

She wasn't actually a wretch and another person might have passed it off as a joke and made a real farce of it, but Archilde was too miserable even to look up. From a mood of high expectation he had passed into wretched embarrassment.

Her name was Vivette, she told him. That was the name that her best friends knew her by.

"Do you not pass through the Rue de Vangirard every night at the same hour? I thought so. I have seen you many times."

He became fascinated by her mouth. It was extremely large and the scarlet rouge she used emphasized its width. The lips were not thick, but they were loose and flabby. When she laughed, she opened her mouth wide.

It was evident that she had been dyeing her hair for many years; it was two or three different colors at once. The ends were a pale straw, almost an ashen color, but nearer the roots it was dark, in places it even looked purple. There were heavy wrinkles in her face and under her chin and her skin had the appearance of chalk. Rouge was smeared on heavily and unevenly. She had a thin, scrawny neck and her chest was flat.

"I have watched you often through my window and knew that you were a fine fellow. But I was always engaged and could not come down to meet you. Tonight I said, 'I will wait and speak to him!' But you are a quiet bird. You are an American, are you not? Good! The Americans are fine! But those English! Pugh! They want too much! Here is the wine. Pour some. Ah, no—you pour it like an Englishman. A drop in your glass first—that is the French way. Well, it makes no difference—only fill mine well. I thank you. What a fine fellow you are!"

She jabbered incessantly, and he was glad that it was unnecessary to answer her. Gradually his embarrassment left and anger came in its place. He looked at her sullenly and contemptuously. He no longer avoided the waitress's eyes nor flushed when she came near. But he made no protests nor did he attempt to leave. When Vivette ordered a second bottle of wine, he said nothing. He ate very little and for the most part sat staring into space.

He left the restaurant in a stupor. He didn't even remember how much the meal had cost nor did he observe that Vivette had taken the five-franc note he had left as a tip. The waitress noticed it however and was cursing when they went out.

Vivette tugged at his arm when they were in the street and wanted to go to a café, but he was sufficiently alert to refuse.

"Ah well," she said, "we can send the porter for a bottle," and hugging tightly to his arm, she led him up the street.

As he went up the stairway in her squalid little hotel, he kept repeating to himself: "What am I doing this for? Am I crazy? Where am I going?" But still he did not protest, and he was no longer conscious of anger. He understood nothing. He was conscious of nothing. She was still hugging his arm, but he was not thinking of her; he felt the pressure on his arm, but it meant no more than the weight of his coat on his shoulders. He could not understand why he was climbing this dark stairway.

In her room he sat down in a chair and did not even take off his overcoat. She had turned the gas flame a little higher and in the dim light she danced around the room, dropping her coat here, her hat there, and unfastening her dress. She rang a bell and through her half-opened door ordered a package of "American cigarettes" and a bottle of cognac.

"The gentleman will leave the money with me."

There was a protest from the other side, but she slammed the door.

"Now, has Mr. Goodfellow a few francs, perhaps?" She crept to him softly and reached for his inside pocket, but he pushed her away. She whined and approached him again.

"Get away!" he said.

She stamped her foot and called him a name, but in a moment she changed her tactics again. She slipped off her dress and paraded back and forth and paced. Again she crept forward and then moved away quickly. He didn't stir. Someone tapped at her door and she reached through to get the cigarettes and bottle, but she was greeted by a girl's voice:

"The concierge says he should have his money before I give them to you."

"Stupid! I will come down in ten minutes!"

The girl walked away without leaving the things and Vivette was in a rage. She walked to Archilde and kicked his leg.

"Fool, give me some money for cigarettes and a drink!"

He looked at her without replying. Finally, he got to his feet and started for the door.

"What are you doing?" she cried.

"I'm going home. Get away!"

"You blockhead! Do you think you will cheat me? I shall ring for the concierge, and he'll drag you before the prefect. So this is the kind of a cheapskate you are!" She was standing at the door with her hand poised over the bell.

"If you come near, I shall ring!" she screamed.

He stood eyeing her uncertainly, and presently he began to feel his anger returning. His senses were clearing and for the first time he realized what had happened. He reached forward suddenly and grabbed her.

The Hungry Generations | 165

In the same movement he gave her arm such a vicious jerk that she went flying across the room and fell against the bed. The next moment she had reached under the bed and hurled a pot at him. It crashed against the wall near his head.

"Enough!" he said and felt sick. He realized what a fool he was. He took a hundred-franc note from his pocketbook and threw it on the floor. He turned and went downstairs.

As he was going through the street, he heard the window open and he was called a dirty name. This was followed by a mocking laugh and then the window was slammed shut.

It was raining again. He passed figures that were heavily muffled and walked with heads inclined to the storm. Never had anything seemed so miserable. He thought of looking for a taxi but remembered in time that he had no more money with him.

He went to bed with a hopeless, dejected feeling. It seemed as if the last spark were gone. For the first time he asked himself what he was doing here. For a moment he was amazed that he hadn't asked the question before. And then he fell asleep.

Chapter Three

That night he had an ugly dream.
He was walking through a street and saw an old woman standing against a wall begging. He wanted to cross the street and avoid meeting her, but for some reason he was impelled to continue until he was quite near. Then she looked up.

She was a miserable creature, dressed in a ragged and faded brown coat that fell to her ankles. On her feet were a pair of men's shoes, large and split open at the toe. Her hair was gray and yellow and hung about her face in strings. He looked at her hand extended toward him and saw that it was caked with dirt and cracked open in places; the fingernails were discolored and broken off. Then he looked at her face and was shocked. Her eyes were only half open, and they watered so profusely that it must have been impossible for her to see. Her cheeks were black; it seemed as if the dirt had become ingrained in the pores, as if she were tattooed. Her mouth was wide and her lips purple in color. Out of her upper lip there protruded a single brown tooth. He stopped before her, fascinated, and could not move.

She smiled and spoke to him and then he realized that she was his mother.

He jumped out of bed and turned on the light with the picture still before his eyes. He sat on the edge of his bed and stared at the floor. Horror and fear were still in his mind, and he was aware that his heart was beating wildly. He went to the window and looked into the pitch-black night.

At first he could not hear a single sound and then far away a trolley rumbled through a street. For some reason that sound made everything normal again; he realized where he was and he smiled at himself.

He sat down and wrote a short note to the Indian agent:

"Don't forget to keep me posted on everything at home. Let me know how Mike and Narcisse are doing in school. Everything is fine with me, but I haven't decided yet what I'm going to do."

He couldn't understand why he had written that last sentence, and he sat for a long time analyzing his thoughts. In the end he tore up the letter and went back to bed.

As he lay in bed he could not go to sleep again, indeed it seemed as if sleep were impossible. His mind kept turning over and over and he realized at last what he was thinking. He was preparing another letter to the agent. Usually, he wrote only a short note of not over a hundred or at the most two hundred words, but for once he would write an honest to goodness letter. He would explain all about himself and then, when it was all down, he would see things more clearly. He would begin like this:

My dear friend Parker:
I sincerely wish that I could talk with you. It seems, as I look back, that I have never talked with anyone in my life except once—that was with my father just before he became sick. In fact, he probably died because of that talk. He already had a chill when I came home from jail and we sat until two o'clock in the morning. We went to bed then, but he never got up again. The next day he was delirious. Even that talk, however, was only an introduction, as I realize. We did not know each other at all before that night. If you knew my father, which of course you did, you understand me. We had always been strangers.

But there was another time that still means a great deal to me—although I can't exactly say that it was a "talk," since I did none of the talking. That was the very same day in your office when you told me a thing or two. I hadn't known you before either. As a matter of fact, I knew no one before that day. You spoke to me in a way that made me glow for the first time with what we recognize as understanding. Perhaps others had spoken to me before with the same seriousness, and I had never listened or hadn't been stirred. On the other hand, I am inclined to think that speech had never been put to such a use in my hearing. This is a long preliminary, but I want especially to emphasize that point. I have, as it were, been born only recently.

If we were sitting here together tonight, there are some things I would like to tell you and I would ask you what you thought.

For instance. Once, when I was in school at Chemawa, I went with two other boys to steal some turnips in a farmer's field. That wasn't the intention we set out with, of course. We were merely walking along the road one afternoon in February. The ground was frozen, I remember, and there was a mild frost in the air. We came to this farmer's field and saw the turnips. The first thought that came to us, naturally, was to jump the fence and pull a turnip and this we did. They were the best turnips I have ever eaten. They had been in the ground all fall and winter and the frost had probably been in them for several months continuously. The effect of the frost was to make them remarkably sweet and tender. I don't know how many we ate, but it must have been a lot, and when we had our fill, we climbed over the fence again with our pockets stuffed. We started down the road again, but we had scarcely gone fifty yards when a young man appeared in the road just ahead of us, and he came up with a pleasant smile and began to talk, asking us our names and where we came from and so on. He was so pleasant that we felt quite happy to think he had even cared to notice us.

Presently, however, we found ourselves in a trap. We happened to look in the other direction and there came the old farmer himself with a long buggy whip in his hand. He had rheumatism and couldn't walk fast, so he had sent his son ahead to hold us until he arrived.

Well, the old farmer marched us back to school, cursing

at us with every step he took. We could easily have bolted and escaped into the timber growing along the road, but somehow he had managed to frighten us to death and we didn't dare.

When he brought us to the disciplinarian's office, he said, "Take these damn Indians and give them a beating that will learn them to respect other people's property. I have never seen an Indian that wasn't a thief, and if you care to make something of these fellows, I think that's the place you can begin. Make 'em learn what another man's property means!"

The disciplinarian, who was a kindhearted man, in spite of his severe military manner, took us into his room and talked to us for a long time about right and wrong and succeeded in making me feel sad and worthless. In the end he gave us each six blows with a strap, more from habit than anything else for all three of us were crying before he even touched us.

The incident is trivial and what the farmer said about Indians is unimportant. But what still riles my blood is the manner in which he executed his "justice." He sent his son to head us off and put on as pleasant a manner as possible in order to deceive us and keep us there until he, the offended Righteousness, should arrive to take us in hand. That, it always seems to me, was a cowardly and unmanly thing to do. I have the primitive notion that justice, to be right, should be absolute. It should not resort to trickery on one hand to accomplish an object in the other hand. There should be nothing two-faced about it.

And that brings me to my point: Is my conception *primitive*? The more I see and understand the more I think it must be.

But that is not all ...

At that point, however, his mind stuck. He could not find the words to express exactly what he meant. He lay tossing to and fro in bed and several times got up to smoke a cigarette and stare through his open window into the black night. He was in a kind of frenzy and he became filled with impatience and nervousness when he could not see exactly what he meant to say. He wanted to express in words the discrepancies he found between men's actions and their principles or ideals, but it was all vague and incoherent.

He was aware, of course, that he was not planning an actual letter. Men never wrote such letters to one another. Why, he did not know, but he could imagine the agent being startled out of his wits if he should receive such a document. That was one of the discrepancies. Nevertheless, he went on pretending. His mind refused to stop, as a matter of fact. Just as soon as he got back into bed he started again. He could see the words written on a piece of paper exactly as he thought them.

I wrote you another letter earlier in the evening but tore it up later because it was vague and untruthful. I had said that I was happy and that everything was going well with me. But that is not so. I am both uncomfortable and unhappy here. Why, I do not know exactly, but I suspect that it started while I was in college these past two years. There are some questions that puzzle me continually.

I would like to know how far I am behind the other young fellows of my age. Such a thought never occurred to me at home, naturally, I suppose. There I lived for myself and the few friends I had thought I was a good fellow and Mike and Narcisse were always pleased with me. In the end my father came to like me too and that seemed to complete it. But, as soon as I came away, things changed. In college people were talking about things I had never heard of or even imagined. It was as if I were looking through a peephole into another world. It frightened me, I tell you, and gave me chills. It seemed that, if I buried myself in books and studied until my eyes popped out, I would still be twenty years behind those fellows. But everybody was nice. When I asked the professor questions that stunned the other fellows because of their simpleness no one laughed. After class the professor would call me into his office and ask about my early life. Naturally, I couldn't tell him much. I couldn't talk to him as I am talking to you in this letter.

After two years I couldn't stand anymore. It seemed that

The Hungry Generations | 171

the further I went the more hopeless it became. I could see
unlimited spaces all around me, like in a huge cave, and I was
at the very tail end of the exploring party. Far away I could see
a light flickering against the walls and I could hear the people
exclaiming and running to look at things—but, when I arrived,
they had gone on ahead and it was dark again. That was the
way it struck me and at last I got very discouraged. I decided to
try it somewhere else. I had heard everybody talking about
Europe—Paris especially. They fairly went into ecstasies over
the word "Paris." It seemed to represent the peak of the world.
Well, I decided to come to Paris. Possibly, I thought, a plunge
in the real thing will hasten things along—like people go to hot
springs at home to get cured of rheumatism all at once.

So here I am, soon it will be five months; that's not long,
I realize, but would you believe it. I haven't met a soul yet!
That's my fault because one of the things I lack, and which
most of the young fellows at college all had, was the courage
or the habit of going up to people and somehow striking up an
acquaintance. That, I can't do. I move around like a lost calf
on the range. I don't know, I have a notion to give up again.

But I haven't expressed half of it. I can't begin to make
you see all these things as they occur to me. I continually lose
myself in a mass of trivial details and lose sight of the thought
I am pursuing. I have even forgotten the questions I was going
to ask you. I must decide something about all this; I can't go on
flopping around like a chicken without its head.

After that he lost the trend entirely. His mind was continually going
back to some thought he had previously reviewed and stating it again
and again until it had lost all sense and he no longer remembered where
it belonged in the letter or what it meant. He had discovered that the
more he said the more that was necessary to say. He had thought for
once to examine his ideas and express them exactly as he felt and
understood them. He wanted to say everything there was to say, but
before long, he found that he was following an indefinite path that led
nowhere at all and ended in confusion.

When he looked out of the window again, the daylight had come and suddenly he felt exhausted. In another minute his body had relaxed and he was sound asleep.

It was no longer raining and the sky was beginning to clear. A cool breeze entered the opened windows and swayed the curtains to and fro.

He had scarcely been asleep five minutes, it seemed, when the garçon came with his cup of chocolate and roll of bread.

"Thank you," Archilde said drowsily, and before the garçon reached the door, he had fallen asleep again.

Chapter Four

He was sitting in the lounge on the first floor later in the afternoon. He had not gone out for lunch but had merely taken a walk. It was bright outside, although there was not a direct sun. Down in the street he could hear heavy drays and trolley cars passing and all the daytime traffic. A vendor was going through the street calling something unintelligible, and gradually his voice was lost among the other sounds.

The piano on the next floor above was silent, so he guessed that the young man with the long head was out. Downstairs the madame was talking in her excited, whining voice to Juliette, the girl at the desk. Archilde always had difficulty getting past Juliette. Every day she called out:

"Ah, there you are, Monsieur Leon! I have watched for you all morning and thought perhaps you had taken a notion to sleep all day. My goodness! How you sleep! But perhaps your dreams are pleasant—is it so?" She would pretend to blush and her heavy breasts would shake with her suppressed laughter.

She couldn't get over that he had taken her to the theater once; he realized that he had made a mistake. She was sure that he had found another "mademoiselle" whom he was taking instead, and she could never miss an opportunity to allude to it. But she had no rancor—she always appeared jolly and tried to make a joke out of everything.

He could hear her chattering with the madame and every moment he expected her to come upstairs. He buried his head in his history and

173

determined that if she should come up, he would pretend not to see her. Maybe she would have sense enough not to disturb him.

He had been reading assiduously for perhaps half an hour when suddenly he happened to look over the top of his book and saw a pair of shoes. It wasn't Juliette, he knew at once, for they were a man's shoes. He looked up in considerable surprise, and there was the young pianist from upstairs gazing at him. Archilde was too confused to speak and he wondered vaguely if he should get up.

They must have been looking at each other in silence for half a minute when suddenly the young man took a step forward and spoke; as he did so he smiled.

"Are you the fellow who plays the violin so beautifully every day?"

"What—? You must be mistaken."

"Oh!" the young man said and his face became utterly blank. "You must excuse me for intruding then. You see, I have heard that violin every day and often I sit with my door open to hear better, but it is two floors above, you know, and I could never determine just what room it came from. But just now, as I was walking home, it suddenly struck me in a flash that you must be the one. Do you know who it is then who plays on the fourth floor?" He was preparing to leave, his interest having been lost.

"Well, no," Archilde said and floundered. "I don't know if there is anyone else in the house—"

The young man returned quickly and he was smiling again.

"That's what I thought—so you *are* the one! Well, that's grand. I had just determined that you must be the one. And so it is true then! Listen come upstairs—no, let me introduce myself first—I am Mitchell Feure—a pianist of no account whatever—if you would believe my friends. But you, I assure you, are a musician. Haven't I listened for weeks now? It is always the same—you seem to have no bad days. Every morning when you tune up I say, 'There he goes!' and after that I cannot practice anymore—I swear. Come upstairs—listen, will you play for me? What is your name—but I haven't given you a chance to say—I am talking like a lunatic—excuse me!"

Archilde had become intoxicated with the young man's words and he was bewildered. Waves of intense pleasure kept sweeping over him,

The Hungry Generations | 175

but each one was followed by an equally poignant wave of doubt. He hardly knew what to say.

"My name is Archilde Leon—but you must be mistaken about the fiddle—I only play a little."

"But you admit that you live on the fourth floor—and no one else plays in the house—am I right? Then there is no mistake. Come upstairs. Listen. I have just taken over a trio—Rachmaninoff's—do you know it? I just got the music last week and I must have it ready for the spring but I have scarcely looked at it. Will you bring your violin and read it through with me? There is a cello too—but never mind that. Will you do it? Then we'll have tea. Archilde Leon—that's exactly the name you should have."

Feure was talking in great nervous outbursts, such as Archilde had never heard anyone but a Frenchman do. They climbed the stairway side by side, and although Archilde said nothing and could think of nothing, his silence was unnoticed. Feure talked for both and didn't seem able to express everything as it was. On the second floor they paused while Feure finished what he had on his chest at the moment, and then Archilde went upstairs for his violin. He climbed the steps in a dream, and it seemed absolutely unbelievable that the young man whom he had been admiring and wishing to meet for so long had actually come forward of *his own accord* and offered his friendship. And in addition, to be praised by that very same young man was too unreal for words. He picked up his violin case with hesitation and took out the instrument with deliberation and care. He turned it over and looked at it as if for the first time. He plucked the E string with his finger, and he could hear the sound throbbing in his ear long after it had become inaudible. Archilde had never been told by anyone that he could play. His teachers had never said anything—except when he came with a poor lesson. Now for the first time, as he stood there alone for a moment, he began to doubt the young pianist. What did he know about violin playing? Perhaps it would come to nothing after all, this "friendship," he thought. When he went downstairs, he was calmer and more sure of himself.

Feure had stopped talking now. He was sitting at the piano examining the introductory chords. His nervousness and effusiveness had left him. Archilde noticed for the first time what large bony hands he had; they were steady and looked as strong as strips of steel. Archilde took his violin out of its case and tuned it. Feure watched him with the greatest attention while he was doing this, only striking the fifths occasionally but all the time with his eyes on Archilde.

"Look," he said, "here's the theme." He played a measure, "Do you get it? Then here you come in—ta-ta-da-de-da. Do you follow?"

Archilde read the piece with no difficulty. He seemed indeed to have a surer instinct for the time and harmony than Feure, although he would never have admitted it even to himself.

"But it is a band piece," Archilde said suddenly when they had gone only partway. "Even the cello will not fill it out; it is a skeleton."

"Exactly!" Feure said and clapped his hands together. "Exactly! Have you heard it performed? No? I have and it is a very weak piece I admit. But this is the way it comes about. My teacher will hear of nothing but Rachmaninoff. So naturally this is the piece that we are to prepare. Tell me, have you done any orchestra work?"

"Yes. I played both in a small orchestra and in a string quartet."

"I thought so. That is why you pick it out so quickly—the defects I mean. You read remarkably well, I must say! But it is as I thought. Come, let's do this last part. There are some better effects."

Later Feure made tea on his alcohol stove and again his tongue was loosened and he talked continually. But Archilde no longer mistrusted his enthusiasms; they were spontaneous and as free as the air. Language with Feure became something different again—it was neither the expression of ideas nor the portraying of a character—it was simply the bubbling up of an ecstatic nature always seeking activity and display. Archilde found it easy and pleasant to relax while that flow of speech flooded the room as with a ray of sun. It wasn't necessary to speak often for each time he did he merely urged Feure on to greater lengths.

"You are from Montana, you say? But where is that for the Lord's sake! I thought I had come from the end of the world myself—can you imagine where—Nebraska! When I tell a Frenchman that he says—'Yes—can it be possible? And is it really in America? What a big country that must be!' But Montana is even worse. Isn't that near—well, of course not! I was going to say the Arctic Ocean—but I meant Canada. But how did you ever learn to play the violin out there? Were your parents musicians? Did you have teachers?"

The Hungry Generations | 177

"No—" Archilde said with an amused smile. He was stretched out on a couch. "No. I played at country dances first. An old fiddler showed me how to make a tune. It wasn't until a long time later that I had a teacher."

Feure looked stunned. He actually stopped with the teapot in his hand in the act of filling the cups and looked at Archilde.

"No! Is that the truth? But I don't see how it is possible! I have been studying continually since I was nine or ten—almost continually, that is. Several years I was too sick to play. But do you mean to tell me that you just picked it up by yourself and had no instructions at the beginning? Well, that's marvelous! I don't understand it. How many years have you been studying then, for the Lord's sake?"

Archilde considered. "Not more than five years altogether and that was not all at one time. There were no teachers around home," he added and was amused again.

Feure repeated again and again that he could not understand. But presently he was off on another subject and he seemed to have forgotten his surprise of a moment before. One subject led to another with him and as soon as he dropped one idea it seemed to go out of his head entirely. He swung to another with the same earnestness and energy, and before long, he would drop that too. He had the faculty of making everything appear out of the ordinary and full of interest—while he was discussing it—but as soon as he had finished, it immediately became the dullest thing in the world.

Gradually the afternoon had slipped away and with surprise they both looked out and saw that evening had come.

"Well, look at that!" Feure cried. "Can it be possible that it is night already?" He went to the window and opened it that he might see the street. "Why, even the streetlights have been turned on!

"Where do you eat dinner?" he asked Archilde, turning back into the room.

"At a terrible place. I'm never going back."

"Good! Then you can come with me. I know a splendid restaurant. Will you come?"

Archilde accepted the invitation eagerly.

After dinner they stopped at a café for coffee. It was one of the liveliest and noisiest cafés on the Boulevard du Montparnasse, and Archilde had often walked past it during the evenings imagining that he was seated at one of the gay tables sharing in the careless talk and laughter. Now, as he followed Feure between the crowded tables looking for vacant seats, he appeared perfectly at ease and scarcely looked up at all. Feure knew almost everyone and he called out repeatedly as he passed along. As soon as they were seated, he leaned toward Archilde and began pointing out various persons and explaining everything about them down to the minutest detail of personal habit. Here was a young American heiress with no sense whatever; she thought herself a wonderful artist and kept a crowd around her all the time who were continually raving and applauding her muddy-looking canvases. Nearer at hand was a young Jew who sponged off everybody and was a perfect beast. Yonder was a young Cuban who claimed to be Spanish royal blood; he was the greatest liar in the *quatre* and people invited him to parties and gave him money just to listen to his outlandish lies and laugh in his face. Farther over was a half-wit who laughed and smiled all the time, and when he talked, the spit dripped out of his mouth. Next was no other than [?] Bess herself—past fifty now, born in Michigan, been in Europe for at least thirty years and a perfect—well, you know what; nobody in the world could tell such filthy stories! And so on and on. He knew a little bit about everybody. He was a perfect gossip. Archilde was amazed and disgusted and entertained; he had no desire to interrupt.

"Tell me," he said suddenly leaning forward and assuming a matter-of-fact tone, "who is the girl who comes with you to the hotel sometimes?. . . Does she ever come to the café here?"

"Claudia, you mean? The girl with dark hair? Yes, that is Claudia. I meant to tell you—she is extremely interested in you. Yes, that's the truth. You are usually sitting in that little lounge reading a book when we come in, and every time she never fails to say—'I wonder who that dark fellow is? He must be brilliant.' Yes. That's the truth! I tell you—shall we go and visit her tonight? That's exactly what we must do! Do you care to? She will be delighted, I'm sure."

"Good! Let's do that!" Archilde said, but a moment later he had another thought. "Maybe she has other guests—or perhaps she is planning to do something else."

The Hungry Generations | 179

"No," Feure said and he was already on his feet, putting down some money for their coffee. "No—they don't have much company— she lives with her family. I must tell you about her family—they're all marvelous. Listen—"

They left the café and were walking down the street, Feure in great excitement.

"Just think of it! She has two brothers who play the piano—and already they have won names for themselves. The oldest boy, Vincent, won the prize at the academy last year—he is studying at Fontainebleu now. But the young fellow—who is only sixteen—may be even better. Every time he plays he is praised to the skies. He composes also and already his pieces have been recognized. You'll enjoy them immensely."

"Is the girl a musician as well?" Archilde asked wonderingly.

"Claudia!—no. She is a poet. Can you imagine! She has had a book published I think. Isn't that a family for you! But wait and see for yourself. Perhaps we can get Vincent to play, although it is improbable. He rarely plays for anyone outside of his practice hours! They have two grand pianos in their flat and they had to pad the walls to quiet the sound. When those two get to going at the same time, they can certainly make a noise! I really believe that Albert, he is the youngest, will make the greatest name. It is certainly remarkable."

Feure talked continually every step of the way. Very little of what he said was of any value or interest, but Archilde was not measuring and weighing the words. Everything sounded equally delightful, and he had no desire whatever to interrupt the chatter or try to get his companion into a more serious discussion. Nothing was serious anymore. His memory was a blank—he could no longer recall what the past months had been like. He was walking toward something *new*. It was all different. He didn't know what it would be—he wasn't even sure that this *new* thing would be enjoyable—but the anticipation made him glow and smile to himself.

They were walking toward Les Invalides and at night this was a strange part of the city to Archilde. He didn't understand how Feure picked his way so assuredly, often passing through narrow, dark streets without even glancing up to see where they were. It had not rained all day and the streets were actually dry. The damp smell had also disappeared and the night air was positively invigorating. Stars were out and the steep roofs and chimney pots stood out clearly. "Never," thought Archilde, "has it been like this before! This is more like it! Now we've got something to talk about!"

"It's up here in one of these crazy little streets. They have an entire flat to themselves. Their father is a sort of invalid and rarely shows himself. He is very thin and tall, and I guess they have difficulty with him. But wait and see for yourself. Claudia will be delighted. You're bashful, aren't you?" he said suddenly and pressed his arm.

"Why—what makes you think so?" Archilde asked with surprise and embarrassment.

"Well, I don't know—you just are. I've often wondered why you didn't try to get acquainted around—if you had even looked up one of those times at the hotel there—I would have come right up and said hello. But you always held me off. And it's a shame—you're so remarkable. But listen—don't be bashful with Claudia. Go right up to her and start talking, that's what she likes." He still had Archilde's arm and they walked closely together.

"So you think me bashful? Well, that's not strange. I haven't met many people, you see, and I have to learn how."

"No! Is that true?" he squeezed Archilde's arm. "You must be a strange person. Will you tell me about yourself—soon? Yes? Well, here we are!"

Chapter Five

The most remarkable thing about the room was its high windows on two sides; they were draped with heavy red cloth. The furnishing was meager and simple. There was a fireplace with a tall, narrow mirror above it; in the grate a heap of coals glowed dully. There was a lounge before one of the windows—near the fireplace there was another lounge and several large chairs. Next to the hall door there were some bookshelves overflowing with books; some were lying on the floor nearby. Excepting a small table near the other window that was also covered with books, there was nothing else in the room, which was quite large. Indeed, it had once been part of the ballroom and was only recently partitioned off into a living room; this was made apparent by the interrupted design on the ceiling and also by the fact that the fireplace was not in the center of the wall.

Archilde was sitting on the lounge near the fireplace, and Claudia was watching him with alert eyes from her chair nearby. Feure was in a conversation with Vincent while Albert, the youngest brother, was reading a book off by himself.

"To tell you the truth," Archilde was answering a question from Claudia, "I have found nothing interesting here. But it's largely my fault, I suppose. I have not known where to look."

"Well, my first impressions were certainly different," she said and smiled. Her face had an expression of calmness, and when she smiled, it became extremely friendly and pleasant. Her eyes were bright and intelligent and gray in color. She had long brown hair that was braided and wrapped around her head. She wore a white woolen dress without a single ornament anywhere about her person. She appeared capable and well balanced and her figure gave assurance of vitality and eagerness. She seemed interested in everything and she talked with a quick, engaging manner.

"I admit now," she continued, still smiling, "that most of my first enthusiasms were sheer sentimentality and had no basis in my real feelings. I had read and heard so much about Paris—everyone does, of course, and I suppose nearly everyone loses his head about silly meaningless things. So I am surprised—and interested—to hear you speak so coolly. Tell me, what did you come for?"

Archilde reflected and found this a hard question to answer, though it was clear enough to himself. Before he could utter a word, however, she interrupted.

"But that is a stupid question. Obviously you came to study violin."

"No. That was what you might call an afterthought. Feure makes too much of my violin playing. Already he is calling me an artist—but he doesn't understand. I am only a beginner in these things. I came to study history and literature like a schoolboy."

She looked at him only half believing his words. She couldn't decide whether he was seriously belittling his own ability or whether he was being insincere and merely amusing himself.

"I see you reading every time I visit Mitchell at the hotel and I thought you were probably interested in a lot of things. Is it true then that you are really studying by yourself? Have you been to college? Pardon my asking so many questions, but every time I see you at the hotel you make me insanely curious. Do you object?"

Archilde didn't object at all. "Yes, I was in college for two years, but it was too learned for me. I didn't know anything—so I decided to go off and study by myself. Now I seem to know less than ever."

She was sure by now that he was putting her off by answering facetiously. Her manner became a little cooler. He appeared to her to be a person inordinately sure of himself and who took pleasure in deprecating his qualities—perhaps for the sake of having others praise him the more warmly. "But am I right?" she kept asking herself. "Isn't he a better person than that?"

"Tell me one thing more," she said, "and then I will leave you in peace. Why are you studying? Are you interested in anything in particular, I mean?"

"I am studying because I never had a chance to before. No, that's not quite it. I hadn't thought much about it before. I was doing other things at home and when I traveled around. But you won't understand this until I tell you a lot of other things—sometime I would like to—if you would be interested."

"Good—that will be a promise! But were you playing the violin at home?"

"No," Archilde said, shaking his head. "I suppose my home was different. Feure has been telling me about you and your brothers—well, my family was quite different."

"Perhaps you are like Michel, then. Let me tell you what his family is like—then you say if yours is the same."

"Do you call him Michel?"

"Yes. He detests Mitchell—so we call him Michel. Listen. Do you know Omaha? It is perfectly terrible; they have stockyards and vile smells. Michel's father died when he was young. His mother is very poor and an invalid, so she can do nothing. But he has a wealthy aunt who is president of the Women's Club and a prominent social worker and society leader. She goes into raptures over poor Michel and declares that he will become the greatest pianist in America. Can you imagine it? He hates her and sometimes he gets depressed, in fact quite sick, because she is supporting him. But he would rather be supported by her and be here in Paris than be living at home where she would be supporting him just the same—at least his mother—and always be making over him. She doesn't want him to work, you see, for fear that he will sacrifice his future—and poor Michel's mother whom he thinks the world of—takes the aunt's part and he always gives in. Now tell me, is your family like that?"

"No—" Archilde said and shook his head slowly.

"Well don't you think," she said in a different tone, "that all families are *different*?"

He looked at her in amazement. Her voice had become cold and haughty. She spoke as if she were finishing an argument and had brought it to a sudden full stop by putting forward a final, unanswerable declaration. He tried to understand what she was thinking and why her attitude had changed.

He didn't have an opportunity to answer for at that moment Vincent came forward and offered his hand.

"I am sorry, but I must leave. I am half an hour late in fact. I hope we will see you often, Leon. Feure thinks there's no one in Paris like you. May I ask with whom you are studying?"

"An old fellow near the opera. Adolf Mercer. Do you know him?"

This announcement met with silence. Feure, Claudia, and Vincent looked at one another and said nothing.

"Why, he's a damned old thief!" Albert blurted out and everybody turned to the young brother who was sitting near the small table in the corner of the room reading. He had his face in his book again and paid no more attention. The rest of them found their tongues.

"Why didn't you say something before?" Feure asked. "No, you can't do that anymore. We've got to get you started right. Who is the violin man?"

"The German, Ritter," Claudia said.

"What!" The young brother broke out again. "He's as dry as sawdust! The best man is in Berlin but go to Cherabov—he's Old Faithful."

"Yes, I think he's right," Vincent added. He had returned to the room with his hat and coat. "Well, I must go. Come and see us Leon. Goodnight."

Feure and Archilde sat down on the lounge, and Claudia went to the chair opposite the fireplace.

"I say, Archilde, you're a funny one! How did you ever pick out this Mercer?"

"I saw his sign when I was walking through the street, so I went in and told him I wanted violin lessons. That was all."

"What did he show you? How does he teach?"

"Finger exercises, bowing exercises, breathing exercises."

"What?" Albert cried and went off into a torrent of laughter. "Breathing exercises, that's good! They say he asked a girl to stand on her head once, and she slapped his face. Muscular control, that's what he talks about. But did you ever hear him play the violin? No—you never would either. He couldn't play a mouth organ." Albert went on reading.

Archilde smiled faintly. Claudia was watching him carefully. The light fell directly upon the lounge while she sat in a shadow. She was smoking a cigarette and saying to herself, "No, I am wrong about him, I have been mistaken. He is really very simple and straightforward. But is that right?"

"Didn't you inquire of anyone?" she asked.

"Where should I have inquired?"

"Why the American consul would give you some advice. They probably wouldn't pick the best—but they would have helped."

"Maybe you're right, Claudia," Feure said on the defensive. "But you or I wouldn't have done any better if we had come over alone, knowing no one at all. No one ever goes to the American consul unless he's broke, and I'd certainly never think to go there to ask for a music teacher."

"Yes," she said. "I just made that up for the sake of the argument. I haven't the faintest notion whether they know anything about such matters or not. I exonerate you!" she said to Archilde and smiled brightly. She had made up her mind to be pleasant again.

Archilde waved his hand. "No, I take the full blame. I admit I was stupid. But tell me something—why such a fuss about a teacher? Is it so serious?"

"That's a fine question. Let Michel answer." Feure looked puzzled.

"Do you mean it seriously?" he asked.

"Yes. When I set out to look for a teacher, I didn't think much one way or another. That was almost the first sign I found. I looked in the paper of course—but everyone made such great claims for himself that I didn't learn anything that way—so I took a walk and saw Mercer's sign and went in. Wasn't that all right?"

"But supposing he has spoiled you! What if he has ruined your hand! Look! See my left hand—how much larger the knuckles are? I will never be able to have it as it should be. It was stretched too severely by an ignorant teacher at home. She had a perfect passion for making people's hands larger. Someday I may regret that even more for doctors have warned me against rheumatism settling in those joints. I never eat meat on that account—can you imagine! A good teacher develops you gradually—only the best teacher can develop you to the utmost—"

"Excuse me," Archilde said, "but I have no wish to be developed to the utmost, as you say. What is the good of that? I am not studying now because I want to make a name or whatever you care to call it. It is only something to do. I like the violin best of all—I wouldn't give two cents to learn the piano—but just the same—"

"I don't understand. You said something like that this afternoon but I thought I hadn't heard right. Really, now, that's no way for anyone to talk who plays as well as you do! I won't have it!"

"No, this is the argument," Albert called across the room. "One does his best. The better you are the more you do."

"I thought you were reading," Claudia called out. "Either you throw away that book and come over here where we can see you or keep your nose where it belongs."

At that moment the mother entered the room. She was a thin, colorless woman, and she walked with slow, measured steps that succeeded in giving her a certain dignity. She wore a long, old-fashioned skirt and waist with a black band around her neck. Her face was pale and her skin was loose and wrinkled around the eyes and mouth. Her eyes were the only thing about her that expressed character and strength. They were browner than Claudia's and equally bright and piercing. She had a nervous, irritable manner and one sensed that she had undergone much illness and physical struggle. Her mouth was pursed as if the lips were drying up and her voice was rather shrill.

"How do you do!" she said when Claudia introduced Archilde. On her lips there was only the faintest flicker of a smile. She sat down facing the fireplace.

"Where is Vincent?" she asked.

"I don't know where he was going," Claudia answered.

"He was going to somebody's reception," Albert spoke up.

"It's time for bed, Buster," the mother said without turning around.

"I wish you wouldn't call me Buster," he replied, and for the first time, he walked over to the fireplace. He fastened his eyes on Archilde. He was a slim boy with light wavy hair that was always falling forward across his face. In spite of his youth there was something very masculine and determined about his actions. He invariably accompanied his words with a slight scornful smile.

"Listen, Mother," he said but didn't look at her. He was still staring at Archilde. "I want to show you a fellow—an American mind you—who plays the violin excellently, so they say, who doesn't want to become an artist!"

The mother looked at Archilde momentarily, and in that one glance, she seemed to have satisfied herself regarding his character and worth.

"Don't mind him if you think he is rude," she said to Archilde in a dry voice.

"No—but isn't that right?" Albert appealed directly. Archilde smiled.

"Partly. First of all I am only a fair player—but it is true that I do not care, rather, I see no purpose in being anything more. I have never before talked or thought so much about it at one time as I have tonight. That is the truth."

Michel began to rave. "I won't stand for you talking that way! Didn't I hear you playing this afternoon? And I tell you," he looked from one to another of his hearers, "it was only a sight reading. I asked him to come down and go through the Rachmaninoff trio with me—and he didn't stop once he started. But that's not what's remarkable—it's his tone—it sings out of his finger. Haven't I heard violinists? I'm no fool! But wait till you hear him and judge for yourselves. Maybe he plays wrong—I don't know anything about that—but you should hear! Therefore, I say it's criminal for him to talk that way. You must help me," he looked directly at Claudia. "We've got to hammer something in his head. Just you wait!" he told Archilde. "You'll never go away from Paris still feeling that way."

"But maybe he is wise in feeling as he does, Mitchell," the mother said. "It's a long, long road."

"That's not the point," Albert interrupted. "You're assuming that he's suffered disillusion. But he refuses to be illusioned. That, you see, is healthy and damn fine, I say."

"Albert, where do you pick up those words?" she asked.

"Mother," said Claudia after a long silence, "don't chide him about a 'damn.' It's a good word."

188 | D'Arcy McNickle

Just then they heard a man's high-pitched, peevish voice calling from an inner room, "Kate!"

"There's Dad," Claudia said.

"Oh dear! It's time to rub his back!" She got up and walked slowly out of the room.

Feure moved over until he was sitting close to Archilde. He put his hand on Archilde's shoulder and looked up into his face.

"You're not really determined are you?" he asked. "Because, if you are, I think it's a shame. Haven't you any desire to go as far as you can—to outstrip all others? Don't you feel that way?"

Archilde was embarrassed that Michel's face was so close. He thought carefully for his answer—instinctively it was not Michel that he cared to answer—it was the others. They were watching him, wondering what he would say. All of these people had bright, piercing eyes. They expected something out of the ordinary. He could tell that they were not easily satisfied and he did not think himself equal to what they wanted. His eyes were on Claudia when he answered; it was to her that he wanted most to talk. Then again he thought: "Shall I really tell them about myself? Shall I try to explain? Will they understand or merely think me of no consequence?"

"What I said a while ago is true—I simply haven't given it much thought. Do you know why? Can you understand why? Let me tell you something of myself—just a short story. Three years ago this month I was sitting at home wondering what I was going to do. There was a heavy snow on the ground and it was cold. My father had been dead almost a week. My mother—well, you wouldn't understand my mother. Only let me say this much: my mother and I have never said more than a dozen words to each other at one time in my life. Does that sound strange?" His eyes had become glued on Claudia, yet he did not see her clearly; he was conscious that he was trying his best to communicate himself, to make his story understood. The others had become completely silent and motionless.

"This decision of mine was to be of considerable importance to myself. My father had a large ranch and he left me some money. It was his wish that I should remain and develop what he had left to me. But there was a certain circumstance that made it difficult for me to remain.

The Hungry Generations | 189

I had explained this difficulty to my father shortly before he died—and he understood and advised me to leave, though it was entirely against his desire. But even after he died I could not make up my mind. This peculiar circumstance, which I have mentioned, was complicated and it involved me in more than one way. A person with more experience and learning might have found it easier—but I haven't much of them. And what's more, I wasn't in the habit of solving problems—we didn't live that way out there. Either you did a thing or you didn't—that was all.

"Another thing I should tell you is that I never played the violin at home—I didn't even have a violin there. Can you imagine why? People would have laughed—yes, my own father. He wouldn't have *then*, if he had been alive, because we came to an understanding just before he died. I used to play for the dances when I was younger. That was different.

"I was at a school long ago and that was where I first heard a violin—and serious music. Even now I remember how it happened and I won't ever forget it. I was lying on the lawn one summer afternoon. It was warm and drowsy. We heard the violin through a window, playing the same piece over and over, slowly, deliberately, as if the player had the greatest desire to attain perfection in that one little piece—you can understand that all right. Well, I always hear that fellow playing and I swear that that is the only thing that gives me a desire to play. I was nine or ten when that happened—but it was several years later before I even had a fiddle in my hands—it was at least seven years later before I ever had a lesson. Is this clear? Or am I rambling around without telling you anything?"

"No!" Claudia said breathlessly. "What was your decision? What a terrible country! I cannot imagine it—but I have a sense of something ugly!"

"You are wrong if you think it is ugly," he said quickly. "But it is true that people don't sit there wondering whether it would be a good idea to become an artist or not," he smiled at Feure who had drawn back and was listening in amazement. "But no, maybe they do, some of them. As for myself, I didn't know what the word meant. The decision? Well, as I say, I sat around the house for weeks until in the end I thought I would go crazy. Finally, I went to town and settled everything. I made up my mind to stop thinking about it and go away. Perhaps I was wrong, but it was beyond me to see where. I came east then, and after talking and begging, I was finally admitted into a college where I have been until last year.

"Does that explain something, a little bit? But I have really told you nothing. I don't know much about words. I am afraid I've been stupid again."

"Whew! That's a story!" Albert said. He got up and left the room. Archilde watched him go and was surprised. He had begun to feel that there was something sympathetic and friendly in the boy and now he couldn't understand what his action signified. He looked at Claudia, but she didn't even notice the incident. She was staring hard into the bed of coals that were slowly dying out. When she looked up her eyes were glistening.

"Can you believe it—I had been thinking all evening that you were quite another sort of person!" she said. "Now I see my mistake and I'm sorry. I was afraid you were a poseur, do you understand?"

"No—I'm afraid not."

"Well, it's an insincere person who tries to make people think he is something different. I really thought that—though I am ashamed to admit it now. But tell me, why did you and your mother never talk? And you say that you and your father had 'come to an understanding'— hadn't you been living together? Or were you utterly uncongenial? My curiosity, you see, gets the better of me."

"I will try to explain that." He had two impulses and he did not know which to follow. On one hand, he wanted to tell everything, carefully and exactly, leaving out no detail; that would be the truthful way, he thought. He was afraid, however, that he would make himself uninteresting and tiresome, and furthermore he knew that it would become too involved and difficult. He would forget what he was trying to explain and in the end his listeners would become as mixed up as he was. He decided to be brief and tell only what seemed essential. "In the end it will amount to nothing," he said to himself. "They will not understand."

"I had some brothers, older than myself, and all outlaws . . . ," he began. He was still talking directly to Claudia. He went on to explain something about them and what their effect had been on his father, how he came to hate them and all his family, how when he, the youngest, was born, his father would no longer talk to his sons or even inquire if they existed. Thus he expanded on his theme, explaining as much as he could. He had a knack of speaking in simple, plain phrases that brought his story before his listeners with the greatest clearness. He was not aware of it and would have doubted anyone who called his attention to the fact. His manner was also fascinating because it was so unaffected and direct. Claudia was making note of these characteristics. He had caught her fancy at last.

"Then you had a reconciliation with your father in the end?" she asked eagerly.

"Yes. It happened shortly after one of my brothers was shot and killed. But that's another story. My father came to like me," he finished without knowing what else to say.

"What a strange person you are! I don't understand at all!" Feure said. He had been repeating those two exclamations over and over. Archilde looked at him and smiled.

"No, you only fancy that. I am not strange. I have lived differently than you—but I probably don't know half as much. That's the truth."

Albert had just returned to the room and had overheard this last statement. He spoke up in some heat.

"You're wrong! There's not one in this crowd knows as much as you! Wait till you're here some evening and hear Claudia discussing aesthetics and the essentials of poetry with some of her friends. Then you'll understand. As for Feure there, or myself—or Vincent—we know something about a piano—but it's mostly rot! We've been kept at it like machines. When I was seven, I was playing little Mozart pieces. Now it's still Mozart. They'll walk me to my grave with Mozart or maybe Chopin. We don't know anything!"

This speech burst upon Archilde like a bomb. He looked with an incredulous expression at Albert. Could it be possible that anyone so young could talk with such firmness and conviction and express ideas so unusual? What was he at seventeen? Why a mere nothing! A stick of wood!

Claudia burst into a jolly laugh. "What's come over you, upstart? You should understand, Mr. Leon, that he's the enfant terrible in our family. He's always knocking things around, finding fault, and sticking his tongue out at us—and usually he's right. It's disgusting."

192 | D'Arcy McNickle

"Ah, get out, *cutie!*"

Claudia crimsoned at this thrust, which seemed to be one of those secret personal jibes that the members of a family employ upon each other at times. Her impulse was to go and slap his face, and if she had been a few years younger, she would probably have done this. Now, however, she controlled herself and merely laughed. Albert left the room again.

"At any rate, Mr. Leon, he's more right than I have the face to admit. Come, Michel, will you admit he's partly right? It will be easier for me then." She was gay and lively again.

Feure was smiling too. "Oh, I think it's true. Can you imagine how we met this afternoon, Claudia? He was sitting in that gloomy lounge again reading a book. I said to myself, 'I'm going to end this silly business right now. I'm going up and speak, and he can give me the cold shoulder if he chooses.' I did that and from the very first moment we got along splendidly. And do you know what? Tonight at dinner he was telling me that for days and days he has been trying to get up enough courage to come and say something to me! Imagine! He has been here almost five months and until today he has not known a soul—except for Juliette! Think of that! Isn't it a crime when we've been passing him almost every day and wondering who he was and what he was like. I'll never forgive myself."

That was Feure all right. Archilde had forgotten what he was like since he had been silent for so long. Now he looked at him as if for the first time. He frowned slightly for a moment but that passed and he turned to his friend with a feeling of pleasure.

"You're a great fellow! Every time you speak you make me feel as if I were somebody. In fact, it seems to me that all of you are trying to make something out of me. But I have too many handicaps—I'm a generation behind you. You'll see—wait till we see each other more—I hope we will see each other?" he turned to Claudia. His eyes were not often away from her, as a matter of fact. He was continually turning to her and allowing his gaze to linger upon her. He could not get accustomed to her fresh, youthful manner.

"Yes, indeed—can't we meet again soon? Won't you bring him to tea, Michel? You see, I am afraid you will not come of yourself. But

The Hungry Generations | 193

Michel will bring you. Positively, this is the most exciting evening I've spent in years!"

In a little while Feure and Archilde got up to leave. The conversation had turned into a light, bantering tone and farewells were said.

As they were standing in the hallway putting on their coats, they heard someone weeping. They became quiet immediately; they even stopped with their coats half on. It was a helpless, pathetic voice, sobbing in a dull, monotonous tone.

"That's Dad," Claudia said in a whisper. A chill ran down Archilde's spine. He looked at her questioningly, expecting her to add something to her words, to give an explanation, but she remained silent. There was a trace of embarrassment that she tried to hide immediately.

"Don't forget that you are to come to tea—and I hope," she smiled brightly again, "I shall have the pleasure of hearing you play sometime soon!"

Chapter Six

Archilde had his friends now. Life was different.
He no longer ate his dinner alone in the Boulevard Saint-Michel; he no longer sat in the Café d'Harcourt and heard the girls making fun of him; he no longer walked through the Rue de Vangirard either by day or by night.

A change was coming over Paris. There had been a final intense week or two of rain and floods occurring in many parts of France, the papers said, but now at last the sun began to appear, not much but a little each day. Archilde's window faced the south, and there he would sit through many an hour watching the increasing patches of blue sky. When it was particularly warm and bright, he sat with his window open and felt the pleasant breeze on his face.

His window overlooked the grounds of a small college or school for boys. Lately, now, they had been coming out of doors to play and as soon as he heard their clamor and shouts in the yard below, he ran to the window to watch. Usually he slept late in the morning and the first sound he heard was the shouting down in the yard when the boys came out for their first recess. He would lie on his back then, and while he sipped his cool chocolate, he would think of the days when he was a small boy at school.

He had been sent to Chemawa at the age of nine. It was the first time he had been away from home and the new country, even a new climate, for the school was out in Oregon where there was scarcely any winter, had made a deep impression on his mind. Possibly there was another thing that had made an even more enduring mark.

At Chemawa he became conscious that he was at *school*, learning something. Formerly he had attended the Jesuit academy at home where everyone treated him warmly and he came to feel that he belonged there as if he were at home—in fact, outside of his mother, home did not offer much warmth those days. But when he was sent away, he went among strangers who measured him coolly and made him show what he was worth. In his three years there he got drawn into many fights and quarrels and he was beaten and cheated out of things. Those experiences stung him into consciousness and taught him to fear certain people, to like some, and to despise many others. That was the beginning of *school*.

He received his first punishment the first week after he arrived. That experience had left a real dent in his brain; he would never get over that. It was something at once so terrible and so penetrating that, even now, he rolled and tossed in his bed as he thought of it, although it was broad daylight and he knew that he was laughing at himself. It happened like this.

He had gone to Chemawa with a group of boys on the train. The boys were of all ages, some being in reality young men. They had almost an entire coach to themselves and they turned it topsy-turvy and made things merry. They bought candy and popcorn and soda water every time the porter came through. They shouted and laughed and climbed over the seats. Archilde, however, had been sent away without a cent of money. His father had not gone to the station to see him off, perhaps he was not aware even that he was going. His mother, of course, had no money. He sat by himself next to a window and watched the boys eating candy and playing games and his spirits were exceedingly low. Several times he was on the point of crying, but shame kept his face straight. Once or twice somebody gave him what was left of a piece of candy after he had eaten until he couldn't hold any more—but that was all. He was out of it entirely, and by the time night came, he was exceedingly dull and lonesome.

That night the director assigned him to an upper berth that he was to share with an older boy—Oswald. Oswald was at least twenty-one and at home he already had a reputation as a ball player and pool shark and all around good fellow. More than that, he had been spending money all day long and he wore a suit of fancy clothes.

Archilde could not sleep. He lay there feeling desolate and forgotten. He hadn't been able to buy a piece of candy even, and boys who were as young as himself considered him an object of scorn. They called him "Straight-Nose" because his nose was unusually long and straight from the tip to the bridge. They had made a dozen jokes about his nose during the day. Although one or two had given him battered pieces of candy that they couldn't eat, there were others who had made a joke of offering him a whole piece with the best of intentions written on their faces—then just as he reached forward with a grateful expression—snatching the candy away and laughing at his dismay.

He lay in the berth listening to the clicking wheels and thinking of the day's awful experiences. Suddenly he was struck with an idea. He turned and looked at his companion and found him fast asleep, or so it seemed. He moved a bit, but there was no response from Oswald. He sat up. Still there was no movement at his side. Oswald was a good-hearted chap too. When he came to bed he had smiled and said, "Hello, sonny! Are you my partner? Well, you sleep on the inside next to the wall—how's that? You're just big enough to roll out of here and fall on your head if the train should shake too much." He had said this with the kindest of smiles. Somehow, because Oswald had been so pleasant, Archilde didn't feel that the thing he was going to do was wrong. If he had been afraid of Oswald, then it would have been different.

He sat up in bed for a long time making sure that everything was all right and gradually working up his courage. Oswald's coat and vest were hanging on the curtain rod on the outside of the bed. Archilde could just barely reach them by partly leaning over the sleeper. His teeth were chattering in his excitement, but he did not falter. He went through the pockets quickly, and just as he was about to give up in despair, he found what he wanted: a pocketful of money. He took a fifty-cent piece and lay down again, weak and happy. Oswald still slept.

The next day he bought a few pieces of candy, just to show that he was able to if he cared, and after that he got on better with the boys and was allowed to join in their games. The incident had not actually meant much to him, although he realized, faintly, that it was wrong.

His greatest, perhaps his only fear, was that Oswald might have awakened and caught him.

The older boys smoked all the time and it wasn't long before they began giving cigarettes to the younger boys. They would go into the toilet and smoke and come out staggering and half sick. Archilde smoked for the first time and Oswald gave him the cigarettes. He had taken a liking to his young bed partner and several times he gave him things during the following day. Strangely enough, Archilde was hardly affected by his first smoke. It made him a little dizzy, but he wasn't even slightly sick. Oswald became more fond of him and paraded him before the other boys as "a man." Some of the small boys had been actually knocked out; they had to go and vomit and then come back and lie down. Archilde had borne up so well, in fact, that by the time they reached their journey's end he had become something of a hero. They were calling him "Stud" now since Oswald had suggested that that was a good name.

"Look what a thick neck he's got. I'll bet none of you other kids have got a neck like that!" It was true that he had a husky neck and shoulders for his age.

Then they came to Chemawa. The first week they did nothing but wander about. The regular term hadn't started yet and only half of the school had arrived. Archilde and his group clung together, particularly the younger ones as the big boys had been assigned to different halls.

Archilde and his friends, of course, had no desire to mix with the boys who were already in school, many of them having been there several years. They refused to notice them even. They wandered from place to place in a gang and played their own games. They called themselves "buffaloes" because they were from Montana, and when they met any of the schoolboys at dinner table or around their beds at night, they told monstrous lies about the "wild and wooly" life in Montana.

They had been warned as soon as they got off the train that smoking was strictly forbidden and that anyone caught offending this rule would be dealt with severely. But the "buffaloes" sneered at this order. Hadn't the big boys filled their pockets with cigarettes just before they left the train? Well, they meant to use them! So that first week passed and they went swaggering around claiming the sidewalks and making fun of the "mudhens" and "webfeet"—who were the native Oregonians.

198 | D'Arcy McNickle

A day of reckoning came. It had been their custom after every meal to go to a swamp that lay in a low place immediately behind the barns. There they would sit and smoke a cigarette or two before making up their minds what to do next. There were always some of the former schoolboys who tagged along, trying to get acquainted and also hoping to get a cigarette. But the "buffaloes" never paid them the slightest attention. This couldn't go on forever. The "webfeet" couldn't put up with being ignored and slighted. Somebody squealed.

Archilde could remember vividly the boy who gave them away. His name was Stanley and he had a whining, nasal voice. In after years at school he was always getting hurt and being imposed on and he never failed to go to the matron.

With equal vividness he recalled the night when he and his friends were brought to justice. That was a momentous occasion.

It happened after supper. Everybody marched to and from each meal. Even the girls, whose buildings were a quarter of a mile away across a broad lawn, marched into the common dining hall. School had begun the day before and practically the full school body had arrived. That night the small boys were marched to their hall in the usual way. But something unusual occurred directly when they reached their hall, and instead of being dismissed, they were told to march into the playroom. Gloom fastened on everyone. Immediately after they were lined up four deep across the large room, the disciplinarian appeared before them. He stood like a soldier and his heavy blue jaws were rigid. The matron appeared at his side and she was almost as tall. She had big breasts and massive hips. The boys had been marking time, and she clapped her hands for them to stop and remain at attention. She and the disciplinarian held a short consultation, then she stepped back and laid her charges before him, as if he were a presiding judge.

"It has been brought to my attention that certain of these young boys have been smoking every day since they arrived in school here. This has happened in spite of the warning I give to every boy as soon as he enters the Small Boys' Home that *smoking is strictly forbidden.*"

"You are sure that they have been warned, then?" the disciplinarian interrupted.

"Positive!" she replied.

The Hungry Generations | 199

"Who are these boys?" he asked and the scowl that had appeared on his face a moment before became blacker.

"They are the Montana boys who arrived a week ago. In fact, I might say that ever since they arrived they have been noticeably impudent and reckless. Smoking is only one of their irregularities. But I assure you that that is especially grave. We owe it to the morale and decency of our home to make an example of these little scoundrels. They must be taught the value of *discipline!*"

"Can you give me their names?" he asked.

"Yes. I will call your names, and as I call each name, please step forward so that the other boys may see you and know who it is that has been violating the *primary* rule of the our hall."

She called the names slowly and distinctly—as if she were reading the roll of fate. The "buffaloes" stepped forward one by one, crestfallen and frightened to death. When they had all been called, the disciplinarian cleared his throat and gave a short threatening lecture.

"Boys, I hate to do this but I am compelled. Small sins lead to crime. In this case your sin is not small by any means. Smoking is a vile, vicious habit. Look at me!" He clicked his heels together and stretched his arms out straight, then brought his clenched fists inward with a snap. He was certainly a giant. "I have never touched tobacco in my life!"

He told them much more and as he talked he seemed to grow more and more angry. He scowled and thumped his hand with his fist and ended up with the following dictum:

"We will absolutely put up with no nonsense here. You've got to learn your duty and follow it. Now I'm going to punish you boys. I'm going to give you a punishment that you will not forget all the days that you are with us. I am sorry that it must be so—but you have brought it on yourselves. Miss Patterson, bring me the rubber hose." She brought him a piece of garden hose, one inch in diameter and about three feet long.

There were benches along the sides of the room and he directed the boys to line up before the benches.

"One word more. You are being punished principally because you dared to break one of the rules of this school. Let each of you remember hereafter that no rule of deportment and conduct thought necessary by our school is to be taken lightly." He turned to the other boys. "This

is to be a lesson to each of you as well. I sincerely hope that this per-
formance will never have to be repeated in the Small Boys' Home. Many
of you are new boys, and I want this scene to sink into your minds.
Hereafter, remember your duty and live accordingly.

"Now!" He bade the boys at the bench bend over. He went along
to make sure that they had nothing in their hip pockets.

"All right," he said to the other boys. "Line up in single file. Your
captain will stand here and give the rubber hose to each of you as you
come up. You are to take the hose and strike the boys at the bench one
after another, then pass it back to the captain. You are to continue this
until the entire line has passed around *two times!*"

There were more than seventy-five, almost a hundred, boys
present.

That night Archilde had the idea of "discipline" pounded into his
body. He never forgot.

As soon as the boys from Petit College Stanislas were called in and
the yard became quiet Archilde got up. The images that had been troop-
ing before his mind faded as soon as their voices died, and once more he
was back in the present. He jumped out of bed and washed his face in
cold water, and as he stood at his window watching the warm mist over
the city and the pale sun, he wanted to shout. Life was different, indeed.

He had a wardrobe in his room with a large plate glass mirror in
the door. He used to stand before this mirror as he practiced his bowing
exercises. Sometimes, as he stood there, he would ask himself, "How
does it happen that I am here?"

Then he would put down his violin and go stand at the window
again. There was melancholy in that question.

At home there was work to do. Spring was coming and his father's
fields were standing idle. The roof of the barn was probably leaking
badly, and the dampness would rot the pine timbers inside. The meadows should be disked or harrowed to loosen the topsoil, otherwise they
would dry out. The wheat fields would be full of weeds that would
spread mustard and wild oats to all the neighboring fields. Undoubtedly,
fence posts were rotting away and stray stock could come and go as they
wished. He recalled that he hadn't looked up the prices of grain and livestock in the Chicago papers for several weeks; he had been following

The Hungry Generations | 201

these prices methodically for a year, not with any particular purpose in mind but simply because he had found it interesting.

Mike and Narcisse were coming home in June. They had been away three years as he had before them. He tried to imagine what ideas they would have in their heads and whether they would amount to anything. One thing he knew. When those boys returned home, somebody should be there to meet them and give them something good to eat for a while and then talk to them, laugh and play with them. When he returned his mother met him in her ancient, shaky buggy. She smiled and grunted when he got off the train and met her back of the depot. Then they drove silently over the dusty hill and home at last. For five years following that he did nothing whatever. He saw no one but his mother, Agnes, and the men who worked for his father. In summertime he fished and rode his horse into the mountains or to town where he played pool or sat in the sun on the sidewalk before the post office. Never did anyone talk to him and say, "What do you intend to do?" or "Why don't you try your hand at this?"

One by one the boys who had returned on the same train with him, who returned dressed in white men's clothes and polished shoes, went back to Indian habits and they appeared on the streets of the village with a blanket wrapped around their shoulders and with moccasins on their feet. Archilde had escaped that—but not because anyone interceded; luckily he had an aversion to such practices. He did not like dirt and smell, but that was accidental.

There was work to do at home and he could not turn a blind eye upon it. Was he standing before the mirror practicing bowing exercises, slowly, rhythmically? A picture of home would flash before his eyes and he put the violin away. Was he lying in bed sleeping soundly? A dream stole into his dormant senses and he saw the sun rising over the black mountains and plows flashing their blades in the sun; presently, he was sitting up staring over the sleeping city and wondering where his destiny lay. Was he at a concert hearing the great artists of the world pluck and pull at his emotions? An image of his nephew Mike rose before him with his sheepish grin and playful eyes, and immediately the music died on his ears and the opera faded away and became a brown hill in spring where the green grass was just pushing through the damp earth.

He, and no other, should be at the station to greet Mike and Narcisse home from school; then give them a fast, stirring ride in a shining new automobile to the big house; then a dinner of roast turkey and pie; then give them hooks with which to fish and a horse to ride. They knew him; they did not distrust him. With a little patience he could manage them and get them to do things for themselves. They must do it for themselves, but it would help to have someone around who could show them what to do. The Indian must succeed by his own effort. Wasn't that what the agent said? But somebody could be at hand who would talk and make things clear. Indians were human beings, and although a grunt was intelligible and often a sufficient means of communication, a word, a short speech, could express things that might never be understood; it also conveyed emotion and made a man out of a shadow. The older Indians, his mother, lived in a world of shadows where a stick or a stone had as much significance as a man.

"Archilde! Archilde!" a voice was calling. He awoke from his meditation with a start and for a second he could not recollect where he was. Then it was clear again and he opened his door and went to the stairwell. Feure was calling him from downstairs.

"I say, aren't you going to eat today? It's almost past lunchtime and we shall have to run if we hope to get served. Are you ready?"

"Just a minute!" Archilde ran back to his room and put his violin away. As he went downstairs with flying feet, he was humming a tune and eager to be with his friend again.

Chapter Seven

The more Archilde saw of Claudia and her family the less he could understand the position of the father in the family. He had been told disconnected facts concerning the father by Feure and Claudia herself at various times and one day he caught a brief glimpse of the old man, but as yet he understood very little. There seemed to be something unreal and unnatural about his relationship with his family, and Archilde never failed to think of him whenever he was in the house or with Claudia.

But one day he understood it all.

He had been asked to come to tea one afternoon. Claudia was not always fond of Feure in spite of being seen in his company often, and of late she had been asking Archilde to come alone, leaving him to devise a means of going off without Feure's knowledge. He came to the apartment that afternoon and was surprised to find that Claudia was out. The boys were also gone and the mother was busy in the kitchen.

"Good afternoon, Mrs. Burness. Claudia isn't around?" he asked after having first gone into the living room.

"No, I haven't heard her come in. She probably met somebody she knows. But take a seat in the living room; she should be here at once. I'm making a cake for Vincent—it's his birthday tomorrow."

"Really! Will you have a party?"

"No—we never have parties. They disturb the boys' work too much."

"Oh!" That was a new thought for Archilde.

He went to the living room and took a seat by the window. Scarcely more than across the street, it seemed, he could see the curving iron legs of the Eiffel Tower.

He was becoming more accustomed to Paris now. He no longer had that dismal foreign feeling. He had gone to Versailles on one or two occasions and rowed a boat in the lake. He had visited the museums and taken taxi rides from one side of the city to the other and through the Bois de Boulogne—all of this with Claudia. Also, she had taken him through dozens of little antique shops searching for rings and unusual trinkets. They went to shows and to the red-plush opera to hear violinists and pianists. Her head was full of anecdotes from French history, and she never failed to point out a building or square or monument without having some story in connection with it. And always she kept promising him something even better—he hadn't begun to see it! He never objected. He went along, admiring her seemingly inexhaustible fund of knowledge and admitting in that naive tone, which was becoming famous, that yes, things were certainly interesting. But only he was aware of the awe and wonder with which he looked upon the shaft that Napoleon had caused to be erected out of the melted cannons of his enemies, or the streets where barricades had been thrown up during the Revolution. He even looked between the cobblestones to see if there might not be some bloodstains remaining. The others never suspected his simple wonder because they could not understand the eyes through which he saw these things. To Feure, history meant nothing. When Claudia had spent the entire afternoon pointing out scenes of former action and drama to Archilde, Feure trotted along with the most pained expression, and when at last they would stop for tea, he looked utterly bored and would not be cheered again until he began talking about his debut which was only a few weeks off. Claudia occasionally had clues to Archilde's state of mind, but she was not capable of following them out—they led away into mists that she had never traveled. She was continually amazed at the revelations he made of himself. Vincent and Albert did not see him often. Vincent was an extremely quiet boy with calm eyes and he seemed to walk in dreams. Albert had a lightning understanding, but he was given to moods and for days at a time he spoke to no one. So Archilde was in no danger of being accepted for what he was; like anyone else he was subjected to more romantic interpretations.

He had been sitting at the window for perhaps five minutes when Mrs. Burness suddenly appeared with her coat and hat on:

"Excuse me," she said, "I must run down to the little shop on the corner as I find that I haven't any flavoring. Do you mind being left alone?"

Archilde got to his feet and in his confusion looked for the proper thing to say.

"Don't mind me at all, Mrs. Burness. I'll wait right here." When she started for the door, after having smiled at him, he was struck with another thought.

"Excuse me, but won't you allow me to go? Yes, that will be much better. What is it you want?"

She turned back and now she was really smiling, almost laughing, though it was still rather cold.

"That's awfully good of you!" she said. "But to tell you the truth, I really must go myself. The little grocer down here is *so* stupid that he'll be sure to give you everything in the shop but what you ask for. I've gotten on to his ways and I can manage him fairly well now. Thank you, just the same!" She smiled again and went out.

Archilde wondered if he should have insisted on going; if, perhaps, he shouldn't have simply pushed her aside and demanded that she let him go. He had seen others do almost that very thing and he was sure that they had been courteous. He sat down again and looked at the roofs across the street.

He was startled suddenly by hearing slow, muffled steps approaching him from behind. A board squeaked. He whirled around and there was the old man, Claudia's father.

"Is the old lady gone?" he asked, standing uncertainly in the doorway.

He was tall, extraordinarily tall and thin as a rail. He stood swaying in the doorway, and Archilde was uncertain what to do. He was afraid that at any moment the old man would totter to the floor on his face, but he hesitated to offer any assistance; he sensed that the old man would resent being helped. He stood watching Archilde and his mouth was continually working. At first, he looked as if he was trying to say something, but it became clear after a while that this was merely a nervous twitching. His cheeks were completely sunken in and his nose stood high above his face with immense nostrils. His shaggy gray hair was profuse and lay matted on his head. His face bore a stubble of whiskers. After his first question he did not speak for some time. With slow, shuffling steps he made his way to a chair and sat down. He wore a ragged dark gray dressing gown and carpet slippers on his long, bony feet. As soon as his chest stopped heaving he spoke:

"They try to make me believe I'm sick, but they ought to know better. Am I sick? Am I? No, sir, I've never been sick in my life. I tell you, I beg my old woman every day to let me work in the garden, but she won't hear of it. She says I'm sick. I haven't worked in the garden for weeks now—" he broke off suddenly and looked quizzically at Archilde. Then he smiled and his huge yellow teeth showed.

"Well, now, you'll think I'm a lunatic. I keep forgetting, you see. Fact is, we've got no garden now. That was at home. I tell you I had a garden at home! There was hollyhocks as high as a man's hand. Every morning I said: 'Good morning Mr. and Mrs. Hollyhock!'

"I hear 'em say you're from the West—is that so?" he asked at the next moment. His breath whistled through his cavernous nostrils.

"That's right," Archilde agreed.

"I thought so," he said and stared stupidly at Archilde. "Yes, you're a Western boy, I can tell." He stared again. "Part Indian, ain't you?"

"Yes—"

"That's right, son. Don't be ashamed of it. I knew lots of Indian boys in my day and they was all right. I had a quarter-breed firing for me for years and he knew his job. I ran a freight on the Santa Fe division for a good many years. Took one of the first trains through. Do you come from down that way?"

"No—I'm from the north. Ever been through Montana?"

"Yes—hell yes! I was there when Virginia City was at her best. I was a young buster then, before I took to railroading. Was your dad a stockman?"

"Yes—he ran cattle for many years in the western part of the state. He had buffalo out there too, maybe you heard of him—Max Leon?"

The old man pondered but couldn't recall the name. When he spoke again his mind had jumped to an entirely different subject, a subject, undoubtedly, that he could never forget for very long.

"What do you think of my old lady—and the boys? How do they strike you? You know, I can't understand it. I was married before—when I was a young buck. I had a son and he was just an ordinary, plain, happy-go-lucky sort like you or me or anybody else. He's railroading himself now—on my old road. He'll probably be an engineer before long, like I was. My first wife died just after Jim was born and then Kate came along. She was just a frail girl with black eyes and pretty as a picture those days—but she had an awful will—I always told myself that she had a terrible will of her own—and others did too, matter of fact. Well we was married in time—I bought a house for Kate in Kansas City—and then we begun having our kids, Vincent was first. And do you know, as soon as he was born, Kate began having notions what she wanted him to be. Right off the bat she said he was goin' to be a piano player. She *knew it*, she was dead certain about it and there was no switchin' her off on another track.

"But Claudia fooled her. She wanted Claudia to be some kind of a musician too, but she just couldn't learn. Why Claudia doesn't know any more about music than—me. They say she's writin' pieces now, though. Do you know anything about that?" He didn't wait for a reply.

"Well, sir, I thought she would let me have the next one to bring up as I thought fit—but there wasn't a chance. She had him playin' the piano almost as soon as he could walk, it seems. But he's a bright youngster in spite of it. You know Albert, don't you? He's the only one ever talks to me—would you believe it? That's the truth, so help me God!" he finished as solemnly as if he had been giving testimony in court.

"It was that damn will of hers. You can see what kind of a fellow I am. Why, Lord! I wouldn't lay down the law to anybody that I'm fond of—live and let live—but not her. No, sir. It was whole hog or none."

His voice suddenly became weak and whining. It was that petulant, high-pitched voice that Archilde had often heard behind the closed door and which never failed to send him home feeling troubled.

"If only she would wear down—but she never will. Do you like this damn frog-eaters' town? I tell you it's driving me loco! No man could like it and be in his right senses! But here I am. I was pensioned off three years ago—and Kate packed up right there on the spot. She hauled us all over here and God knows when we'll ever leave! This rain is killing me. I wasn't bunged up at home—not by a long shot! It's the rain workin' on my rheumatism. But Kate, she's got a will—she'll never listen.

"Tell me," he said struck with a sudden thought. "You're not one of these—musicians, are you?"

"No," Archilde replied.

"No, I didn't think so," the old man said, looking at Archilde through sorrowful eyes that were slowly filling with tears. He pulled out a big blue handkerchief and wiped his face awkwardly.

"It's the rheumatism, son. I ain't cryin'. No, you're a Westerner—I didn't think you was a piano player. What do they get out of it? I've been holdin' on for a long time," he continued after a pause. "But someday I'm goin' to cut loose. I'm goin' to tell 'em all a thing or two. I sort of wanted to know how far Kate would go—I've never said a word. But someday I'll say my say and put an end to it. You'll see. A man can stand just so much—and then you'd better look out. That's what's happenin' to me. You watch!"

Steps were heard mounting the stairs. The old man knew who it was at once and a look of dismay came over him. He glanced from right to left as if looking for a hole.

"Help me up, son," he said finally. "I'm as weak as a cat. Once I could pick up a hundred-pound weight in one hand and heave it. But this damn rheum—"

The steps had reached the top of the stairs and were approaching the hall door. The old man began to tremble and tried to quicken his steps, but this only made him quake more than ever. They hadn't reached the bedroom door.

"She'll be rippin' mad, but I'm glad I talked to you. I feel better."

Mrs. Burness entered and stopped in her tracks. A cry came through her parted lips and then a flush of anger followed. She turned to Archilde and tried to smile.

"I'm sorry—has Mr. Burness been troubling you? Sometimes he gets spells and we can't keep him in his room. I'll take him now."

Archilde was embarrassed and murmured an apology—though one wasn't required.

She helped the old man slowly through the door, but as soon as they had passed into the bedroom she slammed the door with a bang. Her voice could be heard on the other side, first in low tones, but gradually it grew louder and angrier. Suddenly she screamed.

"You bastard!"

At that moment Claudia entered, looking cool and fresh and with her eyes sparkling. Had she heard that word? The expression on her face didn't even waver.

Chapter Eight

After that day Mrs. Burness would never take her eyes off Archilde when he was in the room. She was repeatedly smiling when he looked her way and she often made a special effort to stop and say a word to him. When he had tea with Claudia, she often appeared to be lingering in the immediate background as if she were trying to catch what was being said. All of this embarrassed Archilde and made him feel that he was being watched. He tried to understand why, but it escaped him. He thought possibly that he was imagining it, that he had become more conscious of her since that afternoon. But he felt uneasy.

Things continued on. Feure was every day getting more and more excited about his debut. He worked like a madman and hardly left his room at all.

"My God, nothing is prepared! Can you imagine! Months ago I thought I had these pieces in my very fingertips. But think of it—some days I forget whole passages! It's awful. Why haven't I been working before? Why have I been fooling around? I tell you I'm going mad!" He would beg Archilde to sit with him all day long. When it was lunchtime he would say:

"Oh, please—don't go out! Come, I'll make tea and we have some biscuits left. Please stay! I get so nervous when I'm alone."

Archilde would stay. As he sat hour after hour in the close, stuffy room, his senses would become drugged and he would hear the piano pounding—as if the very hammers were striking on his brain. Strange fantastic images floated before his eyes.

210

He saw a small boy trudging along a dusty road. It was summertime and the trees on either side of the road were gray with dust. The boy was hot and thirsty. A tiny brook ran at the side of the road, but he was in too great a hurry to stop and drink. He was crying and running away from something. Every few feet he stopped and looked back, then turned and ran on again; his feet kicked up suffocating clouds of dust. He couldn't stop to drink. The road entered a city.

He didn't pay any attention to where he was going until he was in the very center of the city. He saw then that he was no longer following the tiny brook—the trees were gone too. He became frightened at first—but in a little while this turned to loneliness. He looked everywhere, but not a soul did he see. For the first time he noticed that the windows and doors in all the houses were closed and locked. Everything was deserted and lonely, although it was still a bright summer afternoon. Archilde knew that this little boy was himself; although he tried hard to see himself in the boy's features, these remained obscure and blurred.

The boy sat down to cry. He was still thirsty. He cried as if his heart was breaking; he had forgotten something, left something behind, and now he was sorrowful because of it. At that moment a small girl walked up and touched his shoulder as he sat on the edge of the sidewalk. He looked up and right away his face cleared, but there were two streaks down his cheeks where the tears had flowed. The girl took him up a hill and showed him a white house with an immense lawn and flower gardens around. She wore a white dress with a golden ribbon in her hair and another ribbon of the same color for a sash around her waist. They stood together on the lawn under a tall rose bush and looked at each other. He picked some berries from the bush and gave them to her. They stood there for a long time after that looking at each other. He had forgotten why he was lonely. As he stood looking at her, he saw a louse climb out onto the loose ends of her hair, and as soon as it felt the hot sunlight, it became motionless. In a minute another louse came into the sunlight. When he looked again at the girl's face, she was crying. She walked away, but the little boy could not move. He stood there staring.

Although Archilde's senses were still dormant, he knew that this dream was to be a prophecy. He was sure of it.

The piano had stopped. Archilde opened his drowsy eyes and saw Feure standing before him with a dejected air.

"Why don't you talk to me?" he said. "Didn't you hear that last movement? How was it? Did I get it right this time? Come, tell me!"

"Yes. That was good! It made me sad."

"But my left hand is so heavy. I swear I'll never be able to move it! Look, see how large the knuckles are? That was what a teacher did for me. How I hated her—I always did—and now more than ever for undoubtedly she has ruined my life. She had pale yellow hair and she kissed me when I gave my first recital as her star pupil. Oh, Archie! What'll I do! I can never, never be ready when *that* night comes! Just think, it's the beginning of everything. Critics will be there from the papers—and from music societies—if I win favor and get good press notices—think what it will mean! I have been here three years now, preparing for just this week—and look at me! I can never do it, I tell you! Talk to me—say something—tell me that that last movement was good!"

Feure walked up and down the room, clasping and unclasping his hands. There were tears in his eyes. He was completely unstrung. Archilde tried to talk in a natural way, but he found it exceedingly difficult. He liked Feure, for some things, but he could not bear to be appealed to for sympathy. He knew also that it was impossible to reason with Feure. Both he and Claudia had been trying it for weeks. He would agree and say, yes, they were perfectly right. There was nothing to worry about and it was imperative that he be perfectly calm and at ease in order to play well. But in another moment he was frantic again, appealing to them, begging them to say that his playing was improving.

Finally, he ceased his pacing the floor and sat down in a chair. He stared at the wall and his face had turned pale.

"Now I see it, now I understand. I was never meant to be an artist. I should have guessed it before. Everyone has been fooling me—they have overrated my talent—they made up stories to cheer me. It's all a mistake. Oh, I hate them! I hate Aunt Grace! She is the principal one— why did she send me over here!" He leaned forward on the bed and buried his face in his arms. He stamped his feet.

Archilde sat motionless. He couldn't possibly have moved. Chills raced up and down his spine and he felt feebleminded—he could think of nothing whatever to say or do—nothing to check that awful hysteria. He had never witnessed anything like it and he could scarcely believe his eyes.

Feure lay with his face in the bed for several minutes. His body became motionless and a painful silence followed. When five minutes had passed, he arose with an appearance of calmness. He seemed to have mastered himself. He walked to the piano and folded up the music on the rack, then he closed the piano. He turned toward Archilde with a pale, set face. Archilde had begun to smile. He jumped to his feet.

"Shall we go out now?" he asked rapidly. "Are you going to quit for today? That's a fine idea. Fresh air and a brisk walk, that's what you want. Then we'll have dinner with Claudia. That will be splendid. You really played that last piece well. You have never done it as good!"

"Shut up! Oh, shut up, won't you!" Feure screamed, but the words were no sooner out of his mouth than an expression of horror came over his face. He put his hands over his mouth and his eyes looked bewildered. He sank weakly into a chair. Archilde got up to go; irritation and impatience had grown acute and he felt that he could not stand another moment of it. He was longing for fresh air himself. Just as he reached the door Feure began speaking in that gentle, pleading voice that Archilde had grown accustomed to:

"Forgive me, please! I didn't mean it. I didn't even realize what I was saying or to whom I said it. Will you go away now? I am so sorry. I would never have said that to you of all persons. You are so kind and generous. Tell me you forgive me—only tell me that! Then you can go—if you want to."

"Pshaw—that was nothing," Archilde said, without looking at Feure. "That's not it at all. I just wanted some fresh air." His voice was quiet.

"You forgive me, then?" Feure's face brightened.

"Sure. Forget it."

Feure had risen too. He hung his head and played with the tassels on his dressing gown.

"I'm glad you're so—kindhearted. I have scarcely ever met anyone who understood me and treated me as nicely as you do. You never question anything—you just smile and take everything as it comes. I—I like you!"

Archilde looked at him amazed. The thought struck him, "Why, he's like a girl! A damn girl!" At first he turned pale and then he felt himself blushing. He glanced about the room, and when he saw that Feure was dressed only in his pajamas and a dressing gown, he became embarrassed. He stepped toward the door again.

"Are you going then?" Feure asked meekly and looked up. Their eyes met. A feeling of genuine repugnance swept over Archilde. He was confused and dropped his eyes almost at once. He couldn't utter a sound. He opened the door quickly and went out.

When he reached the street, he was still confused and ashamed. He felt that his face was red. He walked off at a rapid pace. He repeated over and over:

"So that's it! Why haven't I seen it before? Has it always been that way?" He was completely shaken.

He walked from one street to another without any regard to where he went. For one moment he felt anger, but as another thought entered his head this gave way to disgust, then he was ashamed again. He recalled scenes with [Feure?] and went over them carefully bit by bit for evidence of *that*. Now it all appeared plain as day. He couldn't understand why he had been so slow to catch on. Before he knew it he was standing before Claudia's house. He looked up and unconsciously turned in at the porter's gate. He stopped at once, however, and turned back. "Do I want to go in there?" He walked back to the street and turned to the right. He stopped in a small, dirty café and ordered a glass of beer. His head was confused.

After a while he laughed, softly at first, but there was a sudden outburst that attracted everyone's attention. It had all become ridiculous. He paid for his beer and went out again, still chuckling. The garçon picked up the money and examined it carefully before pocketing his tip.

When he reached the top of the stairs, he found Claudia standing in the doorway waiting for him.

"I was sure it was your step," she said and came to meet him. "Father is very ill. He keeps asking for you. It seems that you were talking with him the other day?" Her smile was extremely pretty and inviting.

"Yes—" Archilde replied uncertainly. He had just climbed the three long flights of stairs and he was out of breath.

The Hungry Generations | 215

"We have gathered something of the sort from his remarks. He wants to tell you something else, I think. He's been delirious most of the day and we've all been on tenterhooks. I called a while ago, but they couldn't get you for some reason. It's good to see you—you're a very sane person, aren't you? Yes, you are. I've often wondered about that." She talked all the time that he was in the hall taking off his coat and only finished as they entered the living room. There was no one in the room, and Claudia led him to the seat by the window. She seemed unusually interested in him that day; she kept studying his face and observing his actions. Nothing appeared to escape her.

"Listen," she said and a slight color came over her face. "Dad said something this morning that interested me greatly. Is it true that you are—Indian?"

"Why, yes—didn't I ever tell you? I thought I had."

"No—" her voice was soft. After a brief pause she continued. "Do you know, I think that's too marvelous for words! It gives me the queerest thrill. Now I understand many things that puzzled me before—your reticence, directness, honesty, your genuine wonder—all that is so unusual and—admirable. Oh, there are a dozen, a hundred things I must ask you about! Listen, let's go out for dinner. I'll give mother a story—something about Feure—she knows he's upset and I'll tell her we're going over to have dinner with him and to cheer him up—then we'll eat alone—and talk—what?"

Her words and manner puzzled him. Inwardly, he felt a growing excitement; something had stirred him, but he couldn't understand her sudden warmth and unusual eagerness. Unconsciously he was wondering if it was real. He didn't actually think about this, of course; if such a thought had occurred to him he would have dismissed it at once. Only he looked at her and she seemed strange. He agreed quickly to the dinner and then Mrs. Burness entered the room, closing the bedroom door softly behind her. For a minute, as the door stood open, they could hear the old man crying softly, monotonously.

"I'm glad you've come," Mrs. Burness said, coming to Archilde at once. Her face looked more rigid and determined than usual; her eyes were slightly bloodshot, but they were cold. Her voice was entirely without emotion and her lips clipped the words off sharply. She was pale, as if she had been engaged in a long, bitter controversy and had been stating her case point by point, demanding every inch, and yielding nothing at all. There was an abrupt, nervous gesture in all her movements.

"I don't know just what my husband talked to you about the other day," she looked at Archilde closely, "but you seem to have made an impression on him. I'm sorry to bother you this way, particularly when I'm sure that it's only one of his childish whims. He has grown very childish the last few years." She said this last softly, apologetically. "But I always try to humor him—if it's not out of reason. He has been asking for you—Claudia has probably told you. Would you mind coming in for just a minute? I want to see just how—*sane* he is. That is, you understand, he's been delirious most of the day, I'm sure. He may not even recognize you. Do you mind? It seems stupid to you, I suppose."

"Not at all. Nothing could please me more than to be of some assistance to you—if I can."

They walked to the door, Mrs. Burness still observing Archilde. The bedroom was darkened and there was a faint odor of medicine in the air. It was a large room, the other half of the ballroom. The great, long figure lay sprawled out in the bed that stood just out of one corner of the room. His shaggy head was propped up on pillows and his hands, which were on the outside of the covers, looked extraordinarily long and thin. The bones stood out sharply. He turned his head and opened his eyes slowly when he heard the door open. As soon as he saw Archilde advancing to the bed, his face brightened at once. It was most surprising and a feeling of intense pleasure shot through Archilde, as if he had been recognized by an old dog or horse.

"Hello, cowboy!" the old man said and the words rumbled out of his chest.

Archilde shook his hand and noticed that he scarcely had the strength to move his fingers.

"How are you feeling now?" he asked. "They tell me you've had kind of a tough time today."

"Yeh, tougher than they think. Half the time they think I'm foolin'. But I'm not. Sit down, Montana, and talk to me. Say, Mother, I want to talk to him alone—will you leave us be?"

Mrs. Burness appeared surprised at such an unusual request. It was evident that she had no intention of withdrawing and was about to frame an excuse for remaining in the room, but at that moment, Claudia spoke up. She was standing just within the doorway and she seemed pleased with the scene.

"Come on, Mother," she said. "Mr. Leon will do him a world of good. See how much quieter he is."

Mrs. Burness looked uncertain. She kept watching Archilde as if she expected him to say or do something that would reveal his attitude, but he sat there smiling and making no comment. In fact, it was rather an embarrassing situation and he didn't know what to say.

"Well," she said, feeling that there was nothing more to be done, "I really feel that we are imposing on you unnecessarily—I'm sure Mr. Burness doesn't *need* to talk to you alone—but if he insists, I suppose there's nothing to do about it. It's very good of you to be so obliging." She turned away abruptly and walked out of the room.

The old man sighed as if he had been released from a great weight. He turned over on his side where he could see Archilde more easily.

"She's breaking me in two, young man. Like you would take a stick and bend it between your hands until it pops. When she's around me I lose my head; I can't even act like a man. If I wasn't laid up with this damn rheumatism, it wouldn't be so bad. I could keep out of her reach, sort of—but I can't move, I gotta lay here and have her wait on me." The words were scarcely audible. Archilde moved his chair nearer to the bed. He spoke in a whisper too, involuntarily.

"Can't you go somewhere—to a hospital or sanatorium—or something?" The old man shook his head slowly and for a long time before he answered.

"No—all the money goes on the boys. She wants 'em to be piano players, you know."

"Don't they understand? Don't they ever talk to you about it? Or ask you what you want to do?"

"They don't savvy nothing. Albert, he comes in and talks to me— but *she* always butts in and says it's nonsense."

"Doesn't Claudia—?" Archilde didn't know what he meant to ask. He dropped his eyes.

"Claudia is a good girl. She sits with me and reads me the news-paper from home. But she doesn't seem to understand, none of 'em do. Then again they don't go against the old lady. We're all scared of Kate. She's got such a will. She makes us all stand around, that's the truth. Do you know my boy Vincent? Well, he broke away once, ran away. That wasn't so long ago. She gave him such a licking that he's never got over it, I guess. You've noticed how quiet he is? That's what started it. He used to be a lively youngster and we got along fine, me and him. But he doesn't come to see me anymore. He plays the piano all day and that's about all. I don't know if Kate ever thinks about what she done to him—but she spoiled a mighty fine young boy."

The old man ceased speaking and a long silence followed. Archilde could scarcely believe his ears yet he knew that this was true. He was stirred by a vague uneasiness that was akin to dread. He had never been comfortable around Mrs. Burness, she was always so intense and out-spoken. Now he recalled her thin, ascetic features and he knew that the old man spoke the truth. What the sick man said next sent a chill through Archilde.

"I can't last much longer. I won't die—I know that. There's still lots of life left in me—but I'll go out of my head. I can feel it coming. Some-times, for a whole day at a time, I keep seeing things, imagining I'm back home or that I'm back railroading. Listen!" He stirred and with extreme effort he raised his hand and put it on Archilde's knees. "This is no way for a man to talk, I know—but things are different now—I'm not on my own feet anymore. I'm talking to you in my right senses now—this is what I wanted to get Kate out of the room for. You see my position, I know nobody, not a soul, I'm like a pup without a home." His voice changed. He had been speaking in a low, easy tone, but now it became high pitched and weak. That was the voice Archilde had always heard behind the closed door.

"Get the kids away! All day long that's on my mind—get the kids away! I don't care how you do it but get them out of her hands! But maybe it can't be done. No—I guess it's gone too far. I might have done it if I had put my foot down years ago—but I didn't realize how far she was gonna go. But try it anyhow. You're not a piano player—I knew that when I saw you—maybe you can do something. I don't know. No, it's too late! You can't do anything. But I'm much obliged just the same. You're a good boy, I can see that—but you can't do anything." He had become incoherent. His hand fell away from Archilde's knee and he buried his face in the pillow. Saliva dripped from his mouth.

Archilde picked up the old man's hand and laid it on the bed and then bent forward until his face was near.

"Listen to me, Frank. I'll try my best. Maybe a word or two will start something. Let me tell you about my father." He went on in a quiet voice to tell him about the misunderstanding that had existed between him and his father for twenty-one years. The hatred and doubt that existed between them. And then how one night they sat down together, and after they had spoken a few words, they suddenly understood each other. Everything else was swept aside and they understood.

"So I'll try it. Sometimes a word or two will start you off. You see things differently and from then on you live in a new way. I'll try it. Take it easy now." He had been talking for some time and the old man had fallen asleep, but even as he slept his lips moved and he seemed to smile. Archilde looked at him for a while. He hated to go away.

He closed the door slowly behind him and tried to keep from looking up into Mrs. Burness's face; he knew that she was standing waiting for him to look up and say something. He turned to Claudia first and then he found it easier.

"He's sleeping," he said and noticed that Mrs. Burness was exceedingly pale.

Chapter Nine

Claudia was still in the mood in which Archilde had found her earlier in the afternoon. She was eager to have him talk about himself, and she was continually leading him on by nicely phrased exclamations and avowals of interest. They were eating dinner in a rather stylish restaurant across the river near the Rond-Point des Champs-Élysées.

"No, you are wrong to belittle yourself as you do. I can understand how you would feel at a disadvantage before people, as myself, for example, or my brothers. But it is wrong. The more you tell me about yourself the more amazing you become. I want to tell you now, for once and always, you lack none of the essentials—indeed you have many fundamental traits that are only given to the few. Perhaps you lack some of the polish and elegance that is occasionally found in men—I only say occasionally, mind you—but that is of little importance. It isn't worth a minute of discussion and you shouldn't waste even that much time thinking about it. What you have got is a new viewpoint. That is what is startling. You cannot realize without having been born and brought up in commonplace surroundings how few people ever have anything new to think or say. And the pleasing thing is that, although what you often say is new—there's nothing really strange or original about it—it is merely the simplicity and naturalness of what you say. Sometimes you seem to use phrases and expressions that I haven't heard since I read them in the reader in the third or fourth grade at school. It's exciting to hear them now—in new surroundings—and find them still true. Think, now, what

220 |

this would mean in your music—for there you carry over the same freshness. Even Feure has remarked on it—and Feure is—you know yourself—a musician only. When he talks he babbles. I don't criticize him—it's simply a fact. In art of all places, there should be freshness. That's why I say you are wrong when you belittle yourself."

Archilde was strangely unmoved by her excited argument. Indeed he seemed to be preoccupied with something else, and if he had followed her words, he gave little indication of it. When he answered it was not to the point.

"Before my father died he told me to travel and find out about things—'and don't stop for anything but the best!'—those were his words. Tell me, is this the best?" He waved his hand slightly as if indicating the room, but all the time he kept his eyes on her.

For the first time she hesitated. His voice had changed and she wondered if he wasn't too serious; that is to say, it sounded as if he spoke in mockery, but it didn't seem possible. She gave a little laugh.

"This is the best!" She too waved her hand, but it was a more definite gesture. "Paris is more than the capital of France—for two centuries, at least, it has been the capital of wit and learning. All the scapegraces in the world come here—and most of the brilliant minds. You've heard that, haven't you?"

"Yes, that was what I heard when I came east. I heard nothing else, in fact." He hesitated over his next words. "Is it so wonderful then? Is it worth sacrificing a great deal to be here?"

She knew that he was getting at something but she wasn't sure what it was. She was more sober, however.

"Yes, some people will give everything—do you know what I mean by *everything*?—just to linger on. Some of those continue to work a little by themselves—but there isn't much left to them. But I think I understand your question. You are wondering just how much you would give, how much it is worth to you? Isn't that it?"

"Partly. In all seriousness, though, I haven't yet seen why anyone should care to sacrifice a single thing of value—such as human relations or emotions—"

"I have an idea!" she interrupted, though it was clear that he had nothing more to add. "Let's take a taxi ride. I want to show you some people—one or two or as many as you wish. The ones I have in mind have sacrificed everything as I just said. Take a look at them and tell me what you think. Would you like to do that?"

"Yes—that should be interesting—perhaps instructive. What I have seen so far has not excited me." Again she looked at him and wondered what he meant.

Many people were on their way to the theater and it was some time before they found an empty taxi. When they hailed one at last, she gave the name of a café on the Boulevard du Montparnasse.

They leaned back in the dark seat and for the first few minutes neither of them spoke. The air had suddenly become exciting, or so it was to Archilde, and he wondered if Claudia felt it. He tried to see her face in the darkness, but it was only a vague blur. She was the first to speak and her voice was low. It suddenly sounded like the most friendly and companionable voice he had ever heard.

"I'm going to introduce you to a man first—he's no longer young— a poet. He was born in Illinois when it was, I suppose, the farthest outpost of civilization. He has been here a long time now—perhaps twenty years. But you will see for yourself. You won't have to talk unless you want to. I will try to lead him out. Sometimes he will talk, but at other times he is as glum as an owl. We'll see how he is tonight." A moment later she added in a disconnected way.

"For a while he was in love with me—so he said. But that's over now," she laughed.

Again he tried to see her in the darkness—they passed a brilliantly lit building and her face was surprising. She was smiling and looking at him with merry eyes. They passed into the darkness again and he became conscious of the odor of her clothes and person. A strange feeling was awakening in him and he couldn't utter a word. Shortly afterward they reached their destination.

As soon as they left the taxi, she went up to one of the waiters and asked if he had seen Dave Marsh.

"Monsieur Marsh?" The waiter surveyed the tables—"Oh yes, a few minutes ago he crossed the street to the café across there. I remember now."

They went to the other café and found Dave sitting at a vacant

The Hungry Generations | 223

table that was somewhat apart from the merrymaking crowd. He smiled as soon as he saw Claudia approaching and rose to his feet.

He was tall and stoop shouldered. Indeed, he would have been an exceedingly big man but for his shoulders, which were rounded and stooped to such an extent that he gave the impression of being a cripple. His hair was long but thin and his scalp could be seen easily. He had a long thin face with a downcast mouth that made him look ludicrously sorrowful. His eyes were exceedingly mild; every gesture and movement of his body expressed mildness. There were many lines in his face and his lower lip hung loosely as if he were an inveterate snuff "chewer," which he was not.

"I haven't seen you for a long time. Won't you sit down?" He spoke in a gentle voice. His large eyes had brightened. His manner was that of a great lazy dog—anxious to express his gratefulness for a kind word.

"No, I've been running to all sorts of places lately. It's good to see you! How are you? I want you to meet a friend of mine—Archilde Leon—this is Dave Marsh. What are you drinking?"

"*Anís*—you don't like it. Have you just come?" he asked Archilde.

"I have been here six months." He liked Marsh immediately.

"What has happened to your book? Will it come out this fall?"

"I'm not interested anymore. The publisher promised it a year ago—then he said certainly last spring—now I don't care. The fact is he's afraid he'll not sell a single copy—which is probably true. That's none of my business." He had a habit before he spoke of looking around at the people and then leaning forward to speak—as if his words were entirely confidential. Also, his eyes blinked continually.

"Are you a writer?" he turned to Archilde again.

"No—I play the fiddle."

"Sometime you must come and hear him, Dave—you'll get a surprise." Marsh laughed softly, as if at himself.

"That's an interesting expression in Paris. Most of these people are doing something or other, painting, drawing, writing poetry, or playing the piano—if you listen to their talk, you will hear them say, 'You must come hear my new piece,' or whatever it is—but nobody ever goes. Or if you do drop in someday and happen to mention it—they've thrown it away and are working on something better. It's always something better.

So many people have asked me to come and see one thing or other—but I never go. And people never visit me, so I don't ask anyone to come and hear a new poem. But it's not the piece or the music—it's the wine and the people. You meet a person and take a drink or two with him and pretty soon you begin to rack your brain for something interesting and friendly to say. So you ask him to come see what you have just painted. Isn't it true? But excuse me!" he interrupted himself suddenly. "I wasn't referring to what you had just said. That phrase happened to occur to me and it made me think of this other thing."

"Listen, Dave," Claudia began, "Archilde and I had a discussion during dinner. Perhaps you can give us a good answer." Archilde was looking at her intently. She had called him by his first name for the first time. He felt himself grow warm.

"Why are people attracted to Paris? Why do they linger on year after year, perhaps letting other things, other connections and relationships, slip away—apparently with no thought or regret? That is, generally speaking, you understand."

He looked at her momentarily and then looked at his foot swinging in the air.

"I can't answer it generally—I can answer for myself," he looked up again and he seemed to inquire if she was sufficiently interested to hear about his own case. She smiled warmly, impulsively.

"I am happy here." He looked at her again. "Isn't that enough?" his manner asked, but he added:

"I don't know how long I've been here now. If I went home, it would be a foreign country. They tell me that Chicago is a big town—second to New York—when I left it was a town of wooden shacks. When I hear about it, I get a sick feeling. Such growth can't be natural—it must be like the papier-mâché towns they build for the movies. Anyhow, I've no desire to go and find out for myself. I'm happy here because there's no hurly-burly—no building forty-story skyscrapers in two weeks or whatever it is. If I come back five years from now, I can sit at this table again and perhaps the same garçon will wait on me or one that looks just like him. A man must take root deeply and he should have plenty of time to do it. Perhaps I was unhappy at home—we went west in a big wagon with oxen—what if I should tell you that my father was a kind of maniac—he killed an ox one day with a single blow with his axe—and did something worse to my mother—we buried her before we built a house even—but there's no use speaking of all that. I've forgotten it. I think my dad is called the 'lumber king' now—what do I care!" A glow had come into his meek eyes. He was recalling things that perhaps he really had forgotten, except for those visions that slip into the brain between sleeping and waking.

"Why should I live in a country that will chain me to its system body and soul! Here every man has his body to do as he pleases. No one bothers you. I've lived in the same house ten years and every morning I say, 'Good morning, Madame Parade! How are you?' It is never any different and it takes so little to live. I have never yet read an American paper that didn't have a news story on some man who had just made his million—and every time this man 'makes a statement'—that is, he gives his formula for making a million. He says, 'I owe my phenomenal success to—' Does anyone want to hear such rubbish? Are they actually mad over there? Do they really read that stuff? They must or it would never be printed. What can you do with a million? What would I do with it? I would have jaundice inside of a week. I am extremely healthy, never been sick—that's because I am always a little bit hungry." He chuckled and his large thick body curled over the table as he picked up the tiny glass and drank.

"In Paris it takes no effort to live—you never give it a thought. 'Success' is a word they forgot to put in the dictionary over here."

Claudia was watching Archilde, wondering if he would object. He sensed this and presently he asked:

"You said a man must take root—how can he do that in a foreign country? Will you ever be like a Frenchman? Is it possible?"

"Maybe not—but what difference does it make?"

Archilde shrugged his shoulders and didn't pursue the question. He knew that Marsh wouldn't answer it.

"Do you really believe that a man works, thinks, understands things as well among strangers—that is, with other people—than those with whom he was born and raised?" Claudia asked and looked at Archilde to see if that was the question he had in mind.

"To me there is a fallacy in dividing men into strangers and those who are friendly—or whatever you wish to call it. The same as there is a fallacy in speaking of a Frenchman or an American. Men do not differ greatly."

"No, you are wrong!" Claudia objected. "I am thinking of foreigners at home. Why is a city always divided into sections—Italians, French, Greeks, Poles—why do they seek their own kind and live together? Why do foreigners always seem affected, unnatural—even stupid—when they may be much more intelligent than we? I have never had a friend who was essentially a foreigner. Have you? I understand French very well—but there is always something that escapes me. I think there always would be. Men are not universal—they form groups naturally and they understand their own group best."

Archilde would say nothing more. He was no longer interested in Marsh. At first he had sensed a familiar spirit and he had thought when they shook hands, "Here is a man I can listen to. He will tell me something. Perhaps we will like each other and I will see everything in a new way." But that impression had worn away. As Marsh had gone on talking, Archilde's eyes grew wider and wider. He hardly believed his ears. It seemed impossible that this man could talk as he did; for all his air of meekness and simplicity he talked bitterly and with unmistakable hatred. It was also incongruous that a man so large and seemingly powerful should want to live easily and at the cost of no effort. What should a man do, then, with a big body and powerful shoulders? Let them rot?

Claudia saw that he had lost interest and she began making excuses to get away. Marsh was plainly attracted to her. He looked at her often and his eyes were beseeching—not for anything specifically, perhaps—but dumbly, in fact. He held her hand a long time at parting.

"I want you to hear a poem I have just written. Here, I have it in my pocket—put it in your purse and read it—later. It's to you," he added in a lower voice.

"Really!" she said with flashing eyes. "That's marvelous! I hope I see you again, *soon!*"

Archilde and Claudia walked down the street together.

"Well, what about it? Shall we visit another one? It's really a shame that you haven't met these people before."

"No," he replied. "One at a time is enough, I think. Is he always that way?" She laughed.

"I knew it! I knew you would be discouraged right away. And Queen Bess would be too much entirely. I was going to take you to her. But we'll leave that for some other time. Have you heard of her?"

"Queen Bess? Yes, I think Michel pointed her out to me several times. She's fat and kind of sloppy, isn't she?"

"I should say she is—but can you imagine she used to be a dancer! They say she was good. Her greatest boast is that she has been the mistress of most of the crowned heads of Europe. She was a gay one. Even now she will not give up. She manages to keep a crowd around her most of the time. But we'll let that go for the time. Let's take a taxi again. I know of a quiet café on Boulevard Saint-Germaine. There we can talk. I'm dying to read the poem. He said it was written for me. Isn't that marvelous! Let's take a taxi."

The poem was stupid. It was manifestly unreal and strained for its effect. Even Claudia could not close her eyes to it, although she was inclined at first to be moved and to overlook its shallowness. He had actually compared her to Octavia, the wife of Caesar, and in another passage, to Lucrece.

"Isn't it disgusting!" she said with a laugh and jammed the script into her purse. "But sometimes his poetry is good."

"What does he write about?"

"Nothing very interesting, it is true. But he gives them interest by a kind of melancholy and gloom that he casts over his subjects. He writes about a leaf falling in the still air, or the silence at noon in a country village, rooftops in the rain—any number of things like that. He is fond of tinkling sounds and gray light. Everything that is quiet and verging on melancholy. Does that sound like him?"

"Yes—he must be a child afraid of his own shadow. His blood is like water. He makes me sick. Are you very interested in him?" This question brought laughter to her lips, but he was so serious that she held it back.

"If I say yes—will you be disappointed?"

"I don't know—I'm probably overlooking many good things in him. I'm not good at judging people and I'm often mistaken." He could not understand her manner. It occurred to him many times that she was laughing and enjoying herself at his expense. She had a habit of asking him a simple question in such a tone of gaiety that he was positive she wasn't interested in his reply—she was sure of it beforehand and was only forcing him to commit himself. Sometimes he was struck with the thought that she took nothing seriously. She rarely spoke without laughing or smiling as if it were all a joke. It happened many times that the merrier she got the more serious and short-spoken he became. That was what occurred as they sat together in the café. He distrusted all her questions and statements. He felt clumsy and dull witted. His only recourse was to speak as accurately and seriously as he could, regardless of the occasion. This made him ridiculous and Claudia could not suppress her mirth.

"What I don't understand," he said at length, "is why these people place so much importance on what they do and how they live. No man amounts to much, I've found that out. Marsh says he feels sick because Chicago has grown too fast. I can't understand that. How does it affect him? What difference can it make? I think it's enough to live and do whatever you can without making any fuss about it. But what is strangest of all is that a man should hate the place he started from and the thing he once was; a boy might do it. When I was small I used to plan awful punishment and revenge for any older person who gave me a licking or took something away from me. But a man shouldn't feel that way. Doesn't it really surprise you to think that a person can continue for twenty years— or whatever it is—still hating the persons you hated when you were a boy? If Paris does that to a person, it must be a strange place.

"However, this may be nonsense to you. I express myself badly and it isn't likely that I have shown you exactly what I mean. The one thing that worries me is this. Perhaps I'm not capable of understanding what it is that attracts people from all over the world—as you said a while ago—to this one city. That thought really bothers me. This is the cream of civilization, you say, but to me it looks like rotten apples. It seems to me, Claudia, that everyone is unhealthy, that is, they're afraid, or they're overly nervous," he remembered Feure all at once and lost the thread of his thought. "How does it seem to you? I must be all wrong—you seem to take it so coolly and enjoy it. Am I kind of a fool, then?"

Claudia was ecstatic—"Archilde, you're a wonder! These people are unhealthy to you because you have vigor. No, I'm not joking you now. All evening you have been sitting here in a rage, thinking I was laughing at you—but I tell you I'm in deadly earnest. I smile and laugh because you're exciting. Is that plain enough? All right. I told you at dinner that you had a new viewpoint. Can't you see now how I meant it! What do you expect of the *cream of civilization*? Life, strength, energy, fierceness—such as you were born into and lived with? No, just the opposite. Here you have polish, smoothness, quietness, decay—rotten apples is a fine expression. Here are the best things in their rarest development and bloom—before it passes out of the race. It must be that way. Freshness is born where things *are* fresh and new and rough. Then it is handed back through millions of hands—when it reaches here it is no longer recognizable. It is split into still smaller parts—it is made into trinkets, freaks, baubles—at last it is cast aside entirely. They do not deal with life here—they put cushions around it and spray scent in the air and hang ornaments on its limbs. Did you honestly expect something different? But of course you did! You had the strength but not the confidence.

"Now you can understand better what I said before. People come here to study art and music. Most of those who come have no blood to start with. They were born in conventional ways and aren't even smart enough to realize it. They study here and you can foretell the result. Are they given the spirit they lack? Is their blood thickened? Certainly not. When you come here, you need unusual spirit and heart because you are coming to be robbed. You are cramped and polished into the mode. Robustness, brutal strength is an insult. Everything that is here strives to refine you—refinement is like cutting your hamstrings. Those who come weak in spirit are rags when they leave. Yes, they understand music as they never did before—possibly! They may even play better—but what of that! They go home, join an orchestra, give a few recitals—but they go into the dust with a hungry look and you hear them gushing at teas and concerts. I have seen them. Some never go away. They have their back broken. Maybe that's what happened to Dave Marsh.

"Do you see what I'm driving at? No? Then I will tell you. You have the spirit. You are the very person, one of the very few persons, who should undertake this period of study and refinement. There may be greater individual teachers at other places, but here you will get the real training. I tell you, you can learn something about music here in five years or even three. And they'll not cut the wind out of you—I know it. When you leave at last, you'll be a wonder! That's true, Archilde, I'm in earnest. Do you believe me? Do you think I'm still making fun?"

He looked and saw that her face was calm at last and a warm, friendly smile was on her mouth. His heart was in his throat; her words had lifted him into such dizzy heights that he felt faint and speechless. He lifted his glass of benedictine, which he hadn't touched until now, and in his excitement he took the whole glass in one gulp.

"No! You're wrong!" he said, gasping for breath after the drink. "I can't play that well. I could never be more than a fair player."

"Oh, but listen! Don't refuse to see the hand before your nose! Your present teacher, Cherabov, doesn't take just whoever happens to read his name in the street and walks into his studio. He made you play for him and don't overlook the fact that he was prejudiced against you when you first approached him. Every teacher is the same. They hate to take on new students. They have enough work—they are paid well— why should they take on a new student? He would have refused you, believe me, on the slightest provocation. He might have protected his interest, yes—but he would have advised you to study for another year or two before you came to him. Did he do that? No. He said, 'I am satisfied that your training is sufficiently advanced'—or something on that order. Didn't he? Of course. Well, what more do you want? Can he make it any plainer? But just wait. He will."

Archilde felt weak. "Well, I can't argue anymore. You beat me every time. Let's go home. I've been drinking too much and everything is mixed up. Some other time I'll give you an answer to all that—but not tonight. No, it's no use. You've mixed everything up."

"Why, you sound really drunk!"

"I am!" She laughed and took his arm as they went out into the street.

Chapter Ten

When Archilde returned to his hotel he felt completely tired out. A great deal had happened that day and the excitement had been intense at times. As he paid the taxi driver, he was already half asleep and he turned into the hotel door with a feeling of relief. But he was not to sleep for a while yet. Someone was waiting to see him.

It was quite late by now and the lights were turned out in the entranceway. The only light that burned on the ground floor was in the small clerk's room at the bottom of the stairway. Juliette had gone to bed long before, and the garçon who cleaned Archilde's room every day was taking his turn as night clerk. He lay on a short lounge back of the desk, sound asleep. He woke up, however, as soon as Archilde entered and he smiled at once. He was a pleasant-natured fellow and he had taken a liking to Archilde.

"Did you get your letter, monsieur?" For the first time Archilde noticed that there was a letter in his box.

"Sure enough!" It was from the Indian agent. He was anxious to open it at once and had already started to tear open one end of the envelope when the garçon spoke again. He was grinning.

"I think you had better go at once, monsieur. There is a madame waiting for you upstairs in the salon. She has been here already two hours. She would not go away though I told her you might not return at all. You had better see."

Archilde was surprised. "A madame? What kind of a madame? Is she short?" He had already started upstairs and didn't wait for the reply. He had shoved the letter in his pocket, forgetting it for the time.

Mrs. Burness was waiting for him in the lounge. She wore a dark gray coat with a small purple hat and a veil that fell down over her face. She did not draw this up at once, and Archilde couldn't divine the expression on her face. Her voice, however, told him her state of emotion. She was exceedingly sharp and acrid.

"You certainly keep unhealthy hours for anyone pretending to study music!" she said at once.

"I am awfully sorry! Have you waited long?" He looked at her and at the room uncertainly. He stood before her without even thinking of sitting down. "Did you want to see me?" He couldn't imagine why she was there.

"Yes. I had expected to have a talk with you—I came considerably earlier. But I made a discovery that has so interested me that I haven't minded the wait at all. Please sit down."

He remembered that there was a second room just off the lounge— it was used as a tea room and it had a door. He sensed that the conversation was going to be exciting, and he thought it would be better to go behind a closed door. People were sleeping only a few feet away.

"Excuse me," he said, opening the door to the tea room. He found the switch and turned the light on. "Would you mind coming in here? There we shan't disturb anyone." His drowsiness had left him, but his body was exceedingly weary. He sank into a chair gladly.

"Can I assist you in any way, Mrs. Burness?" he asked.

"We'll discuss that later. First of all, I want to ask you something. Why did you get Claudia to lie to me today? Never in her life has she told me a lie—and now you have very plainly influenced her to do so. Have you any reason for this?"

"A lie? She told you a lie? How is that?"

"Oh, why sit there like that, pretending you don't know or understand anything about it! That's the first trick of every cheap hypocrite." She had thrown her veil back as soon as she entered the room, and her eyes flashed with hatred and distrust.

Archilde was totally at a loss. Her manner was so resolute and firm that he experienced a sense of guilt almost immediately. But he couldn't understand what she was referring to and managed to say so in a bewildered, hesitating tone.

"Then I will remind you. When you left my apartment this afternoon, Claudia told me explicitly that she was coming to have dinner with Michel. She is not often away from home for dinner and never without giving me a reason. She mentioned the fact that Michel is in a very nervous condition owing to his approaching recital, and she expressed the deepest sympathy and said that she planned to come here with you and take him to dinner and try to divert his mind. Isn't that so? Weren't you standing there beside her when she told me that?"

"Yes—that is so." He saw at once what she was referring to.

"Then how do you account for the fact that Michel has seen neither of you this evening? Come on, tell me now. What are you up to? What is your purpose in coming into my family and winning the confidence of certain members? What do you hope to gain? I repeat that never in her life has Claudia told me a lie. Yet you seem to have influenced her to do so at last. Surely you must have a motive."

"If I had an evil design, you don't actually think I would tell you, do you?" he had gotten over his first bewilderment and her sharp words and ugly allusions had made him respect her considerably less so that he felt freer to answer. His manner was no longer apologetic.

"Claudia and I had no other purpose than to discuss a matter quietly by ourselves. And this is what we have been doing."

"She has nothing to discuss with young men that can't be done openly in our house. You have not yet explained why you got her to lie to me."

"That, I assure you, was unintentional and I take the full responsibility for it. I apologize. I didn't realize how it would affect you. We had a matter to discuss that I will explain to you fully if you desire. I asked her to have dinner with me, but since she was afraid you might refuse her, I suggested that she tell you we were coming to see Feure. That is all there was to it."

"And what right, young man, have you to *suggest* to her that she lie to me? Isn't that impertinent and nasty? Never mind giving me any explanations of what this important matter was that you wished to discuss. Claudia shall explain the whole matter to me. But understand this, there's to be no more of it! If you can't come to my house like a gentleman, I don't want to see you in it! You are Indian, aren't you?"

"Yes—I am!" His face had turned pale.

"I thought so. I never entertained Indians at home and I don't see why I should now. We're here on business. My sons are studying hard and Claudia should be. I'll see that she does hereafter and has less time for running around at night. So I'll beg of you not to interrupt us. Now there's another matter." She paused and considered her words for a moment. During all this outburst she had scarcely changed her expression. It was evident that she had tried to control her high-pitched voice to keep from shouting, but in every other respect she was perfectly calm. Archilde could not help noticing this. It was such an unnatural, deadly calm.

"I came here on a somewhat different matter—though I realize now that they are not so different after all. For some reason you have taken it into your head to interfere in my family—but I am totally at a loss to understand your purpose. Do you mean to thwart me deliberately?" Without realizing it, certainly without intending to, she had revealed herself utterly. She had probed to the quick and uncovered the source of all her fear and doubt as well as the secret of her unquenchable desire and energy. She had been so jealous of her purpose and had guarded it so fiercely that she had come to believe, actually to believe, that everyone she met was designing to frustrate her. Everybody was against her and plotting the downfall of her dreams and plans. She noticed almost at once that she had showed her hand too plainly and her manner changed. She put aside the sharp, bitter tone in which she had been speaking, and now she actually attempted a pleasantry. She leaned forward slightly.

"Young men are all alike—you've got to keep a bear-trap in front of your door all the time if there's a girl in the house! Don't I know! Enough." Again her speech had betrayed her, and she had been too pleasant. Now she became sharp again.

"I'd like to know what your object is in appearing so friendly with Mr. Burness. He acts as if he had known you all his life—and I presume he tells you things in the same way. I would be greatly obliged to you if you would tell me what he had to say to you this afternoon that was so important he thought it necessary for me to leave the room. Of course,

I can hardly expect you to be truthful in this matter either." She was evidently satisfied with this thrust and she watched him expectantly.

Archilde had grown angry. He had been watching her face intently, and now he was aware of the cruelty it expressed. She was ugly, he was also aware. Her face was like mud and there were a few stiff black hairs growing on her chin. Within himself he was raging. He had gone beyond that stage where people frightened him by assuming a positive air. He knew that underneath there was something that could yield and give when it was attacked. He was no longer the Indian boy who ran behind a bush when another man appeared on the road ahead.

"You are telling me to my face that I am a scoundrel and a liar! I don't know what kind of a woman you are—but you must be half mad. Is it necessary that I sit here and listen? Not at all. I am very tired. Besides, I have a letter from home that I am anxious to read." He started to get to his feet, but she protested at once.

"Please don't go for a minute yet! I realize that I am often too hasty and outspoken. The fact is that I am worried to death by my husband, Frank. I lie awake nights worrying about him, and lately my nerves have begun to give way under it. That's the whole truth. Don't you understand now? I was afraid, you see, that he was telling you things about his condition that I really should know. The fact is that he has always been obstinate and headstrong, and now that he has become unwell he is almost insane in his perverseness. As an example of this, he will tell me absolutely nothing about his condition. I bring in doctors, but he pretends to be delirious or he has a lapse of memory when they come and makes faces at them. He is making himself worse every day, and now I am almost at my wits' end. If you can help me I beseech you to do so. Has he told you what is wrong? How he feels? What he wants? Anything at all? Surely you understand now?"

He looked at her sharply and felt sure that she was lying and playing a game. He did not attempt to answer with her own weapons. He was not equipped for that. He tried merely to tell her what he knew and as directly as possible.

"I suppose I do appear like an imposter to you; I can see how you might feel that way now—though it had never occurred to me before. Your husband has become interested in me because I'm from the West;

he came out and talked to me that day when you went down to the grocer's and he seemed tickled to meet someone from out West—it was almost as if he had known me before—he was so enthusiastic. I won't deny either that he has told me how he feels and what he thinks about—naturally, he would say something about himself.

"I think," he continued after a short pause, "he is unwell because he is unhappy—pretty much. Please, Mrs. Burness, don't think I'm giving you an opinion or judging this matter one way or another. You asked me to tell you what he talked to me about, and I intend to tell you as exactly as I can recall it—not his own words but what he meant. He believes first of all that his principal—in fact, his only—ailment is this rheumatism, and he is sure that the dampness of this country is making it worse. No—let me tell everything at once and then I won't get mixed up. He said something today that scared me; he's afraid he may go out of his mind because he can't do anything but lay still all day long and think about himself. Something else is bothering him, however, and it is this other thing that seems to give him the most pain and uneasiness. He is worrying about the boys and about Claudia. He doesn't want them to be piano players—he says that over and over—he's afraid that it's not good for them—or that they're doing it against their will. That's not quite right, I've said it wrongly—but he feels something like that. He thinks that you took them in hand before they were old enough to know what they wanted and have kept them at it—so to speak. Anyhow, he keeps worrying and thinking about the matter and never gets any rest from it. Frankly, I don't know how much of this is true and I'm not anxious to find out—by that I mean that I have no intention of trying to verify what he has told me or sticking my nose anywhere it doesn't belong. I have told you the facts as he has given them to me, and you know best how true they are. Are you satisfied? Is that what you want to know? Or do you still think that I am a liar and trying to push myself in where I don't belong? If you do I'm sorry, but I don't see what else can be done about it."

"The idea! The very idea!" She had hardly restrained herself until he finished speaking. "Can it be possible that he would say such things? Has he gone out of his mind already? What an irresponsible old fool he has become! Can you possibly believe such things? Don't you see that he

The Hungry Generations | 237

has made that up? He is feverish, sick, crazy—something! He doesn't know what he is talking about. Rheumatism! A fine way to put it! He has drunk himself to death! Don't you see it in his face? When his nose is red as a beet and swollen like a sponge. His face is splotchy. That's a drunkard's face! Don't you know anything at all? I brought him over here, possibly to save his life. I couldn't control him at home—he was an absolute disgrace! God only knows how I managed to keep him together as long as I did. Haven't I gone to the superintendent of his division—not once, at least half a dozen times—and begged him, yes, on my knees, not to fire him. And they would have years ago. Just think he caused a wreck once—yes, killed people! Because he was drunk and disregarded his orders. Wasn't there hell to pay then! I tell you, I was sick for months afterward. And all the time I was trying to educate my children, provide for them, make them fit for other things—for better things. You say he's worrying about them—why—he has never given them a thought in his life. He didn't know they were alive when we were at home. He wouldn't look at them when they were born. He didn't come near me when I was in the hospital, and I almost died when Albert was born—where was he? Drunk. They found him the next morning, lying just outside the roundhouse. After he put his engine away, he went on one of his usual sprees with that gang of gamblers that were always hanging around there. No, sir, he didn't even get home—as for me—and the children—my child being born—what did he care. And do you know what? He actually wanted to make the same kind of people out of my children that he was. He made his own son a worthless gambler and drinker—already his reputation is as black as his father's. That's what he wanted to make my children into! And because I put down my foot and fought him tooth and nail from the moment they were born up to this day, he has never forgiven me. He even resorted to mean petty tricks to get them away. Only three years ago, just before we came over here, he took Vincent out one night and got him drunk—yes, *drunk*—and then talked him into running away. Can you imagine anything more despicable! But the worst of it was that, when Vincent explained everything to me later, he actually was low enough to turn on his own son and call him a liar! How's that for filthiness! And now he explains everything to you—makes out that he's abused—ill treated—martyred! God, such a man! No, sir—the only thing that's upsetting him now—*absolutely the only thing*, I tell you, is that he can't swim in booze anymore. I made up my mind that I was going to make one last attempt to cure him before it was too late. He might at least live a sober old age and not disgrace his children when they were old enough to take their place in the world. Do you know how I got him over here? It wasn't simple I can tell you. I kept him drunk—dead drunk—until we were on the boat. Even then he thought we had gone to Chicago and taken a boat for a trip on the Great Lakes. I'll admit it's rather hard on him just now because we are sobering him up after a lifetime of booze—fighting. I let him have a little wine—but only so much each day. And it's an absolute fact that he's improving! Does he look bad? You should have seen him when we first came! And this is my thanks! But what else should I expect— he will probably curse me the rest of his life. That's to be expected from his kind. Look at me, then! Do I look like I've lived a sweet life? Have I had a bed of roses? Isn't it plain? You're not blind! And you actually believed him. Yes, I knew at once that you had taken his word for everything. That's a man for you! They're always willing to believe the worst about a woman. We slave for them from the moment they are born, trying to make them amount to something—trying to make things easier. Do you know, I often go out of my head almost at the thought that my boys may forget me someday—cast me aside, after I've lowered myself in the dust before their father trying to hang on to him and get him to provide for them. I tell you I've had many humiliating moments in my life with that man! I know what it is to eat humble pie and keep my face straight before the world. But my children will never know it. Not if I can help it. They're going to travel in a different world and live like human beings—I've promised myself that—and I mean it! Now, are you satisfied? Have you seen the truth at last? Will you believe me?" She was nearly shouting at the last.

Archilde stared at her in utter bewilderment. She had routed his senses. His mouth dropped open, but not a sound came at first.

"I am sorry—awfully sorry. I've wronged you—" he started to speak in a wavering voice, but at that moment the door to the tea room began to open slowly. He and Mrs. Burness both turned and looked. At first the knob turned, then the door moved slowly inward. At the next moment Claudia was standing before them.

She was pale and completely sober; there was even a suggestion of fear in her face. She carried her hat in her hand and her hair seemed to be mussed up. Her coat collar was fastened tightly around her throat. As soon as she entered the room, she fastened her eyes on her mother at once and for a long time during the ensuing conversation she didn't look away. She was conscious of Archilde, her hand fluttered once in a kind of salute, but she didn't turn her eyes to him.

Mrs. Burness gasped when Claudia first appeared, but her mouth tightened immediately afterward and she became motionless. She was fascinated by her daughter's stare and she could not turn her eyes away. It was a long time before anyone spoke.

Then Claudia said, "Mother! What have you been saying! I came and heard you speaking—it was so terrible I couldn't go away or come in—I couldn't move. It—it was frightful!" Her voice was surprisingly soft and calm. Archilde knew now that she was frightened as if something ugly and terrifying had risen before her.

Chapter Eleven

"Where have you come from? What did you hear?" her mother asked sharply.

"I just came from home—you weren't there. Dad said he had a hunch you were coming here from something you said. I couldn't understand why on earth. Now I understand. Oh. I could hear—you were shouting. Everyone must have heard." Her voice was stronger. She was surer of herself.

"What business is it of yours! Why do you have to come for me? I'm able to take care of myself. Why are you so surprised at what I have been telling this young man? What's wrong with it?"

"What's wrong with it? What's wrong—"

"Yes, that's what I asked you!" Her eyes were piercing, and it was evident that she hoped to silence her daughter, to force her to back down. Claudia didn't move.

"You've been lying. That's what's wrong," she said quietly.

"I lie! You tell me I lie!" she screamed.

"Yes—Dad has never been a drunkard. He has never wrecked his train. You know—"

"What! What are you saying? You dirty little beast!" She slapped Claudia across the mouth and her body was quivering with rage.

"I repeat it," Claudia said without flinching. "You've lied to him."

The mother became violent. She squealed and flew into Claudia, scratching and tearing her clothes. She kicked and bit and sobbed in a broken voice.

"Archilde!" Claudia called out, feeling herself overpowered.

For the first time Archilde could move. He had been standing absolutely still, no longer able to think or feel anything but a kind of sickness in his stomach. He grabbed Claudia's mother, but her body was quick and her strength was astonishing. She turned to attack him as well, and she kicked his legs and covered his face with scratches. She was quite mad.

"We must get her into a taxi!" Claudia called. "Can you hold her? Pick her up?"

Archilde was trying to do something of the sort. He finally lifted her like a child, but she had one hand so tightly wrapped in his hair that he could not get it out. As they started to carry her through the door, she began to scream and Claudia pressed her handkerchief into her mouth.

The garçon had come upstairs and stood in the lounge with wide eyes.

"What is wrong! My goodness, the whole house is awake!"

"Yes, yes. Never mind now. Go for a taxi. She is ill—a fit." Archilde called and began carrying his kicking, squirming burden downstairs. He was afraid she would throw him off balance and he would fall. Claudia walked alongside, holding her head and trying to get her hand loosened from Archilde's hair. Several heads popped out of doors through the hall and surprised voices called—"Mon dieu! A crazy woman!"

As soon as they were in the taxi Mrs. Burness became quiet. Her strength had deserted her. She was still grinding her teeth however. Before they reached the apartment, she broke down and began to sob. She rolled her head from side to side on the back of the seat.

"Ah, God! Deliver me from such ungrateful children," she cried in a broken voice.

Claudia looked across at Archilde and tears were in her eyes.

"Forgive me!" she said. "I'm so ashamed—" she could not finish and hung her head.

"What? What's that you say?" the mother said, as if hearing something in a delirium, but she did not pay any further attention. She rolled her head from side to side and moaned to herself. Once or twice she tried to free herself from Archilde, but he clung to her desperately. His face was smarting from her scratches and his head ached violently.

"Don't be ashamed, Claudia. It's—nothing. I'm glad you came." He didn't know what to say. Every thought that came to his head was stupid and meaningless. The awkwardness lasted only a moment however for they were soon home.

When the car stopped, Claudia tried to talk to her mother and arouse her to her senses.

"We're home now, Mother. We mustn't make any noise. We will walk upstairs in a perfectly natural manner, and no one will know anything about it. We mustn't wake the boys. Do you understand?"

Mrs. Burness made no indication that she even heard. She had grown listless and relaxed. Tears streamed from her eyes, and now and then, a sob came through her lips. She mumbled words over and over, but they were incoherent. Archilde took her in his arms. For a moment she seemed on the point of reviving into violence when Claudia pounded on the gate and called her name to the porter, but this passed away. Archilde carried her upstairs like a child. She was very light in his arms.

Claudia became frantic momentarily. "What will we do with her? Oh what can we do? Will she stay in bed or must someone sit by her all night? We must wake the boys. But what will we tell them? Will she be sick, do you suppose?"

"I think she will sleep. She is very quiet."

Archilde laid her on a bed. "Wait outside," Claudia told him. "If— I need you I will call. We won't wake anybody else."

He paced up and down the carpet in the hall. His thoughts were in confusion, but underneath everything else he felt a warm glowing sensation. It was at once so pleasant and so disturbing that he was continually smiling as he walked up and down. He recalled the hundreds of things that he and Claudia had done together, and at each picture of her his feeling of pleasure increased. He was not thinking of the evening's happenings at all, strangely enough.

Claudia came out in about ten minutes. She was no longer frantic or uneasy. She had arranged her hair and clothes and now she smiled.

"I really believe she is going to sleep! Does it seem possible after—

The Hungry Generations | 243

that! Ah, Archilde, you are scratched terribly! Come to the bathroom and I'll put peroxide or something on."

She brought him straight to the bathroom without the slightest hesitation and made him take off his coat and tie. She bathed his face and all the time he was afraid to look at her. She put disinfectant on the scratches and begged his pardon all the time. At times she laughed softly and to herself.

"I can't understand. It simply leaves me speechless!" she said. "Wasn't it awful? Aren't you really ashamed of me?"

"No—why?" he answered.

"You're a good one," she said and squeezed his hand. "Will you go and sit in the front room for a minute? I must put on a different dress—see how this is torn! Then I want to look in and see if she's asleep."

Archilde sat and stared into the fireplace where a few coals still glowed. The day had been too full of events—his senses were turning groggy. He was extremely tired and his bones ached where he had been kicked. Presently he remembered what he had promised the old man, Claudia's father, he would do his best; an understanding might be brought about by a few words. He smiled but with no feeling of pleasure. "What is it? Why is it so different?" he asked himself.

Claudia returned, looking pale and serious.

"She has recovered. She has gotten out of bed and is walking the floor. I think she realizes what has taken place though she won't talk to me. I am sure, however, that she has full control of herself. I don't think she will be violent again. You have been awfully kind and thoughtful. I can never thank you. I think you had better go now—it is frightfully late and I can see that you are tired."

"Are you sure everything will be all right? I don't like to go if anything should happen—"

"Not at all," she smiled confidently. "To be frank, if she sees you— if she realizes how we brought her home—and what happened before that—she may lose control of herself again. I can always call the boys if necessary. I don't want to. It has always been the tradition in our family to keep unpleasant things away from the boys. It interferes with their work. Even now she is probably aware of that and will stay quiet." She spoke these last sentences with a peculiar emphasis and there was a smile of mockery on her face.

"Yes, I understand, I think. It is strange," he answered. "I will go then." She took his hand.

"I will come to you tomorrow and tell you a few things. I think somebody should offer you an explanation. And perhaps you will give me your argument. You should have a good one now," she smiled dryly. "Tomorrow, then?"

"Yes—tomorrow. Good night, Claudia."

"Good night, Archilde."

When Archilde returned to his hotel again, he was utterly exhausted. Never had there been a time that he could remember when he had felt so tired. His body ached as if he had been thrown to the ground and jumped on. He managed to slip into the doorway without awakening the garçon and he went upstairs clinging to the banister. He mounted slowly to his room, and while a few minutes before dozens and hundreds of impressions had been whirling and tumbling in his mind, now everything began to slip away and an oppressive, dull blankness came instead. He frowned and closed his eyes, but he could no longer recall what had been happening.

He stood before his door a long while before entering. He was catching his breath after climbing the stairs. He fumbled with his key in the lock and only after many attempts did he get the door open. He turned on the light mechanically and fell straightway on the bed with all his clothes on. In a minute he was asleep.

How long he lay there he never remembered. After a while relaxation and calmness came to his body and he breathed easily.

He awoke with a start. The light was shining directly into his eyes. The windows were closed and the room had become stuffy. He looked up and blinked and for a long time sat on the edge of his bed in a stupor. He could not realize where he was. When he stood up he heard a paper rattle, and involuntarily put his hand into his pocket. He took a letter out and only after looking at it for half a minute did he realize that it was the letter from the Indian agent. At the next moment a gleam of intelligence lit up his face and he smiled. He started to take the letter from the envelope that he had previously torn open. His mind had cleared and the blood seemed to flow once more to his head and feet. He shivered and felt the warmth stir into his veins.

For the first time he saw an envelope lying on the carpet; someone had evidently shoved it under the door while he was out. He stooped and picked it up, and for some unaccountable reason, he laid the agent's letter aside and began to open this second letter. He tore the envelope open awkwardly. As he read it his face reddened.

> Forgive me! Are you still angry with me? Will you never come to see me again? Please do! I will wait for you tomorrow morning. We will have lunch together. I've had a change of heart and now I don't care what happens to the old debut! Hereafter I'll be quite different—you'll see! Please come tomorrow morning! I'll be expecting you—Michel

The name was underscored three times. The handwriting was large and very regular. There were also certain flourishes and embellishments to the letters that gave it all quite an air of originality.

For the longest time Archilde could not appreciate the significance of the note. It seemed as foreign and unrelated to his life as if he had picked up a letter in the street written by an unknown to another unknown. At last it all came back. He remembered the scene of the morning and he burned with shame again. He glanced hastily through the note once more, then crumpled it and threw it into the corner. It sounded indecent. He went to the window and threw it open. The cold air rushed in and stimulated his senses. He inhaled deeply and once more remembered the agent's letter. He smiled.

He went to the bed where he had laid the letter and unfolded it with some eagerness. Here was news from home! A real breath of air!

What were those words? Why did they jump about? Why did he read one sentence over and over and make no sense of it? There were only a few sentences to be sure, but he read them many times before he knew their meaning.

> I have bad news this time and it is with sadness that I hand it on to you. Your mother is dead. We are burying her tomorrow.

Agnes says she talked to you a lot lately! She thought you had come back.

We will be putting in our crops in a few weeks. I hope you are doing well. Be assured that my sympathy is with you at this time.

Faithfully, Parker

Archilde remembered nothing more of that night—nor of that memorable day.

Chapter Twelve

"I never knew my mother before," Claudia said the next day. There were traces of anguish in her face and shame in her voice. She had not slept during the night.

They were walking together in the princely gardens of the Luxembourg, speaking only at intervals; after the adventures of the night before they were weary and preoccupied.

"More than that, it was the first time I, or anyone in the family, opposed her by even a word." She became silent again and they walked on.

It was a bright day and children were swarming around the pond with their sailing boats and some were riding on donkeys with red saddles and in carts pulled by goats. A vendor passed through the lively crowd with two bunches of rubber balloons flying above his head, and a nearby cart was stacked high with sailboats that were for rent. Mothers and nursemaids moved continually among the children, keeping their charges in sight. It had rained overnight and there were occasional puddles of water, but the sun was warm. Banks of white clouds moved rapidly across the pale sky. Pigeons were flying overhead in a closely formed bunch, and as they wheeled in the air, the sun flashed from their wings.

Archilde had never seen Claudia as sober as she was that day, and much as he wanted to say something that would at once cheer her and reveal his own friendliness, he found it difficult to make even the simplest answers to incidental questions she asked. Words were always perplexing, but shyness, even more than words, was the vigilant tyrant that ruled his emotions. He walked at her side, alert to the many feelings hidden in her words and expressions, but saying little.

"I suppose we've been afraid of her. Strange, wasn't it, that last night I didn't even think of fear? Do you know why? I believe it was because you were in the room. I hated her for being so shallow and ugly. I forgot to be afraid."

They sat down on some collapsible chairs near the Rue de Médicis and were silent until Claudia spoke again.

"It's amazing how thoughtless one can be. I suppose there are few days in a lifetime when one really lives, conscious of all one's obligations and shortcomings, as well as one's power and peace of mind. If we have peace of mind, we dodge all the other things.

"I was thinking of my father," she continued after a pause, in which she had occupied herself with making designs in the sand with the point of her umbrella. "For several years I've scarcely thought of him. The awful things mother said last night made me realize that he's been the goat in our family for a long time."

"Is it true, then," Archilde asked wonderingly, "that she made up most of that?"

"Yes, of course. Dad used to drink, but he was never like she painted him. I know why she talked that way, though. When we were at home, people criticized her and even made fun of her for her ambitions; I've heard women who came visiting give her advice about how children should be brought up. She put us at the piano as soon as we were able to walk, it seemed, and every day of our lives we did our little bit, taking turns. She had been a music teacher once. When the boys got big enough to give public recitals and win scholarships, the criticism of the neighbors became even sharper; they were sure that she was hoping to raise herself above them. They probably hated her. The remarkable thing is that in all those years she never spoke a word in her defense; not once did she open her mouth to explain herself. As I recall her, she was always tight-lipped and determined, as if every day she made a fresh resolution to achieve the hopes she had set for us.

"Father did nothing to oppose her—but neither did he help her; he thought the same as the neighbors, I guess. In his easygoing way I don't suppose he ever realized the depth of her passion. We kids knew more

The Hungry Generations | 249

about it than he did, but she had to overcome our stupidity and natural stubbornness. She wasted a good many years over me before deciding that I would never learn, and she feels resentment toward me to this day, I believe, because my stupidity was greater than her will. Can't you just see what sort of person she was? She was furnishing the energy and willpower for all of us and, more than that, withstanding the attacks of the spectators and managing the household on Dad's salary. We had no rich relatives, you know, and no influential friends. I don't suppose Dad got a large salary, yet she found it possible to send the boys to high-priced teachers.

"Last night she heaped on your head all the wrongs, real or fancied, that she has suffered all these years. She had never paused to justify herself to anyone before; why she chose you I don't know. I have an idea, however."

She looked at Archilde and became aware that he had been watching her for a long time.

"What are you thinking?" she asked.

"Well, it's funny. You understand your mother, but you don't say a word about your father. He told me all about himself the first time I met him, about your mother too. He sounded so sad and all the time he was in pain. Once, when he was talking, tears came in his eyes because of a pain he had. I wondered if you knew that he was suffering. Every time I saw you or went to your house I thought of your father. But you never mentioned him."

"Yes, that's what I meant when I said he's been the goat. We'd all forgotten about him. Vincent is always dreaming; one can't tell what he thinks about. Albert is bright and sometimes he has real fire, but he loses it too quickly, and I've been thinking too much about my peace of mind. We've gone our own ways, trusting that everyone was as happy as we were.

"Let's take a walk again. I can't sit still today.

"Dad is a good soul. He used to give us kids each a nickel and send us out to buy candy when he knew we were supposed to be practicing. Ma would discover what he had done, of course, and didn't she call him down! My! All the time that we were young there was a silent understanding between Dad and us kids. I expected it to continue, but I guess it has gradually died out. I never knew until now how remote he had become the past few years.

"A rather curious thing happened a few years ago, to show how he influenced us. A few years before we came over here Vincent went down to play for some benefit at the state fair and Dad went with him. I don't know how it happened that Mother let them go together for usually she won't let the boys out of her sight, especially before a recital of any kind. They must have got very chummy for it seems that Vincent confessed to Dad after the concert that he was sick and tired of trying to be a pianist and he wanted a regular job. Dad, I guess, was tickled and he went to the offices of his railroad there in St. Louis and got Vincent a job as a clerk. Vincent sent a wire to Mother telling her that he wouldn't be home; meantime Dad's leave had ended and he started for Kansas City. Mother didn't meet him, they must have passed each other, and it was lucky for him. She blamed him right away, naturally, for influencing Vincent. She went to St. Louis, found out at Vincent's boarding house where he was working, and went straight to the office. Believe it or not, she slapped Vincent's face four or five times before a room full of people and made him go home! And that was that."

"Holy smokes!" Archilde exclaimed. "That gives me the chills. Where did she get these ideas? What made her decide to make musicians out of everybody?"

They sat down again. A half-grown chestnut tree stood nearby and its large swollen buds were beginning to burst.

"Wait till I tell you about her father. He was a queer one too. He was a preacher and he went west with his young wife to do missionary work. He also wrote poetry; Mother has over two hundred of his manuscripts, some of them remarkable. He went west, as he put it, to spend his forty days in the wilderness—but I imagine it was too much for him. He found so little spirit for such vast space—hardly a spark. He ended up by preaching to the open air, hoping to infuse his spirit into the emptiness. He'd go into the middle of the timber and shout—and listen for the echo of his own voice. He wanted to reach to all ends of the wilderness. His poems show the growth of that idea. It's a remarkable study. He was quite mad in the end.

"I don't know exactly how Mother spent her childhood, but it was terrible enough. Both parents were dead before she was very old, and she was handed from neighbor to neighbor and ended up in an orphan asylum.

The Hungry Generations | 251

"Why are we sitting here? Let's go and have a glass of beer!

"So Mother has spent her life doing missionary work too. It's a terrible frame of mind to be in."

"Yeh. It makes me want to go home right away and start planting potatoes."

"Two beers, garçon!" she called out before they even sat down at the café. "Maybe you're right, but it's a shame. There's nothing wrong with you and you'd be a winner."

"I might lose too. Anyhow I don't see any sense in it."

"Tell me this. Wouldn't you like to become a real master of the violin and go from town to town giving concerts and receiving praise and honor from the high-ups? Wouldn't you enjoy being a sort of king among your kind—if you were reasonably sure that you could do it?"

"I can't imagine what it would be like at all. I never thought of it that way."

"It's a queer business. Any number of people would give their soul and body to any junk man to do that. Of the ones I know, none have the stuff, no matter what they do with their souls. I have a hunch you could go the farthest of any, but you don't care. Isn't it funny?"

"How about your brothers? Albert, now, he's a wizard."

"No. I used to think so. But he loses his fire too quick. Anyhow, Ma has ruined both of them already. She took their backbones out and put sawdust in. That time she slapped Vincent was a memorable occasion, you might say."

"Jesus!" Archilde said and shrugged. "Let's have some more beer."

"So you think you'll go home then. What do you expect to do when you get there?"

"There's lots to do. I'll be busy for a year just getting ready."

"You mean you've got a job waiting for you back there?"

"Sure. The barn needs mending. I want to buy cows and plant more alfalfa and break new land—"

"Well, that's all very well; but I mean what are you going to do for humanity?"

"Should I do something?"

"Of course you should. Everybody does. Some start revolutions, others become cooks, and still others musicians. You've turned down the chance to be a musician, so you'd better make sure you'll be something just as good."

"I'll tell you what I'm going to do. I've got two nephews, one is twelve, the other fifteen years old—in ten years, if nobody looks after them, they'll be perfect Indian bucks wearing blankets and long hair. I'm going to make white men out of them. How's that?"

"You mean you're going to be like a Baptist missionary? That's a hell of an ambition!"

"No, I'm not a missionary. All I want is to be around and talk to Mike and Narcisse—that's their names—when they come home from school. I don't like to see them get fat and lazy. I came home after three years in a government school and for a long time I did nothing but sit in the pool halls and gamble a little; there was nobody to talk to, nothing to do. One night we got in a fight and somebody cut me up pretty bad. I guess that scared me and I never went back. But the boys might not get cold feet and go on the way I was for the rest of their lives. Everybody's got to have a friend when he wants to talk about something. I'd like to have my nephews talk to me."

"So that's what's in your mind! Is that why you're giving up your violin?"

"Partly. Also because my father wanted me to build up the ranch. We have a big place and just now it's standing idle and everything needs repairing."

"Maybe you're right, Archilde. I laugh at your ideas because I confess that, up to now, I've found more interest and stimulation here than I've ever had before. But maybe you're right and perhaps I should get out too."

"You've really liked it here, then?"

"I've adored every minute! But I confess it seems different. What's more, I've never tried seriously to earn my own living. I sell an article to a newspaper or magazine once in a while; otherwise I've lived at home and given it no thought. Dad paid the freight.

"I guess I'll have to go and see how Mother is. If I drink any more beer, I won't be able to make it. She hates beer too and she'll smell it on me. So much the worse for her.

The Hungry Generations | 253

"I say, you haven't had a very good time in Paris. Everybody you've met turns out a fizzle."

"I've had the best time in my life! I've never known anyone like you before—"

"Go on! They grow on bushes!"

"No, it's a fact! I've never known anyone like you."

They stood together on the sidewalk for a minute without saying anything and when an empty taxi appeared, Claudia hailed it.

"Well, I've got to go," she said, watching him. "I guess you hadn't better come. Ma may be in a bad temper."

"Yes. I guess you're right."

"Well—good-bye. We should have had another beer." She got in the taxi and drove away while he was still standing in the same place.

[Editor's note: a page of the original manuscript is missing here.]

. . . the yard bringing black, rich-looking soil and manure. Each time the cart came upon the scene the gardener in his long smock would stop his work and engage the drayman in conversation. Together they would stand before the pile of manure and talk quietly and earnestly about things. Their voices scarcely reached Archilde, but he could tell that their conversation was serious and dignified. He watched them and seemed to understand perfectly every word they uttered. He agreed or disagreed now with one—now with the other. When the drayman took his horse by the bridle and led him away at last, Archilde all but gave him a farewell salute. Then he bent his gaze on the gardener once more.

He saw him spread a layer of soil over the bed and rake it evenly over the surface; next he put a layer of manure and raked it long and thoroughly until it was completely mixed with the soil. At last his beds were built up, high in the center and with the utmost regularity in shape. Finally, he brought his plants from the hotbeds and set them out with painstaking care. It was a great day, this day of planting, and the gardener did not finish until it had grown quite dark. Darkness did not bring a chill with it any longer; now there was a soft warmth and freshness in the evening wind. When the lights came on in the city, a few stars had already made their appearance overhead. Archilde continued to sit in the window until the last glow of daylight had faded out of the sky and the night was at hand. When he arose, he was extraordinarily happy. It was as if he had been working in the soil himself.

His two trunks were standing near the doorway, packed and ready to go; one trunk was full of books. He looked at them in the shadow and felt an overwhelming excitement. He was going away at last.

He turned on the light and went into his little lavatory to shave. When he looked at himself in the mirror he was smiling broadly. "I am going away, do you understand!" he said aloud.

During the past four or five days he had been on the go every hour of the day. The excitement had been at work in his blood for a long time, and now it was surging into the open. He hardly knew what he was doing anymore and he could not keep the smile from breaking out on his face. In the street he walked rapidly with his coattails flying. Every day he had gone to the American hospital to see Claudia's father. Only there, when he stood at the sick man's bed, he did not smile; his excitement disappeared too. When he shook hands with the long, thin figure, Mrs. Burness stood by, pale and speechless.

He had been at the hospital during the morning, and when he was leaving the room, Mrs. Burness spoke for almost the first time.

"I hear you are going away. That will be pleasant!" She forced a smile into her colorless features that made her look unpleasant. She did not offer her hand.

He had just finished shaving and was dressing to go out when he heard a knock at the door. He looked up in surprise and had just bade "come in" when the door opened and there stood Feure, smiling and looking very friendly.

"Let's go to dinner together, or have you other plans?" he said in a casual tone.

At once Archilde felt foolish and unmanly for ignoring and avoiding Feure who seemed at that moment good and generous. A warm friendly light shone in his eyes.

"Feure! That's a good idea!" He was awkward and tried to apologize but couldn't think of the right thing to say. In a little while Feure put him at his ease by talking in a very ordinary way and as though they had been meeting every day as formerly.

"Claudia tells me that you were pleased with my recital. I'm awfully glad because I really think it went off well. Did you read the reviews? Weren't they excellent! Except the one in the *Paris Times*—I hate that fellow. He's a Jew, a young American who goes around puffing himself up all the time. You've seen him. But I don't care! It went off very well and I was surprised more than anyone else. And just think, I haven't played for a week since, only for an hour a day! I feel good, I can tell you! What do you think of Claudia's father? Isn't that a shame! Have you been out to the hospital? I was there yesterday and Mrs. Burness looks like a ghost. I've never seen anyone take anything so tragically. I told her she would be in bed herself if she didn't stop worrying. She said yes, she wished she were in bed. I had a letter from Aunt Grace this morning, congratulating me and urging me to come home in June. But I'm not going to do it; I've made up my mind to stay in New York. I'll take some pupils and live by myself. No, I'll not go home—I'll starve first—unless Mother needs me. Then I might go for a while—"

The same old Feure talking himself out of breath and saying nothing. Archilde smiled when they were in the dark street.

A curious incident took place just as they were entering the restaurant. They had started to go through the doorway but stood to one side to make way for three young Americans who were coming out. The first fellow had his head lowered and was putting money into his billfold after having paid the cashier. He stumbled into Feure and looked up to apologize; when he saw who it was he smiled, almost laughed.

"Well look who's here!" he cried. "Mitchell Feure. Mitchell F-e-w-e-r! Where have I heard that before? Oh, I know! I was thinking of *mich less!*" Everybody within earshot burst into guffaws. Feure turned pale and walked to a vacant table quickly.

"That's the swine!" he said under his breath. "That's that Jew who wrote the piece in the *Paris Times!* Isn't he hateful! Let's not eat here. Everybody is looking. What'll I do? Oh, I hate him!"

Archilde had laughed too, but now he felt rather sorry for his companion. "No, don't go away," he said, laying his hand on his arm. "That will be more noticeable. They don't mean anything bad. See, they really look friendly and several over there are saying hello. No, just sit here and we'll talk in a natural way. That will be best. I saw Claudia's father too. Tell me, don't you think he is better off in the hospital than

256 | D'Arcy McNickle

at home? In the hospital it will be quiet and at least he will be alone part of the time, at night anyhow—and he can rest. That's what he needs. He hasn't rested for many years. Don't you think?"

"What's that? Yes, I suppose he needs rest. What do you think of that swine talking to me that way! Isn't it too awful for words? But that's a Jew for you!"

"What is a Jew?" Archilde asked.

"Don't you know what a Jew is? Really! Do you mean you don't know?"

"No. Are they any different?"

Feure was too astonished for words. Even now he couldn't believe that Archilde was serious.

"Do you really mean it?" he paused a moment. "They're Jews that's all; you can't mistake them; they're rude and coarse. You can always tell one on sight. They look greasy and they always push themselves in front of you. You're certainly funny if you don't know what a Jew is! Don't they have them where you come from?"

"I guess not. You really hate them then? Is it true that they are all alike?"

Feure could not get over it and exclaimed every few moments that Archilde was a wonder. He developed his ideas on Jews at length until Archilde became tired of hearing it. There didn't seem to be any reason or purpose in his attack, and he tried to change the subject.

It wasn't an enjoyable meal, and he began to regret his friendliness of a moment before. He was amazed that he had ever enjoyed Feure's company and also surprised that scarcely an hour before, when Feure appeared at his door, he seemed to have forgotten his former dislike. He determined to get away. He'd had enough of the silly business.

Feure wanted him to go to a café for a cup of coffee, but Archilde said he had to pack his trunk.

"To pack your trunk? What for?"

"Why I'm going away—didn't I tell you?"

"Going away? Well, of all things! No, you haven't told me a word. When are you going?"

"Tomorrow. I must bring my trunks to the station first thing in the morning." Feure was overwhelmed.

"Going away tomorrow! Good Lord! Then you aren't going to stay and study? You're coming back, aren't you?"

"No—I don't plan to come back."

"But that's so silly! I've been telling everybody about—I know a dozen people who want to hear you play! I can arrange a recital for you at once—if you will say yes—I know several organizations that would be only too glad to have you."

"No—I've given up that. I'm going home to work."

"Work? You mean study? Don't you think you're good enough? You're crazy!"

"No, I mean work—on the ranch. Fix the roof on the barn, build fences, plant crops—all that."

Feure's eyes grew wider and wider. Finally, he gave in and didn't try to argue. "Well, you certainly are strange! Let me come help you pack, then. Everything must be in a mess. Why didn't you say something before? I think you're mean!"

Archilde flushed. "As a matter of fact, I'd like to be alone tonight. Everything is in a mess, as you say—my mind is too. I want to sit down and think—by myself. Will you pardon me for being rude?"

"Oh, why—certainly." Feure was at a loss. For once his speech failed and he merely stared. His face slowly reddened.

"Yes, I see. I'll leave you alone. I suppose I bother you with my talking. Will you knock on my door before you leave? I'd like to say good-bye." He turned around quickly and walked away. Archilde stood watching him and he felt ashamed.

He was going away, but he wasn't excited any longer. Unaccountably, the magic of the thought had slipped away. He felt tired and he dreaded the feverish hurry and confusion of the next day. He had been thinking for months of the joyous moment when he would make up his mind at last to go back home. As he had thought of it in his mind, this decision would entail nothing more than taking the train to the boat, getting on the boat, and going home. But he had been attending to the details for almost a week, and as it seemed, everything was yet to be done on the next day. When he reached his room, he had almost decided to cancel his passage. His room was barren looking and no longer cheerful. Everything was packed. He was sorry that he lied and acted so unfriendly to Feure when on this, the last night, he could easily have put his grudges out of sight. "But why isn't he different?" he thought at the next moment.

Someone knocked on his door and he started violently. Surely Feure hadn't come again!

"Who's there?" he called.

"It is me," his genial garçon replied. "Someone wants you on the telephone at once!"

"The telephone? Who is it?" he asked, already starting down the stairs.

"It is a mademoiselle, I think." The garçon smiled and could offer nothing more.

"This is—" said the voice over the wire, but the name escaped him entirely. The voice was utterly strange. It sounded old and tired.

"Who? Who's talking?" he shouted, for the voice had already started to say something else.

"Claudia! Don't you know me. I had been planning all week to come and see you tonight—and surprise you—but I can't. Something terrible has happened. I can't speak. I must hurry back—" somewhere, he didn't hear. He had missed a complete sentence.

"Claudia!" he shouted. "I can't hear! Please say it again."

"Good-bye—maybe I won't see you! Good-bye—" her voice broke off again and her receiver hung up.

He was irritated, half angry. Everything was conspiring to make these last hours unpleasant and gloomy. He put on his hat and coat and went downstairs again. He walked through the street slowly. People strolled along leisurely, couples had their arms around each other; one couple stopped abruptly to kiss and he nearly ran into them. He turned off the Rue de Rennes and without thinking, started down the Rue de Vangirard. He observed his position when he came to the Boulevard Raspail, but he turned neither to right or left, he continued across the boulevard and disappeared again into the dark Rue de Vangirard. He walked slowly and without thinking. He came to the iron fence around the Luxembourg gardens, passed the Senate building, and came to the Odeon. Stars were overhead and the street was pitch dark. He went on, down the short hill that ends in the Boulevard Saint-Michel. He expected every moment that someone would step out of the shadows, but the street was empty. When he stepped into Saint-Michel, he saw the traffic whirling past. He crossed the street and went to the Café d'Harcourt.

The orchestra was playing and the room was full of smoke. Talk and laughter were everywhere. He took a seat in a corner on a leather bench. Some girls were seated several tables distant and they all noticed him when he sat down. He ordered a liqueur and looked several times at the girl on the end of the table. She was young, fresh looking. She was not haggard like some of the others. Her hair was dark and her lips and cheeks brilliantly rouged. She let her eyes wander in his direction. He did not look away. She crossed her legs and turned more directly toward him. One of the girls said something and she laughed gaily, showing her teeth and swaying her body. She turned again to the table as if her interest were in something else. As she looked in the other direction, she pulled her dress up and fixed her garter, which was above the knee. She stretched her leg out straight before her and then slowly brought it back, letting her dress fall from her fingers. When she looked again, Archilde was reading a paper; he sipped his liqueur and never once looked up. His face was perfectly calm. When he finished his drink, he got up to leave; as he passed her chair, she leaned back to laugh at something and her elbow poked him in the hip. He didn't look to right or left, only murmured "pardon," and walked on. At the doorway he thought, "Shall I look back?" but again he moved straight ahead. He went to another café and ordered a liqueur and sat out under the awning in semidarkness.

"Is it true that people like this?" he said half aloud. "They suffer to come and enjoy it? They make each other mad to live here? They become artists here?" The garçon gave him a look and came forward to ask if he had ordered something else.

"No," he said and smiled. "What damn fools!" he muttered and walked away.

Chapter Fourteen

He was going away! Excitement had returned to his blood and he walked up and down the train platform in the Gare Saint-Lazare impatiently. He had too much clothing on and perspiration covered his face. He could hardly breathe. What confusion and noise there was everywhere!

Americans were arriving in one taxi load after another. They had their arms loaded with packages and the porters who hurried after them were staggering under bags and more packages. It was a quarter of an hour before train time. Parties had become separated, and fat women in gray coats moved through the throng looking worried and frantic. When they found whomever they were searching for, they spoke angrily and in loud voices; French gendarmes paced serenely up and down, their hands resting on their belts and their eyes fastening now on one person now on another with shrewd, appreciative glances.

Everything had been done that morning with the utmost precision. Everything had become simple when he actually took hold of it. He had only a small bag and a light overcoat to carry. He smoked innumerable cigarettes and waited. Now it was only twelve minutes. He decided to start toward the track; the gatekeepers were getting things in readiness; they would open the gate presently.

"Archilde!" he heard his name called, but it seemed too unlikely to be possible. He didn't even turn.

"*Archilde!*" He turned quickly and found Claudia almost at his

260

side. She had been coming in a hurry and her face was flushed. At once he saw her bright eyes and her smile seemed somewhat self-conscious and confused.

"I never thought I'd make it! I swear I didn't! I gave the taxi driver ten francs as soon as I got in the cab, and he drove like the very devil. Oh, it was awful! I'm a wreck! But you aren't gone, isn't that swell!"

"No, I just started for the gate—but there's lots of time. Where did you come from? Oh, and that strange telephone call last night, I couldn't understand anything you said! Only when you said good-bye. And then I almost fell over—that was the first time I realized I was going away."

"Yes, I know I sounded like a nut. The truth is everything was upset. Just as I was getting ready to leave and come to your hotel—it happened. I was going to surprise you. And then do you know what else I was going to do? I was going to sit there in your room and for a whole hour—longer than that if necessary—tell you, tell you straight out and to your face, what a fine fellow you are and how glad I am that you have chucked us all out of your life and are going back where you understand life best and where—no doubt—you will be a master in your own way. Yes, I had thought it all up in a pretty speech and I was going to let you hear it to the end. My, how your mouth drops open at that! You are a barbarian, you will never permit flattery. Isn't it flattery that distinguishes a civilized man? Does a barbarian know how to accept it or how to give it in return, as a smooth polished weapon that pierces every armor and cuts the heart cold in a flash? No, a barbarian doesn't have armor and when he wants to make an impression he throws a rock. But his bare chest is there to be hit with a rock in return. What nonsense I am talking." She stopped to tuck her hair under her hat.

He had noticed immediately that she was unusually excited; as she talked he became more acutely aware of this and it made him uneasy. She talked almost as if she were drunk or on the verge of hysteria. Also he knew that she had been talking about mere whims—as if she feared to tell him the real thing.

"What—what is it?" he asked her, standing very near. "Why are you so—excited?"

"Am I excited? No, really I'm not. It was the fast ride and the thought that I might miss you. No, that's not it. Archilde! Mother has gone mad! My God—yes—" she swayed and fell against him. She whirled around quickly to look the other way, but he had seen in a flash that her eyes were red and swollen. He turned pale and walked to her quickly, taking her arm.

"Here, let's go away. I'm not going on the damn train! Where shall we go. Let's go have a drink or a cup of coffee." She put her handkerchief to her face and for a while could not speak. Her hand gripped his arm.

They had moved to the opposite end of the platform where there was no one. She leaned against him and dabbed at her eyes with her handkerchief. Suddenly she smiled.

"What a goose I am! Don't be foolish, Archilde, you must go and in another minute. Look the crowd has almost all passed through the gate. It's only temporary. The doctor assures me that she'll recover. You'll never get a seat, now. Poor boy, you'll stand all the way to Cherbourg." She powdered her face nervously.

"No, Claudia, I don't want to go! Let me stay. I'm no good at helping people when things happen, but I want to be around just the same. No, we'll walk away now and that's all there'll be to it. Then we'll go have a drink."

"Please, Archilde—you are tearing my nerves! You must go! Look—the last of the people are going through the gate. The guard is giving the signal. Run, Archilde. Only, listen! Think of me, that now I have a job too! I must work now! Good-bye, Archilde! Run!"

Why, he did not know, he never understood afterward—he turned and ran! Someone had stolen his bag, but he did not stop to look for it. The guard closed the gate as soon as he passed through.

The train was rolling down to the sea. Evening was approaching. He had forgotten to ask the steward for a ticket to the dining car and he hadn't eaten a bite. The excitement had frozen in his heart and he was numb and lethargic. Claudia had been right. He didn't get a seat and he had been standing in the narrow passageway all the time, staring through the window. He watched the dull, flat countryside slip by and a mounting sadness filled his chest. He was tired. Thank God! There would be mountains soon!

Part Three

Montana

Chapter One

Archilde was a farmer now. He arose every morning at daybreak and put on his heavy boots and overalls. As he went downstairs, his steps echoed loud and firm in the quiet house. He walked through the shadowy barnyard and the cool air drove away the last traces of drowsiness. Down by the creek the trees were coming to life, a sharp, brisk wind swayed the dark pines, and as their shadowy tops moved from side to side, they soughed in slow rhythm. The cottonwoods were more rigid; they had the limbs of old men and they could not yield easily to each vagrant wind. Tiny leaves hung on the cottonwoods, giving a meager covering to their barrenness. For spring had come.

Archilde had built a milk house over the creek. A small cart with two large wheels stood by the doorway. Inside there was a strong odor of milk. A dim light entered the windows, revealing the deep trough where he washed his cans, and on a wide, sloping bench, his cans and buckets were standing upside down where they had been left to drain. There was also a stove with a big iron kettle in which he heated water. The stream could be heard tinkling and gurgling beneath the floor. At one place there was an opening left in the floor and a box had been built down into the water. In this box he kept his cream cans and the cold water flowed around them, all but covering them. He took two large cans and a bucket from the draining board and put them in the cart by the door. Then he started for the cow barn. It was growing light quickly,

| 265

and he could see the nearby fields. Agnes had gotten up by now and a light burned in the kitchen. A heavy odor of wood smoke filled the air.

The cow barn was small and of recent construction. A few chips and shavings were still to be found nearby, and the white paint with which it had been painted was still fresh where it had spattered on the cement foundation. A small ditch had been dug leading into the barn, and water from the creek could be directed to flow through the barn and flush the gutter. The hired man had just finished feeding the cows as Archilde entered. There were only six cows and they milked three apiece. The hired man was a full-blood Indian with long hair, braided and hanging down each side of his chest. He always wore a blue coat and a low-crowned, broad-brimmed hat. He and Archilde only exchanged a word at long intervals. The barn had a hayloft overhead and it was built wide enough to have another row of stanchions when the herd got bigger. At the front end there was a feed room and granary with a gasoline engine for grinding feed. In this room there was the musty odor that is given off when oats and barley are ground.

As soon as the milking was over, Archilde sent his helper to run it through the separator while he went at once to the machine shed. He opened the door and pulled the long red seeder into the open. It was dusty and there was chicken manure on the lid of one of the grain boxes. That morning he was to start seeding his grain. He worked on the drill for half an hour, and then Agnes opened the kitchen door and said that breakfast was ready. Even then he did not stop at once but continued to piece together one of the chains that drags behind to pull the soil over the planted furrow. At the kitchen door he spoke to Tom, his helper, who was washing his hands at the bench outside:

"Are the horses harnessed up?"

"Yeh—all ready."

Inside it was warm and pleasant with the smell of cooking. A table was set in the kitchen covered with a red and white checked cloth. Just as they sat down to eat, Narcisse came downstairs. Archilde frowned.

"Where's Mike?" he asked.

"I think he slept at Pete's house," Narcisse answered indifferently and went outside to wash his face. Nobody could eat with Archilde without washing. Narcisse returned to the room in less than a minute and slipped into his place at the table without a word.

"Why didn't you bring Mike home with you?" Archilde asked.

"He wouldn't come," Narcisse replied.

"What were you doing there? I told you before not to go."

Narcisse shrugged his shoulders. "We met Pete in town. We rode back with him." He offered no further information and Archilde had to pursue his questioning.

"What were you doing? How long did you stay at Pete's?"

"We ate supper then I came home. Mike stayed."

"Did you ask him to come with you?"

"Yes. Pete told me to shut up and get away."

"Oh, he did! Was Pete drunk?"

"Sure." Archilde paused for a moment, then asked:

"Were you and Mike drinking?"

"I took a drink because Mike laughed at me. He got drunk I guess."

Archilde shoved his chair away from the table abruptly and got to his feet. He was pale with anger. He turned on Agnes.

"Why don't you watch these boys like I tell you! I'm working in the field and can't see everything that goes on!" He walked out of the room without another word and with his breakfast unfinished. He went to the barn, cursing under his breath. He did not pause for a moment. As soon as he entered the barn, he went to his horse and threw a saddle on him. He led the horse outside, sprang on his back, and went down the road at a gallop. He was without a hat or coat.

Trouble was on the horizon. For a long time clouds had been gathering. They would not go away. The choicest land on Max Leon's ranch belonged to his children. It had been given to them by government allotment. During his lifetime he had been virtually the renter of their land— though none had ever dared to demand it of him. The agent favored this arrangement because under Max the land was put to good use and his sons received benefit from it—he paid a regular rent for it each year. When Max died, the land continued as part of his estate and the rent was still paid as formerly. This arrangement continued during the years that Archilde was away. As soon as he returned, trouble began to develop. The older brothers came and demanded their places. Their claims were legitimate and nothing could be done but concede their wishes. Pete built a shack on his ranch and imported his gang of hood-lums. He was supposed to be farming for Umbert and Big Blase as well—but he did nothing. He had a half-hundred head of cattle, and they roamed all over Archilde's ranch for Pete would build no fences; he had torn down Archilde's fence on one or two occasions. Moreover, these allotments were in the very center of Leon's holdings. Several large springs arose on one allotment, fringed by cottonwood and poplar groves. The soil on every side of the spring was deep and rich. Max had started his grain raising there. But Pete wasn't the principal aggressor in this matter. It was a far more subtle attack. Someone else was inspiring it and advising Pete, perhaps even financing him. Now they were trying to win Mike and Narcisse too so that Pete could rent their places.

Pete's home was built hastily out of rough, unpainted boards. It had been built less than two years ago and it was already dark and weather stained. Dark brown streaks marked the rows of nails. The roof was cov-ered with tar paper that was becoming loose and torn in places. In the yard everything was confusion and dirt. Two mowing machines and a wagon, new only the year before, were backed under a large pine tree. They had been standing there all winter—and the summer before that. A hay rake stood by the barn, there was no more space under the tree; it was heavily rusted. The barn was built of straw stuffed between poles that were placed close together; the roof was also of straw. This had not been repaired for a year or so, and large holes began to appear where the wind had carried away some of the straw or where the cattle had eaten holes during the winter. A pile of manure stood immediately in front of the door—but inside there was much more. There were four stalls, two of them occupied. These stalls had not been cleaned for so long that the horses stood with their hind quarters slightly higher than their front; the smell was acrid and the underfooting was soggy. There was nothing else on Pete's "farm." A pile of tin cans and refuse lay outside the door of the house—saddles and bridles lay on the ground where they had been pulled from the horses. A set of harness lay across the tongue of the wagon, stiff and cracked with weathering. Archilde knew all these things. He had been here before and observed each item with disgust. When he rode to the house on this morning, he looked neither to right or left. More than half a dozen dogs had been trailing him for a hundred yards, setting up a terrific howling. They were thin, cowardly beasts. They scattered as soon as he looked at them. He dismounted before the door and left his horse standing with the reins trailing on the ground. He pounded on the door with the wooden handle of his quirt. Everyone was sound asleep. He knocked again, and presently he heard a sleepy grunt. He pushed the door open and looked into the dim interior.

People were sleeping on the floor. Archilde could not see how many nor could he tell who they were. There was only the one room. Back in the farthest corner was a stove. Pete slowly rose to a sitting position and looked at Archilde. He was fat and greasy looking. He slept in his clothes with a blanket rolled around him. A dull grin came to his lips and he started to roll a cigarette as soon as he sat up.

"What do you want, chicken?" he asked.

"Where's Mike?" Archilde was still pale, but in his voice there was no sign of emotion; it was grave and serious.

"I don't know. Didn't he come home?" Pete finished his cigarette and grinned as he lit it, shielding the mouth with his hand.

"That's a lie!" Archilde said quietly.

Pete shrugged his shoulders and lay back on his elbow.

"Who've you got in here anyhow?" Archilde stepped inside and peered down at the sleepers. Pete's squaw and another woman were over by the wall. There were two other forms nearer Pete. Everyone was asleep or feigned sleep. There was one form that aroused Archilde's suspicion. The blanket was pulled over the head completely, and he couldn't tell whether it was man or woman.

"What you doin' in here!" Pete asked sharply. "This is my house. Get out!"

"Shut your mouth," Archilde said without looking up. He went to the suspicious form and kicked the feet. The figure didn't stir.

"If you don't get the hell out of here, I'll give you a slug in the jaw," Pete growled, though he didn't move.

"If you get up, I'll bust your head!" Archilde said and looked quickly and sharply at his brother. He knew that he was a coward. He reached down and grabbed the blanket; he gave it a quick jerk—and there was Mike. He was laughing softly and looked up with a roguish grin.

"What are you doing here? Get up!" Archilde's voice was sharper.

"Go on! It's too early. Can't you let a fella sleep?" Mike countered in a bantering tone. Pete was chuckling to himself.

"Get up, I say!" He didn't wait for any more words. He took Mike by the shirt and pants and dragged him to his feet. A scuffle ensued in which, either purposely or accidentally, Mike hit Archilde in the face. Without a moment's hesitation Archilde drew back and hit Mike square in the mouth and sent him flying toward the door where he fell in a heap. The breath was hissing in Archilde's nose and his anger became apparent in the nervousness of his movements. He had never before struck either of his nephews.

Mike got to his feet slowly. His mouth was bleeding and his lips began to swell. He looked at Archilde with flashing eyes and slowly went outside. At the doorway Archilde turned to Pete.

"If you'll step out here, I'll give you the damnest threshing you ever got in your life!"

"Ho! Is that so! No, you like to pick on little boys! No, don't try to bluff a man—you might get hurt!"

"Yeh—well, come out and do it! You bag of manure!" He called him a string of foul names, but Pete merely lay there and grinned. Archilde walked away.

Mike was leaning against the side of the building staring at the ground and his hands in his pockets.

"Where's your horse?" Archilde asked.

Mike didn't answer.

"Did you turn him loose?"

"None of your business!" Mike answered without looking up.

"Well, go on home now. The horse will come of his own accord. Take your saddle then."

Mike didn't stir. Archilde walked up close to him and took his arms in his hands with a sharp grip.

"Look here, Mike. I'm boss, do you understand? I'm going to make you obey me if I have to break your neck!" he tightened his grip. "When I tell you not to come to Pete's, you're not to come or you'll take the consequences. When I tell you to go home now, I mean it or I'll whip you every step of the way with this quirt. Do you understand me? Pete is a coward and a dog. Ask him yourself to come out here and fight me.

The Hungry Generations | 271

He won't move. You know it yourself. Do you care for cowards? You're not one yourself. You're strong and afraid of nobody. You should pick a man for a friend. Come home now. You can ride my horse. I'll walk."

Mike went home. He wouldn't ride Archilde's horse, however, so they walked side by side and Archilde led his horse behind.

Chapter Two

Mike would soon be fifteen years old. He was getting tall and broad shouldered. In a few more years he would begin to fill out and then he would be quite a man. He would have a deep chest and a long straight limb. His arms would be powerful. In his mind, though, there was a dark, ugly twist. He was resentful and, at times, mean. He scowled and had a contemptuous sneer when Archilde spoke of certain things. Some days he worked, even willingly, then he would undergo a change and for days do nothing but lay around, useless and irresponsible. He was a good rider and had already made a reputation for himself at the fall rodeo show where bucking contests were held. He even took in a horse once in a while to "break" for some rancher nearby, but he didn't stick with it for long at a time, though Archilde encouraged him. He was growing rapidly enough, but he was growing crooked. Archilde watched him and was not happy.

Archilde rode the seeder back and forth across the field. Behind him lay the straight, even furrows into which the wheat grains were deposited. When he reached the end of the furrow, he turned his horses carefully so that the inside wheel should not move from its position and leave a gap in the seedbed. Returning down the other side, he kept his horses well against the previous drilling. It was a slow, sedative process. The wheels left a broad, smooth track in the soft earth; a fine dust rose from the planters and at times flowed over his head. The sun was growing warmer each day and by noon a good, comfortable heat held over

272 |

The Hungry Generations | 273

the land. Up in the mountains the snows were just beginning to move and the creek below the house could be heard for a long way over the fields. The sky overhead was intensely blue and the sun wandered across its space alone, unencumbered—a god in glistening brass. There was not a cloud anywhere. Far down, near the edge of the timber, a meadowlark called at long, drowsy intervals. Archilde went back and forth across the field with his cloud of dust.

Archilde, now, had grown into manhood. Some would say that he was late at arriving there; perhaps he was. Things did not turn over rapidly in his mind. He came at things with hesitancy; he was never sure that he was in a position to give credence to his first impressions and reactions. It was only long afterward that he looked back and saw his experience in all its significance and importance. He could never deal summarily with facts and ideas as they were presented; nor could he trust himself to say what he thought at any given moment. He would never have made a good gambler. He might have been reckless enough, but a gambler is not thoughtlessly reckless; he deals in fleeting whims and "hunches" that are good judgment at least 50 percent of the time.

He was a man because he no longer feared his thoughts and emotions, such as they were. He was straightforward and peremptory in his attitude toward himself and his family. In other matters he might waver until he had time to think them over, but eventually he chose his course and then he could be found bearing straight ahead. But he was young. Many things were yet to happen before wrinkles came to his face. In a certain sense he might always be a child—if it is childlike to wonder and be amazed at the eccentricities of a natural world.

Sometimes, when he thought of the bright, quick eyes of Claudia, he slowed his walk or looked up quickly from his task. For a moment a heavy sensation came over him as if he had truly lost something or had gone along the wrong path. A moment later he would return to the idea on hand and continue as before. Such things could not be known. Here, he was at home, and that seemed to suffice.

He rode his seeder back and forth across the field and was totally unaware of the cloud of fine dust that enveloped him from time to time. He had a grown face now, though it had always inclined to be serious. Distinct from his brothers, he had few of the features of the Indian; most people who were accustomed to seeing breeds were genuinely surprised when they learned that he was a half-blood. He had a long, thin face with a full crown to the head. His chin was tapered finely and stood before a full jaw. His eyes were not black but a dark brown and deeply set. He had heavy brows and high temples. His cheekbones only slightly suggested his race for they were quite broad, emphasizing the eye cavity. His hair was jet black but fine, not thick and wiry. It almost seemed that he was his father's sole inheritor. As he grew older, this contrast was heightened; unconsciously, as his latent qualities developed, he went nearer to the one parent and farther from the other, yet in many respects, he differed essentially from either. He was only partially aware of this.

Archilde had a problem in his nephews. Mike and Narcisse returned from school, apparently untouched by the experience. He tried to draw them out, to get them to talk about their school days, but they were not interested in recalling a single detail—except those dealing with raids on neighboring fruit farms and smoking behind the horse barn. They had no recollection of their teachers, except that most of them were distasteful. As to learning anything, they protested vehemently that it was foolishness; they had learned nothing. Archilde knew that this wasn't so. He detected certain habits or mannerisms that could only have been acquired at school—he had picked up similar ones himself. When he drew their attention to these matters, they denied it at once and, thereafter, studiously avoided similar actions. Mike was most pronounced in this attitude. Indeed, he was in every respect more positive and definite in his character than his brother, Narcisse. The latter was a lackadaisical, slothful Indian breed, fond of squatting on his heels and talking in guttural monosyllables. He had unsteady eyes and an obscure, suspicious nature.

Mike, on the other hand, was teeming with energy and activity. He was vain and nothing pleased him more than fancy cowboy rigging and a spirited horse. He always rode at a gallop and he could sit a horse with perfect grace. Riding through the streets of the town, he held his horse's head high and made him single-foot. He broke and trained horses with remarkable skill and ease. He taught them to trot easily and to handle their feet with lightness. It was a trick he had. Yet, he was cruel to them; he used quirt and spurs viciously at times. He was only a boy.

Archilde barely kept him under control. Unwittingly, he had assumed the dream of his father. Here in this valley, where his brothers lived so miserably and were known to everyone as utterly worthless, he hoped yet to establish a firm name and to warrant the honor of his neighbors—not individually, but as a group. He wanted to deal honestly and prove a good farmer and business man. In a word, it was confidence in himself that he wanted to establish. He would not have that confidence until others were aware of it and reflected it back upon him. That is what every man wants.

There were many obstacles in the way of this. In the first place, he wanted to have his nephews with him. Single-handed, his handicap would be too great; if he could win Mike to living steadily and peacefully, then he would no longer doubt and be uncertain of the outcome. There was another matter that he was facing. His brothers had already returned and demanded their allotments of land for their own use. That wasn't serious, beyond the fact that these allotments were situated in the very center of the ranch, and Archilde had been compelled to build a new road as they had taken possession of the old one and closed it up to him. They were also bad neighbors, and he had to exercise ceaseless vigilance or he would find a herd of cattle tramping down his half-grown wheat crop—as had happened, not once, but several times. The serious problem that was facing him at the present time was that now his brothers, through an unscrupulous lawyer, were demanding a share in their father's estate. Max had kicked every one of them out of his house years before his death and did not even mention their names in his will. It was true, likewise, that they were incompetent and a court had declared them so—yet the case was still hanging fire and a fresh appeal was pending.

His brothers hadn't taken these steps on their own initiative. There was ingenuity back of it; Archilde was not fooled. Moser, the storekeeper, was the guiding spirit. He had even advanced money, Archilde had learned indirectly. He had an enemy there.

The faint notes of a bell drifted across the field. Archilde looked up in surprise and then saw Annie standing down at the house waving to him. It was dinnertime. He drove his seeder to the end of the field and unhitched his horses. Trudging along behind them in the noon heat, he went to the house, watered them, and gave them a feed of oats in the barn.

Things had not changed greatly on the ranch. The wild cucumber vines that in summer clambered over the screen porch across the front of the tall white house were beginning to grow again. The fence posts around the house had been whitewashed recently and the sagging "hog" wire repaired. His mother's cabin, sole remnant of the early days, stood untenanted; the mud plastering was falling from between the logs and the grass was springing up anew on the sod roof as it had done for almost forty years. A gentle push would probably have sent the whole structure crumbling. Archilde had bought a few more pigs and chickens. He had built a fine house and runway for the latter, and they no longer roamed the alfalfa fields and sheds at will, laying their eggs wherever they took a fancy. The horse barn had a whole roof again and a coat of red paint. The cow barn was the latest building, but it wasn't of any great size. There was no mill down by the creek. That dream had passed on to the grave. Archilde never thought of it. The job of taking things in hand, repairing them, planning, altering, erecting new buildings, was tedious and slow. If he went to build a cross fence in his pasture, he must determine how rapidly his clover grew and to how many cows it would offer pasturage. Planting time brought endless calculations about the dampness of the soil; farmers on the flat had their grain in a full two weeks before he dared set his seeder to work. Frost lingered near the mountains. He had been told that his alfalfa must be three-fourths in bloom before he started cutting but, when he walked into an alfalfa field, he was at a total loss. From the time the first bloom appeared he was in a state of anxiety. If he happened to return from town or another field after a particularly warm day and found that blossoms had appeared magically all over the field, he was all excited and ready to go at once to get together a haying crew. If he started to dig an irrigation ditch through his field, he found it necessary to know something about surveying and to have a few instruments. When he tried to use his eye, he ended up with furrows all over the field. He usually found, at last, that he couldn't get the water where it was most needed. One winter he had gone alone into the mountains to cut cedar posts and then realized that he had never in his life measured a fence post. He brought back the largest posts that had ever been used in the country. When he went to build his cow barn, he discovered that there was only one man in town who knew how to mix cement; this man refused to give his information unless he could build the barn. He was an old German carpenter with a reputation for his stinginess and gruff nature. Archilde hired him to build the foundations and feeding troughs. Usually, he had no other help than old Jim who had been a friend of his mother's. He offered no comments whatever, though many of the things Archilde did must have filled him with amazement. He was not a full-blood and did not disdain work, though he was too old to do much more than milk and care for the horses. When the barn was painted, he sat nearby and admired the brilliant red coloring matter. Perhaps he was dismayed that so much good paint should be wasted.

The task was endless. This was the third year starting and nothing had been done, as yet. He was not putting in a larger crop than he had started with, he had not seeded fresh alfalfa fields, he had not bought more stock, he had originated no new and startling policy in the valley. For the time he had to copy ideas from others as rapidly as he could assimilate them. He was like a man still balancing on one foot after jumping from one edge of a crevice to the other; he wasn't sure yet where he would come to rest. But he was fierce in his determination.

After lunch it was his habit to sit on the front porch and read for half an hour. Reading was almost the only habit he brought back with him from the outside. He read incessantly and on many subjects. Learning had become a personal thing at last; it was no longer an eccentric robe placed upon the shoulders of favored individuals by kind gods. It was an attainable quality that was not forbidden even to him. But the world of knowledge was still vast and uncharted, though of his own accord he had picked certain landmarks. Not yet had he gotten over the astonishment of discovering that, coming up from the edge of the world, as it were, he had encountered the main stream that went flowing into unimaginable distances, with a calm, unhurried wash and flow. In his childhood he had fashioned worlds of his own as he sat by the banks of the creek or lay over a pile of brush and watched a great bull trout undulating with the slow current—but what impoverished worlds they must have been! The elements at his command were few and simple for world creation; a stick and a stone symbolized, in turn, many things. Now he knew them only for what they were and no more. History was his fascination. He was enthralled by the romance of civilization and men standing shoulder to shoulder until they faded into mist and became once more clothed in barbaric skins and the filth of a savage's cave or hut. He stood at the threshold of one such hut and, after gazing long enough at the pomp and pageantry of brilliant civilization, saw himself again. Instead of gazing through a telescope, as he expected, he was merely looking into a hollow cylinder with a mirror fixed at the other end. Such thoughts made him ecstatic. He was not unmoved by the gargantuan spectacle of a savage stepping through two thousand years of space and appearing fully clothed, mannered, and equipped and speaking the language of the new age. The difference was infinitesimal if it was there at all. The only person Archilde had utterly failed to understand was the girl who threw the pot at his head in that shabby room. He could form no notion of her at all. She was at once a monster and a phantom.

Claudia, he understood, or so he thought. This understanding was twofold. He had sometimes seen in her a warm, human, perceptive quality that had never failed to set him stirring and throbbing. Her attitude toward her parents, particularly her father, was of that quality. She was sympathetic at such moments and possessed an infinite capacity to forgive and befriend. Also, she was confident and courageous then, for she was taking guidance from her deepest instincts and roots. Then there were other times. Above her friendliness stood her intellect, bright eyed, impersonal, making jokes, and above all, striving to accomplish things outside of herself. She was not content to grow. She was impelled to disregard all emotions, ties, relationships in order to go forward unencumbered and free of distraction to her chosen end. She took a leaf there from her mother, willful, voracious creature. When he confronted that side of her nature, he was left cold and uncommunicative. His understanding took a deceptive turn and left him groping. It had another effect on him too: it made him cognizant of the great distance between their lives. He withdrew immediately into himself and realized how near he had come to disclosing his emotion to her. Several times, during those months in Paris, particularly the last few weeks, he had almost ventured to speak of love; in a word, to ask her to be his wife. He had actually gone that far in his mind, and when he sat and talked to her with that thought lying there ready to appear at any moment, she seemed to become aware of it, so it had struck him at the time, and she led him away to something entirely different. He was sure that she had done it

The Hungry Generations | 279

knowingly, no doubt it gave her a certain enjoyment. It wasn't likely that she would ever have considered marriage with himself—a savage—an Indian. She was too well under the dominance of her intellect for that. Such was his understanding of Claudia.

Thus it was that Archilde weighed and reflected. His mind worked slowly, and it was necessary to recall things many times before he was sure that he understood. When he sat reading a book or performing a chore around the barn, he would look up suddenly and smile, or maybe swear under his breath, as he recalled some incident in all its clearness and was either made happy or embarrassed by the recollection. He relived that moment as actually as if it had occurred now for the first time. When it passed, he felt foolish and looked around to see if he had been observed. He had become a thinking animal. He was no longer content to live things the one time in physical reality; they must pass through his mind as well. The digesting stomach was in his head and there, as he went from place to place in his corner of the world, he called up the miscellany of his life and chewed it over. He was a ruminant and life had multiplied his interests.

Before returning to the field that afternoon, he went to have a word with Mike who had not been at the noon meal. He found him down by the barn, spinning a rope. Narcisse lay in the shade of an old corral with his elbow resting against the ground for support. Mike was expert with a rope. He started with a small loop, scarcely more than a foot in diameter. As he spun the loop before him, round and firm as the hoop of a barrel, he gradually fed more rope into it until at last the loop had grown many times its original size, and then he would jump through it or whirl it into the air above his head and let it settle down around his body, still whirling, still round and firm. Archilde stood watching, smiling in admiration.

"That's fine! But can you catch a pig?" he asked when Mike let the rope drop to the ground at last.

A short silence followed.

"Who wants to catch a pig?" Mike responded dully and sat down near Narcisse with his back against the corral. His lips were swollen. He took a package of readymade cigarettes from his shirt pocket and began to smoke, not once did he look up at Archilde.

"That was just a joke. What are you fellows gonna do this afternoon? Why don't you go over in the granary and blue stone the rest of the wheat? There's only about twenty sacks and the tank is ready. I'll finish seedin' the wheat that's already fixed this afternoon. How about it? You'll be through in less than an hour."

Narcisse shifted his position, rolling over on his stomach where he could look at Mike. The latter smoked his cigarette in resolute silence.

"Come, are you deaf?" Archilde asked with a slight frown. "What do you say, Mike?"

"Who, me?" Mike asked. "I thought you meant old Jim. As for me, I'm gonna ride to Saul Steuger's pretty soon. He's got a brown filly he wants me to break. I said I'd see him today. Maybe Narcisse can do it."

"No," Narcisse replied, "I feel pretty sick. I'm gonna ask Agnes for some pills."

Archilde stood before them, his legs wide apart and his hands in his pockets. His mouth sneered and taunts were already on his lips, ready to burst forth. But he said nothing. He spat on the ground and walked away. As soon as he turned his face a different expression came over him. He was pale and his whole person shook. As he was untying one of his horses in the barn, the horse stepped on him, and in a burst of rage, he struck him savagely on the soft muzzle and the horse reared back in pain. He had never struck a horse before. As he drove to the field shame and anger made a tumult in his breast.

Chapter Three

The first of May came. Brighter and warmer were the days. The hill before the house was blanketed in soft green. The creek awoke each day with a louder voice and already it was threatening the tops of its banks. A chicken hawk appeared in the sky from time to time, sailing majestically overhead, viewing the countryside where the flocks of chickens once more roamed the fields and barn lots. When his shadow drifted across the yard, terror seized the mild hens and with flapping wings, cackling voices, and racing feet that scarcely touched the ground, they ran for the shelter of their house and the friendly bushes growing in their yard.

One noon hour, shortly after the first of May, Archilde went to his mailbox, which was placed in the county lane a quarter of a mile above the house. He found two letters there and the first one made him flush with excitement. It was from Claudia. Several times before he had received a word from her—he having written first. Her letter was only a short note, covering the first page of a folded piece of stationery. She was in New York and wrote that her mother was seriously ill, had been for some time. Vincent had given several concerts during the past season, and Albert was in Europe at present. His symphony was to be performed in New York the following season. Vincent was teaching in Boston and she was alone with her mother. She was curious to know how he was getting along. Did he have any good friends to talk to? She knew no one. She was working in a store. That was all she wrote, a

| 281

short, matter-of-fact note that was neither jolly nor depressed. But there was a hint of unhappiness that he did not miss. She had written the year before that her father had died. At that time she had been at home, "alone," too. Both brothers were in Europe then. He walked the entire distance home before he even thought of opening the second letter.

A bill from the Moser Mercantile Co. was the next thing he saw. He had sat down in the faded wicker armchair on the front porch that had been old and rickety in his father's day. He stared at the sheet of paper in his hand and slowly the image called up by Claudia's letter faded away. A bill from Moser? He had never charged a single purchase at the store! How could that be? The amount was two-hundred-seventy-odd dollars. For what? A saddle and bridle, chaps, spurs, and lariat. There were other items listed, cigarettes, hat, two silk shirts, silk handkerchief, etc.

"It is a mistake!" Archilde thought at last, and felt easy at once. The bill was meant for someone else. He got to his feet and looked out over his fields. He had finished his planting the day before. His fall wheat was already well above the ground; he had only a small field of it. He decided to put the bill aside until the next time he went to town, but on a sudden impulse, he determined to go at once. It had struck him as very peculiar that his name, which shouldn't have been on the books at all, should become mixed in with the regular list of debtors. If he were on the books it was conceivable that they might have sent him the wrong bill, but since he wasn't the mistake seemed peculiar.

He went to the garage and started the engine of his little delivery car and drove it to the milk house where he found one full can of cream. There was no flashy blue automobile on the ranch now, the delivery truck was all he had. As he drove down the road, he stirred up a faint dust cloud.

Moser wasn't around the store. Archilde looked everywhere and, finally, found him in his grain elevator talking with several men. Archilde stood off to one side for five or ten minutes. Moser didn't look up even once or in any way indicate that he had seen Archilde approach; he continued his conversation and, presently, motioned the men toward the store and began to walk with them in that direction. Archilde spoke up.

"Mr. Moser, are you busy for five minutes? I'd like to speak to you about something."

Moser stopped but as he was in the middle of a sentence, he went on talking. When he had finished, he held his hand as if requesting his companions to pardon the interruption.

"My office is the place to see me on any business matters. I suppose it is business?" he asked without in any way changing his tone.

"Yes, but as you weren't in your office, I decided to look for you. I haven't time to wait today."

"Why not come tomorrow then?"

"Because it's a matter that won't wait. Can I see you as soon's you're through with these men?"

"Are you sure George Eagen can't take care of you? These men are from the Bitterroot and they're leaving pretty soon."

"I'd like to see you personally. I've already spoken to Eagen."

"Oh, all right then. Come over to the store. I can spare a minute, I suppose, if it's so important." He turned his back on Archilde and continued his conversation with the other men. They were both tall, well-dressed men, apparently not farmers. He walked between them, occasionally grasping one by the arm and pointing at various objects before them, his house and lawn, his gasoline station in front of the store, his warehouse at the back of the store, his two large trucks that happened to be standing before the warehouse—all these he indicated with gestures expressive of pride and ownership.

Archilde stood on the platform of the grain elevator and rolled a cigarette, waiting for the storekeeper and his party to proceed. When they had almost reached the store, he followed. He began to feel excited.

There was a side door that entered directly into the office, which was in the back end of the store. This entrance had a screen door. Archilde stood on the concrete stoop for a minute until he finished his cigarette, then he entered. On his right were several desks finished in natural oak. There was also a high sloping desk where the cashier, George Eagen, was working, perched up on a high stool. There were several windows on this side. On the left was a blank wall with a single door leading into the store. There was a map of the United States on this wall with several large calendars from a harvester company and a large manufacturer of plows.

Directly across the room was a door leading into a smaller office, which Moser used only for privileged visitors and on special business occasions, when, for instance, a destitute family were signing over the last of their property and income to him and he wanted to put a good face on the deal, or when an aged Indian came with a government check that he wanted to cash. As the Indian couldn't sign his name, Moser wrote it out for him and then showed him where to make his mark; next he would take him into the store and introduce him to a new shipment of blankets and silk shirts. Moser's smile was broad and affable at such times.

Archilde waited inside the door for five minutes while Moser was seating his two guests inside his private office and telling them a joke. Presently, he turned back to the outer room and his face ceased to smile immediately. He stopped at one of the desks to look at some papers placed on it and without looking up he asked:

"Well, what is it? I'm in a hurry."

Archilde walked across the room and took the bill that he had received that noon from his pocket.

"I'd like to know if there isn't a mistake about this," he laid the bill on the desk. Moser glanced at it and his face underwent a complete change. He looked utterly scornful.

"Is that all you're bothering me about! This has nothing to do with me! See Eagen there—he's the cashier. He knows all about these things. Didn't I tell you I was busy?" He turned away and started for the half-open door but Archilde stopped him.

"Just a minute. I've already seen Eagen, as I told you. He can't do any more than show me the books with these items written down against my name. What I want to know is who the devil bought these things?"

"Who bought 'em? Who do you suppose? They're charged to you on the books, you say, so you must have bought 'em. That's simple enough, isn't it?"

"Say, what do you mean? I haven't bought a saddle since I've been back and I haven't a silk shirt to my name. So what does all this mean?"

"You haven't, you say? Well, why don't you take it up with Eagen. I can't be bothered with the silk shirts you buy or don't buy! What's this got to do with me? I'm busy, haven't I told you already." He started for the door again, but when Archilde followed right at his heels, determined

The Hungry Generations | 285

to say what was on his mind, he contented himself with closing the door and then walking toward the center of the room.

"My God, you'll give me an explanation of this right now and in your own words or I'll bring the sheriff over," Archilde thundered at him.

"Not so loud, son," Moser cautioned, assuming a lower tone himself and also appearing more patient and forbearing. "Now, just what is it you don't like? Is there a mistake in our bookkeeping—or what is it?"

"Your bookkeeping has nothing to do with the matter. I want to know why you're charging me with articles I never bought. What's your explanation?"

"Don't exaggerate. That is, don't make out that we'd deliberately charge you for things you didn't buy. If the articles are on the books, you must have bought 'em—or someone did for you, I don't know. Have you seen the books? Here, George, what do you know about this? Where's the book?"

Eagen had the journal spread out on his desk. He turned his bloodshot eyes from Archilde to Moser and presented the book to the latter. Archilde waved it aside when Moser shoved it toward him.

"I've already seen it, I tell you. You say someone might have bought these things for me—well who was it? That's what I'd like to know. It's a damn cinch I didn't!"

"Who bought 'em? What do you mean? You certainly aren't going to insist that you don't know anything about buying these things? You can't back out of it as easy as that, my boy."

"Well, who bought the stuff? Answer that."

"Why, now that I think of it, I believe your nephew Mike opened the account."

"Mike?"

"Yes—I believe it was Mike," Moser continued in a quiet tone. He had laid the journal down, face upward, and with his hands clasped behind his back, he rocked back and forth on his heels. "Yes, Mike came to me the first of the month and said you had given him permission to open an account for himself. Wasn't that all right? Is that all you want to know?"

Archilde was dumbfounded for the moment and made no immediate reply. A little later he said:

"See here, Moser, there's to be no more of this, do you understand?
I'll not be responsible for such debts hereafter, and you'll have public
notice to that effect. So you let Mike open an account, did you?" He
spoke absently and in a calm voice. But his paleness betrayed his excitement. He turned and walked out of the room slowly without paying any
more attention to Moser or his bookkeeper, as if his mind had become
occupied with other matters.

That night Archilde ate dinner with Agnes and Annie, his niece.

"Where're the boys?" he asked when he came in from the front
room to take his place at the table.

"I don't know. Fishing, maybe," Agnes replied.

"At night?" he half growled.

"Annie saw them start up the creek this afternoon. They haven't
come back."

The meal consisted of vegetables boiled with beef, the meat not
being boiled long enough to make it tender. It was Agnes's favorite way
of cooking meat. Of her own accord, she would have added only potatoes; Archilde had planted carrots, turnips, rutabagas, and onions in the
garden and he persuaded her to use these as well.

Annie was a quiet girl, dark and heavy featured, but not ugly. She
was shy before Archilde and never looked him directly in the face. She
was taller than Agnes, as tall as Archilde, and noticeably awkward.
Archilde spoke to her every day, at every meal, but she never grew at
ease before him. Once, only a little while after he returned home, he had
said, "Annie, put on a clean dress two or three times a week. For supper, especially." Now she always wore a clean dress. He bought her
dresses at the store and they were neat. She braided her hair and let it
hang down her back. Her face had a stupid expression because of its
immobility; that was characteristically Indian. Sometimes Archilde
asked, "Don't you ever laugh?" In reply her head dropped a little more.
When something was missing from the table and Archilde asked for it,
she got up quickly and fetched it, without a word or look. Somewhere,

underneath, there was undoubtedly a person with certain likes and dislikes, fears, hates, inclinations, hopes, like any human being that breathes and lives from day to day. If there was such a person beneath her dark skin, it was imprisoned deeply within a stony, nerveless, listless body. She was like a dead, sapless tree that stands almost immovable in a storm. Yet she did everything her mother asked of her, and Archilde never spoke to her twice before she fulfilled his request. That much could be said for her.

Agnes grew lazy as she grew older; she was five years older than Archilde. She was quickly becoming the old lady of the house, though everyone called her Agnes as in the days when she was much younger. Sometimes she could be quite jolly. She had a soft, pleasant voice and one of her front teeth was of gold; Max had this put in for her. Since then many other teeth had decayed, but she would never go to a dentist again; she had her gold tooth. Perhaps she learned to smile because of that tooth. She had never scolded her children, now she never asked them what they were doing. She looked out before their doings and was content to sit in her kitchen and say nothing. Formerly, she had not gone to pick berries or fish, but now sometimes she would go out and leave Annie to cook a meal. More and more she was growing like the old lady, Max's wife; she was getting broader and more and more fond of sitting in the sun. But her gold tooth and jolly smile made her a different person.

As his father had done before him, Archilde was constantly asking Agnes for information and often he would relay advice or a general hint through her to his nephews.

"Has Mike got a new saddle and riding outfit?" he asked toward the end of the meal.

"A saddle? I have seen none."

"No? But Moser tells me he bought chaps, bridle, and saddle, besides some clothes. I have not seen it either." He remained silent for another moment.

"Why should he buy these things and not use 'em?"

"How could he buy? He has no money," Agnes interrupted.

"He didn't pay. He told Moser I would pay. Was he mad because I hit him at Pete's house?"

"Sure. You shouldn't do that."

"No? Then tell him to be careful next time! I will break his neck!"

Agnes shook her head from side to side. "No, that is bad. He will get even with you, he said so."

"He did? All right, we'll see!"

"You be careful!" His sister answered with a peculiarly ringing, challenging tone. Archilde looked up and studied her face, but she glanced away at once.

"What do you mean? Can't I make him do what I want—if I have to kick his pants to make him mind? I've been too good to Mike and Narce. I used to give them presents every time they did what I told them to—that was wrong. Now they won't work at all—until they find out they've got to. You'll see, a blow now and then will help."

"No—you watch out for Mike," she repeated.

"You keep saying that—what do you mean? Is he such a devil then? Or is he just a boy that I can turn over my knee and spank?"

"He is a hothead and you be careful," she persisted.

"What can he do? Cut me up with a knife? He'll have to get up early."

"No, he knows about something that you have forgotten, maybe."

"What? What's that? He knows something? What?" It was no use to ask her questions. She became silent as a stone and as undemonstrative. The meal was ended and she began to stack up the dishes, moving around the table noiselessly in her moccasined feet. Archilde shrugged his shoulders and walked into the front room.

The front room held a pleasant atmosphere. The tall heating stove with its nickel trimmings stood in the corner. Here, before this stove, he and his father had talked one night, and the memory of it was fastened permanently in Archilde's mind. Every time he entered the room, more particularly at night when he came in leisurely and with a certain turn of meditation, he was met with a kind of presence and pleasant atmosphere. In this room too he found it easier to think and plan his days. There was a spiritual reassurance in the lamplight and the worn leather-upholstered furniture.

He passed through the room and stood for a while on the few steps before the screened porch entrance. The last of the twilight had faded from the sky and there was no moon as yet to ease the darkness. The heavens, however, were thick with stars that glinted as heavily and sharply as black velvet sprinkled richly with cut diamonds both large and small and also diamond dust. The air was cool. A single dog was barking several miles away. Archilde could see the outline of the hill that he had climbed as a boy and upon whose rounded shoulder he watched for the first signs of green in spring. Off to his right, a distance of half a mile, was the land that his brothers had usurped. There stood Pete's shack and teepee. He could see the reflection of a campfire down there. It shone on the top branches of some pine trees and looked nearer at hand than it really was. An obnoxious feeling of despair came upon him as he stood there. He had a suspicion that his two nephews were visiting Pete again, drinking, no doubt—but he had no desire to find out. For the night—for a few hours—he would let his conscience rest. He faltered, and momentarily, he had an impulse to turn his back upon everything that troubled him. Life was undeniably growing more difficult day by day. He had a portent of extreme difficulty and ugliness lying in wait somewhere near. He recalled how eagerly he had returned over a quarter of the earth's surface to be in this place again—and how cold his reception had been. No one was stirred; people greeted him casually. There had grown an undercurrent of opposition, so it seemed to him, to the young Indian buck who was traveling abroad, raising himself above his birth. Was this so, or did he imagine it?

Tonight he had an impulse not to face the hurdle. He could go away quietly, with explanations to no one. No one would care that he had dodged the issue. That fire burning down there against the timber, rising and falling against the darkness of the night, bred hatred and disgust in him—also despair. Wasn't it enough for one man to build himself? Was it necessary to blow life into others too—and be kicked in the face for it?

Peace, serenity, and a majestic fullness lived in this night. Where was the key to that calmness? Why did a man encourage passion, welcome hatred, face opposition, make demands, and stand by their fulfillment when that was so contrary? Tonight he would maintain silence. If Mike and Narcisse were down there drinking—well, they could go to hell!

Chapter Four

Mike and Narcisse came home early the next morning. They had gone to see a wrestling match in town.

"Where did you stay?" Archilde asked.

"With Charlie Moise," Mike answered.

"Well, you'd better go and shake the lice off," he said, looking his nephews over carefully.

"Naw, Charlie hasn't got any. He eats 'em," Narcisse said soberly.

Archilde made a face. "Did you see him?"

"That's a lie!" Mike pointed out. "Charlie don't but his grandfather does. He's blind too. We slept in the barn."

Mike was feeling gay that morning. He spun his rope and danced in and out of the loop. When he spoke, he let the rope die down and said what was on his mind, then started the rope all over again. They were standing by the corral that was near the cowshed. Old Jim was running water through the barn and cleaning it out. His broom could be heard sweeping across the heavy plank floor.

"Tomorrow I want you to plant potatoes," Archilde said. Mike looked up.

"How many potatoes?"

"Not much. You will be finished by the afternoon. The ground is all ready. I'll plow the furrows and you two come along and drop them in."

"Sure, we'll plant potatoes."

"Today, you'll have to cut them. They're all sorted out in the cellar.

The Hungry Generations | 291

Take the big pile in the middle of the floor and be sure you leave an eye in every piece."

"Ugh, that's a hell of a job!" Mike grunted, spinning his rope fast and furiously.

"No, it's a good job for you. You can sit on your behind all the time."

"Narcisse is good at that; let him do it."

"No, sir! You're best for sitting on your behind! If I hit you on the jaw, I guess you'll be sitting there anyhow."

"Pooh! You couldn't sock a flea on the jaw."

"All right, my prizefighters, go down and get a stranglehold on those potatoes. You saw a wrestling match last night, so you should know all about that."

"Ah, I don't want to cut potatoes!" Mike said, standing listlessly with his rope in his hand.

"You'll have to do it just the same, so you better decide to like it."

"I don't have to if I don't want to!" For a moment he looked ugly and obstinate. Archilde didn't hesitate a second. He grabbed Mike by the neck and twisted his face up so he could look him in the eyes. Bloodred anger flashed before him, but he controlled it instantly. He spoke with a smile on his lips.

"Look here, little chicken. Do as I say and avoid trouble around here. If you don't work, I'm going to put a dress on you and make you wear it. Yes, by George, you'll wear it too! I'll bring you to town that way. So get busy." He took him by the arm and started toward the cellar. "Come on, Narcisse!" Narcisse followed behind, looking curiously at his brother. This seemed to be an unexpected turn in events. Mike went along with his feet half dragging, but he made no open protest.

At the cellar door Archilde stopped and turned his nephew around to face him again.

"By the way, how about that saddle and stuff you bought at the store? Where are they? And the silk shirts?"

"I didn't buy them!"

"What? You didn't buy any? But Moser sent me a bill yesterday!" Mike and Narcisse looked at each other.

"Moser give me that!" Mike said with a tone of surprise. Now Archilde looked surprised. He glanced from one to the other.

"Why did he give you such things? Is he such a good friend? What did you do for him? Did you promise him something?"

Although Mike's face was turned toward Archilde, he hadn't been looking at him. He continued to gaze through the corners of his eyes, and for a moment, he was silent.

"Naw, I didn't give him nothing."

Archilde gave him a shake. "Why don't you look at me if you're not lying? Did Moser take you into his office?"

"Sure, me and Narcisse, eh Narcisse? He said, 'You're a good rider, Mike, I'll give you a saddle and a whole outfit.'"

"He did? But did he say I'd pay for it?"

"I don't know."

"What? Don't be stupid! Of course you knew! What did he say, Narcisse? Weren't you there?"

Narcisse hung his head and scratched at the ground with his foot. "I don't remember."

Archilde looked exasperated. "I'll be damned! Such blockheads! Tell me, where is the stuff? Have you used it? I'll go shove it down Moser's throat." Mike didn't answer at once, but finally he said:

"I sold it—the saddle and bridle. All I got left is the chaps. Charlie Moise bought it."

Archilde exploded. They were such-and-such blockheads and damn fools! Thieves and liars to boot! "Get down there in the cellar and set to work!" He grabbed them both and gave them a shove. He was angry, but at the same time he was half-inclined to laugh.

At that moment a motor car appeared in the lane that led toward the house. He turned and gazed at it. The car was familiar. The next moment he recognized the little Ford from the agency. It was his friend, the agent. He walked toward the gate to meet the car. A surge of good feeling swept through him and he began to smile in earnest.

The agent left his car and walked around the back of it to enter the gate. He seemed taller when he walked in the open air. His dress had not varied in years, the same khaki breeches and leather putties; the same dark coat, white shirt, and black tie; and on his head a soft Stetson of medium brim. He carried a briefcase in one hand. He took off his hat to let the air get to his head for the morning was already quite warm.

Archilde greeted Parker with a genial smile but was struck at once with the agent's cold, unresponsive rejoinder. He had never before seen him in such a mood and he became serious at once, sensing that his friend was probably in difficulties over some matter.

"Did you come up from the agency this morning?" he asked, and led the way toward the house.

"Yes. It's getting warm."

"Shall we go inside or do you want to sit on the porch?" Archilde asked as he held the screen door open.

"The porch will do. Have you got a drink of water?"

"Sure. I'll go get some." He disappeared into the house.

The agent took a chair and sat motionless. He had a grave face but a kindly one. He had the air of a man of good breeding—a man of conscience and understanding. His hair was sandy colored, and he combed it over from the side so that it stood in a large wave over the top of his head. His eyes were gray. On his forehead, where his hat shielded his face, he was freckled, the lower part of his face bore a heavy tan and was all of one color. He took a long, thin cigar from the breast pocket of his coat and was carefully biting the end off when Archilde returned with a pitcher of water and a goblet.

"I thought we might have some lemonade, but Agnes tells me we have no lemons." Archilde poured a glass of water and handed it to his guest. Then he sat down, half-expecting the agent to open the conversation.

"Is it true that you have been back three years, Archilde?"

"Yes—it is three years at the end of the month."

"I hadn't realized it." The agent spoke absently. A brief silence followed. Parker took several brisk pulls on his cigar and, finally, blew a heavy cloud of smoke and watched it float away against the screen where it hesitated, appeared to break, and then was lost in the bright air. As the smoke drifted away, he sat up straighter in his chair and his absentmindedness left him. He looked directly at Archilde, the first time since they had met.

"I have an unpleasant task, my boy, and I must get it over with at once. I have just been told, Archilde, that you know more about the death of the game warden than you admitted to me. That you were, in fact, present at his killing and—possibly—involved in a disagreeable way. I was informed this morning, in fact."

He had spoken softly, without hesitating, and with no sign of emotion in his voice. As he stopped, his eyes were still on Archilde, studying his face with critical eyes, but betraying nothing of his own thought or judgment.

A slow heavy blush came over Archilde. Something died within him like a lantern that falls into a well. He sank heavily under a wave of despair and in that moment there was no light of hope in his heart. He had gone forward to meet the agent under such a different sun that this sudden disclosure was too violent in its contrast. He gazed at the floor and did not utter a word.

"I don't know how reliable my information is," Parker continued, looking away at last, "and I hope you can add something to it. It is a strange case. It has popped up to my notice several times during these years. While you were away, several men were brought in to the county attorney and questioned. The body has never been found." He went on talking for a while longer, looking out over the countryside, waiting for Archilde to offer a reply. He checked himself presently and changed his manner.

"But I haven't asked you anything definite yet. Tell me, did you and your mother see the game warden on your hunting trip?"

"Yes, we did. I lied to you." He did not look at the agent.

"You did, you say?"

"Yes, Louis was with us at the time, alive." After a brief pause he told the story in its bare facts. He gained a little composure as he talked, his voice grew steady. He spoke with a feeling of futility and did not seek to hold anything back. At the end he explained why he had lied when he was first questioned.

"You wanted to shield your mother, I understand. But she has been dead three years, Archilde. Why haven't you come forward and told me this of your own free will? Why did you wait until it was disclosed, Archilde?" His voice was exceedingly gentle.

"I haven't an answer to that, I'm afraid. I wasn't afraid. I hadn't forgotten. Perhaps I did forget the disgust that I felt when it happened, maybe I forgot too my responsibility in the matter—I can't think very clearly about it just now. I don't know what my thoughts have been."

"Did you forget that your first story was a lie? That you weren't square with me?"

"No—I didn't forget that. But afterward you trusted me and were kind. I never could make up my mind to come to you and show you your mistake. And at bottom, I was worth trusting, I think. In the end I expected that it would be even. I haven't lied since."

Another car appeared in the lane. It came up from the low creek bed in a haze of dust and proceeded rapidly up the lane. Archilde recognized the car as Moser's. He felt the hair prickle on his neck and the mild hatred he had felt for the storekeeper during the past years increased with a sudden, vicious surge.

"Is that Moser's car?" Parker asked.

"Yes."

The agent got to his feet. "Now what does he want? I told him to stay away."

"He knows then?" Archilde asked sharply.

"Yes—he came to my house before eight o'clock."

Moser's dusty car came to a quick stop before the gate and he shut his engine off at once. His face was glistening with excitement.

"Have you got him? Is everything all right?" he called in a high, sharp voice and did not move from his car. "I phoned the sheriff, but he wasn't in. A deputy is coming to my place at once."

Parker flushed angrily. He left the porch and strode vigorously toward the car. In a loud voice he commanded:

"This is none of your business! Keep out! I told you so before and I repeat it. Keep out!" After that he spoke more quietly and he could not be heard. Archilde remained on the porch as long as he could, but when Moser did not turn to leave at once, he got to his feet and went to the steps where he stood a moment, then he sauntered across the yard.

"Hello!" Moser called out, seeing him approach. "How do you feel?" he asked with a grin. Archilde ignored the question.

"I'd like to know what your object was in giving Mike presents and charging me for them afterward?"

"Presents? Did I ever give Mike any presents?"

"That's what he tells me."

The storekeeper was suave and smiling.

"He must have had a dream. He came and wanted to buy a saddle. However, if he really had that impression, why I'm willing to let it go that way. The stuff only amounts to a few dollars, doesn't it? I like Mike, he's a darn smart fellow at his age. He'll probably amount to something."

"Your opinions aren't worth a damn, Moser, and you can keep them to yourself! There's something two-faced about this deal that I'm going to find out, and I'll see you about it as soon as I do find out."

"Archilde!" The agent broke in, "you'd better go back to the house. Moser had just agreed to go away." He turned to the storekeeper. "You've done your duty and it's useless for you to butt in this way. In fact, you're being damned impertinent. Kindly leave this in my hands."

"All right, Parker. But the sheriff is going to have a look-in on this. I'd like to see the courts handle the case this time, that's where it belongs." He had already started his engine and a minute later he turned his car and drove away.

On the porch Archilde was standing, pale and shaken. He remained standing after Parker had sat down again. The agent spoke immediately.

"Archilde, we'll have to go to Missoula with this thing. My hand is being forced. I don't know exactly how the prosecutor will act in the matter, but I have an idea he'll stir up as much stink as he can—as you can see, there'll be somebody there to stir things up. But I'm not afraid of the outcome. You've got to face it."

Archilde whirled around, and he called Moser a vile name. "He's got the mind of a rat!"

"Forget it, my boy! Forget it! This is what I wanted to tell you. About a year ago there was a piece in the paper about that game warden's family. I don't know whether you saw it or not. I cut the story out and I was going to bring it along to show you, but I couldn't find it this morning. Perhaps you didn't realize that he had left a family? He had a wife and a daughter who is twelve years old now. They live in a little town out of Missoula. A year ago the school authorities pounced on the mother because the little girl was being kept out of school. The reason was that they had nothing to live on, and the girl had to stay home to help with the washing. The mother has made her living as a scrub-woman and by doing washing for her neighbors ever since her husband was killed. An older daughter died soon after that happened, and since then, there have been just these two. They are very poor and the mother is sick. I tell you this to show you the other side, and perhaps it will be easier to understand why you should face the situation and tell everything you know before the court. The state, Archilde, is organized to protect its people and to ensure at least approximate justice for each person. This man was killed and it would be bad enough if he was the only one harmed—but you see his family has suffered considerably too. I don't think we can estimate how far the harm reaches. What will the effect be on the twelve-year-old daughter who can't go to school? She was about five at the time her father disappeared—what effect did that have on her? These people have a right to ask the law to aid them—at least to tell them as much as possible about the disappearance of the man who was husband and father. Justice, Archilde, is a profound subject, and you have been wrong in frustrating it so long. I know you are innocent, I believe you implicitly, but you have wronged two people at least, possibly more. Did you bury the man?"

"Yes—" Archilde had taken a seat. He was looking through his eyes in a mist.

"Wasn't it horrible to do?"

"Yes."

A silence fell between them.

"Haven't you ever thought of the meaning of the state—how dependent we are on the intelligence and humanity of one another to make happiness possible for each of us?"

"No—"

There was another silence and then Parker got to his feet. "Well, let's not talk anymore. Wisdom comes slowly. By the way, did you say that Moser had given Mike some things as a present?"

"Mike says so—a saddle and bridle, chaps and things. I don't know who to believe."

"Supposing I go around and see Mike—and I guess you ought to go up and change. We'll go to the agency first. I'll keep you out of the sheriff's hands. Tomorrow we'll go to Missoula."

"They're working in the cellar," Archilde said, still seated. Parker had gone outside, and as he turned the corner of the house, he called back:

"They're not working now. They're sitting out here by the corral."
He disappeared around the house.

Archilde went upstairs. He entered his room and threw himself across the bed for a moment.

As Archilde drove away with the agent, Mike and Narcisse were standing idly in the yard, watching curiously but not approaching. They would have no master hereafter.

They sped past the fields of his diligent labor. They left the meadows behind where his small herd of milk cows were grazing on their first grass. The sun spread his splendors over the land as far as the eye could see. Nothing in the world was beyond the reach of the sun.

Chapter Five

Somehow, there has come into the practice of justice a notion that, as quickly as a man comes at variance with the law, it is permissible for him to be subjected to indignity and vile offensiveness until such times as he is able to show that he is no longer at variance. When that time arrives, if luckily it does, the law relinquishes its claim and allows the man to return to orderly society and "justice" has been served—no apologies offered.

The first morning after Archilde had been lodged in the county jail, he was hailed before the "kangaroo court," a mock court session held by the prisoners themselves, no sheriff, deputy, or jailer being present. This took place after breakfast.

There were two tiers of cells, the lower tier being completely filled with prisoners, Archilde was put in the upper story entirely by himself. He had arrived after nightfall the day before. In the morning he lay outstretched on the iron bunk with his eyes wide open. He had not slept all night, but he was not sleepy. He didn't want to move. The prisoners on the floor below had been moving around for an hour or more, talking, laughing, eating; he didn't stir. He didn't want to see anyone or talk with anyone. When he stretched his head a little, he could see the top of a tree through the barred window in the wall that was ten or fifteen feet from his cage. There were leaves on the tree half an inch long. Presently, one of the prisoners below began calling to him.

299

300 | D'Arcy McNickle

"Say, mister, ya better come and eat! There's a spud or two left an' they'll take it away in a minute. You, up in nigger heaven, I mean." Someone else added:

"Are you laid out up there or what's the matter?"

"What's he in for?" another voice asked.

"He killed a guy, the jailer says."

"Killed a guy, eh? Must be a tough bird. Better go up after him, Shorty."

"Yeh. Go after him yourself!"

"Hey, toughy! Don't ya wanta eat?"

Archilde turned his face to the wall and made no response. He lay there for a long time with his eyes fastened on the names and dates and lewd pictures drawn on the steel wall. For the first time he looked with conscious eyes on his surroundings. Pictures of prizefighters and an actress or two had been cut out of newspapers and pasted on the walls. Names and initials were scribbled everywhere. He had not slept under the covers during the night, though it had been uncomfortably cold and even now the sun had not penetrated the stone building enough to drive the chill away. He lay in his cell for fifteen minutes longer, but at length it dawned on him that he was being needlessly reticent. He would have to eat sometime and he might as well start now. As soon as he got to his feet and started to walk, he was astonished at the noise he made on the steely floor. He walked to the end of the passageway and went down the iron stairs.

Contrary to his expectation, no one spoke to him at first. The inmates were busy cleaning their cells and making their bunks; some were shaving while in one cell a game of cards was in progress. He walked to a table near the door to the jailer's office and found a large gray pot in which there was a little lukewarm coffee. He poured a cupful and took a drink; it was almost impossible to swallow, so bitter was the brew. In another pot were boiled potatoes. He ate one, determined to accept everything that went with his condition; the potato was soggy and unsalted.

One of the prisoners stopped beside him, leaning on the broom that he held in his hand. He had been sweeping the floor outside of the row of cells, which was built in the middle of a fairly large room.

"What they got you in for, kid?" the man asked. All he had on was an undershirt and a pair of pants.

The Hungry Generations | 301

"Manslaughter," Archilde said bluntly and picked up another potato.

When he turned around again, he saw that nearly all the prisoners had left their cells and were forming in a group around him.

"How's the cold potato?" a tall prisoner in waist overalls asked.

"Fine!" he answered with exaggerated pleasantry.

"That's all you get here—and nothing more until five o'clock! Don't forget that!" the tall man added.

"If it's potatoes again, I don't mind," Archilde said.

"Let's call court," someone said. "He looks like he ought to have some jack."

"Go ahead, Slim, call the court to order."

"All right," the tall man responded. "The kangaroo court is called to order. Shorty, you're the prosecutor, and Winky is the defense lawyer." The two men designated stepped forward. Shorty was the man in the undershirt who had been sweeping. Winky turned out to be a cross-eyed half-wit who was continually smiling.

The judge had taken a seat on the table with the coffee pot.

"First," he said, "I will state the charge to the prisoner. Prisoner to the bar, you are charged with breaking into the county jail. What have you to say, are you guilty or not guilty?"

Archilde had no notion what mood the men were in; on the surface he assumed it to be mere horseplay and he laughed at the judge's pronouncement. Strangely enough, there was no echo to his laugh, and he had a feeling that it was something more than a jest.

"Are you guilty or not guilty?" the judge repeated.

"Well, here I am. I must be guilty," Archilde replied jovially.

"The prisoner pleads guilty. We'll dismiss the prosecution and defense. I will now pass sentence. All right, kid, I fine you thirty dollars for breaking into the county jail and for which you plead guilty."

"Thirty dollars! Who the hell gets the thirty dollars?" Archilde asked. For the first time it dawned on him that they were enacting a hoax to get money out of him.

"The money goes to the kangaroo court to pay for our noon meal and to buy tobacco, salt, and butter."

"But what if I'm only to be here a few days or a week—you still want me to buy you thirty dollars worth of butter, do you?"

"That's the fine the court imposes."

"What if I don't want to pay it?"

"We'll attend to that all right," the tall judge said with an air of threat. "How much money you got with you?"

"He left a wad with the jailer," someone spoke up.

"It'll stay with the jailer, too!" Archilde put in. He didn't know whether the jailer was in sympathy with the prisoners and would turn the money over to them or not. Slowly he was growing angered by their attitude.

"Pay us ten dollars and call it quits," the judge granted.

"Nothing doing. I'll pay whatever it's worth per day but no more."

"George, fill the tub," the judge directed.

"Righto!" A fat Dutchman left the group and waddled through the door leading into the cells. A moment later water was heard pouring into a tub.

"I give the prisoner five minutes to think it over. Ten dollars is the sum."

Someone called him a "damn cheapskate" and a "rube." They drew away from him and scattered around the room. Even the judge walked off and joined a group. Archilde remained standing near the table. A pile of dirty, worn books were piled on one end of the table and he began looking through them. He half supposed that the matter had dropped. The water continued to pour into the tub.

The matter hadn't been dropped. When five minutes had passed, the judge and half a dozen others approached him once more.

"Are you ready to fork over the ten bucks?" the judge asked.

"Not a cent when you demand it!"

"All right boys! Do your stuff!"

They all grabbed him at once. But it was unnecessary. He made no protest, though he was strongly inclined to put up a fight. He was deeply roused and it was not easy to keep a tight lip. He walked straight through the passageway without a word.

The room containing the bathtub was a filthy hole. A foul toilet stood nearby and a vile stench almost stopped the breath in his nostrils. The cement floor was wet and moldy. The water pipes were rusted heavily and the bathtub, which was more than half full of water, was stained and unclean.

"What do you say now?" the judge asked. "It's ten bucks or a ducking. Which do you choose?"

"Go to hell!" Archilde said in a low voice.

The words were no sooner out of his mouth than four men grabbed him, one on each leg and arm. They lifted him and for a moment held him suspended over the tub.

"Your last chance!"

"Oh, go ahead!"

They let him drop and he sank head and all under the icy water. When he climbed out of the tub, with water streaming from his clothes and shoes, the men had returned to the cells without another comment. He went through the passageway and up the iron stairs to his cell, streaming water and shivering violently. He took off his trousers and undergarments and for a long time could not untie his shoelaces. He crawled between the rough, coarse blankets, forgetting the dirt and dust contained in them.

Endless, irrelevant images drifted through his mind as he lay in his cell. The sounds of the city reached him faintly and caused him to speculate, first on one thing and then another. The gong in the tower of the court-house a stone's throw away boomed the hours with a terrific clatter that made the steel walls of the cell vibrate. Trolleys passed to and fro with rumbling wheels.

Surely, he thought, the world had forgotten him. Even that little world of which he was a part had dropped him out of its sight without a ripple of interest. Once, not so long ago, only a matter of days, he had played the part of a lord, demanding what should be done in his house and in his fields—but now he couldn't so much as say what he would like to eat. He lay there on a bleak isle with unknown waters drifting idly past. He tried to recall the grandiose thoughts that he had filled his head with and that had warmed his blood, but he could not cheat or evade the great maw of emptiness that was drawing him down. Passion had gone from him, hatred too, purpose and determination were no more. He lay in stagnant waters and for days he had not moved.

He had brought an armload of books into his cell and he read them one after another with greediness and abandon. The stories were cheap and tawdry and could not enliven his failing senses. He had read the last of the books and tossed it aside. In the cells below someone was singing a bawdy, monotonous song of "The Lone Star Trail"; others were playing cards and disputing from time to time; one man was walking the concrete floor, tirelessly from end to end of the room. Oaths drifted upward, grunts and broken sentences, and from time to time there was a loud, mechanical laugh. Archilde watched the tree outside from hour to hour and from day to day. In the morning it was in shadow and in late afternoon again. The leaves had grown longer, soon they would be full size and the brown branches would all be hidden.

He no longer knew what stage his case was in; Parker was attending to everything, two or three times a week he came to see Archilde and encouraged him about the strong defense his lawyer was building. Archilde showed only the slightest interest. He could not feel shame or unrest in his position any longer, all that had passed away. From day's end to day's end he sat in his cell pondering weightily—but when a ray of consciousness entered his mind and he groped for the thing over which he was brooding, he realized it was nothing, absolutely nothing.

When he went down to eat, the prisoners looked at him askance. At the end of the first week the tall, dark fellow who had presided as judge over the kangaroo court said:

"Well, kid, the week has passed and you're still with us I see! Yes, you'll have a chance to rot here yet!"

The others ignored him as completely as he did them, but at night, when the lights were turned out, they lay in their bunks and talked about the "queer mutt upstairs" in voices that he heard plainly. More than once he had been cursed as "a damn sissy without the guts to take his medicine." Nothing stirred him.

Since he had contributed no money to the kangaroo court he did not eat a noon meal; coffee and potatoes for breakfast and boiled meat and potatoes for supper was all the food he had. There were days when he scarcely ate even that much. When Parker asked him what he wanted, he replied, "Nothing at all." It was true. He desired nothing. He was slipping out of reality and drifting far to sea on a sluggish, murky tide. Driftwood and jetsam entangled him in their pallid froth and he went on, never once stirring or beating back against the urge of indolence. Under this indifference and lethargy a force was working that he did not recognize.

He stood arm in arm with his mother those days, breathing the unhealthy mist of a hundred generations before his day. Inhabitants of a bleak world into which the sunlight had not yet penetrated, there were his people. They gazed into the sky and scanned the earth, picking their food from under the rocks and in the meadows. They feared the passing shadow of a bird overhead, they stood in awe before a blasted tree, they worshipped the wind that howled at night. They murdered their enemies, who were no more than their brothers, casually. They wrought hideous distortions on their own bodies in deference to savage pride. On all these faces, not a laugh or smile. They walked grim faced through life and passed out amidst a burst of wailing. When opposition and adversity overtook them and threatened death and starvation on the snowy flats of winter, they sat in a huddle before a sick fire and, with blank eyes, awaited the hand to fall. They fought when the hand of the spirit pushed them forward—when it turned against them, they bowed their heads before the wind of wrath. Dull, naked, savage, the breath of their nostrils was fatalism—these were the hundred generations who stood behind Archilde. In his sad days they came upon him and feasted on his strength, drawing his blood away and thinning the marrow of his bones. He lay on his iron cot and was scarcely aware that the days passed. In his body there were no passions.

Into the dark cavern a ray of light fell at last. One morning after breakfast the warden called Archilde to the heavily barred opening within the iron door leading to the jailer's office and handed him a letter. Archilde took it and walked slowly back to his cell, climbing the iron stairway and passing the entire length of the passageway before he looked at it a second time. It was a letter from Claudia. He looked at the handwriting on the envelope for many minutes before he opened it. With the first words that he read she came into his cell and stood before his cot. His head was lowered so that he could not see the wall before him, but there she stood against that wall; her mood was gay and lively. When he looked up and saw no one there, he did not mind. A moment was long enough. In her letter she wrote:

You have not answered my letter—that is too bad! I had expected greater things of you—greater attention to my demands, etc. Is it possible that I am writing a second time? Yes, so I am.

New York is a rum place. In another month it will be hot—such smelly heat they have here. Where are my brothers? Scattered around. Albert has a medal now.

But I sat down with another purpose. Mother just died. I have not slept for some time. I was going out to take a walk in the park; it is dawn and the sky is gray. Instead of walking, however, I have opened my window and here I am, reminding you that you have not written to me.

In my fancy I see you walking over your broad fields casting seeds like the old patriarchs. Do you still plant that way or is there a machine for it now? Is it true that the air is pure and fresh out there? Do you have creeks and springs of clear water? Are there mountains with white snow on top? I'd like to come and have a look at your fairyland. Here, the enchanted tale has worn thin and stale; there is not much to amuse. I have, as I say, a growing curiosity to come and see your god-what-a-country. Supposing I should?

But now I must go out after all and send cables and telegrams to my little brothers. One at least should come and have a look at his dead mother.

Don't forget to write this time.

Archilde read on and on, heeding neither beginning nor end of the letter. He pondered over words and phrases, extracting their full meaning with a slowly kindling intelligence. Sparks began to fly before his eyes and tingling senses told him that the numbness was slipping away. Warmth came, mounting slowly. Blood surged through his body. He looked at himself, at his wrinkled clothes and soiled hands. He was unshaven. He jumped from his cot as a bright burning excitement mounted in his breast. An exultant shout hung in his throat and at any moment it might be released. Strength and pride rushed into his limbs so mightily that a slight dizziness made him reel against the wall. Laughter was on his lips, his face beamed with a great smile.

Life had returned. Purpose sat upon its throne with a clear brow, such was the magic of the spoken thought.

Chapter Six

When Archilde was called to trial, he felt for the first time the contempt of an outraged society. During the first week in prison he experienced something of this feeling, but it wasn't until he appeared in court before a mass of upturned faces that he got a full sense of certain phrases that he had often heard and considered meaningless. The "state," empty word heretofore, became a calm, menacing judge in black robes and a caustic voice; a prosecuting attorney who shouted and screamed and turned red in the face with the exertion of denouncing his prisoner in the blackest words he could call to mind; beyond these two there were the court officials and the jailer, putty-faced men who moved mechanically and with frozen emotions. "People around," the "great public," these, too, were figurative expressions that had come to life and sat in the benches beyond the railing, and though not a sound came from them, he fancied that expressions of satisfaction and malice came over their faces each time the prosecutor made an accusation; this public had emotions that he never dreamed existed, hideous, cruel, spiteful; individuals might be kindhearted but in a mass a dark spirit entered into them and made them grin and applaud the torture applied to a wrongdoer.

Before, in his days of freedom, he had considered that he had a right to decide his own actions, that he could live as he pleased and dictate his own conduct. Now the reverse seemed nearer the truth. He took whatever rights and privileges law and society granted him. He was responsible to the "authorities" first of all. He had been guilty of ignoring the

308

powers above him—that was his greatest guilt. Indeed, a feeling of inexcusable guilt and shame swept over him; more than once during the process of the trial he had trembled on the point of breaking his reserve and admitting everything of which he was accused. Much of the accusation seemed to be true, more than he had dreamed. Was it possible that he had lived in the borderland between right and wrong all his life?

"We have seen that he has shown ingratitude; we know him to be willful, headstrong, spoiled by an easy life. Hasn't his father lavished a fortune on him? What did he do with it—did he engage in respectable business or farming? Nothing of the sort. He set out for the cities where he could spend it easier. He spent a year in Paris like any other dandy. Has he shared his legacy with his brothers? Not at all!"

Thus it had continued. The proceedings had lasted three days already. In jail at night a wave of deep and bitter resentment swept over him and set him raging. Through the black night he lay in torment, cursing the malice of a man who could turn his actions and purposes so topsy-turvy. But, when he returned to court the following day, he was swept under again by the awesomeness of the sour-faced judge, the cold, mechanical officials, the shouting, blaspheming prosecutor, and the upturned faces of the spectators with their hundred staring eyes. So he had learned what it meant to offend society; he felt the wrath of the unseen horde.

The trial was drawing to a close at last. The prosecutor stood before the jury, summing up his evidence with all the venom and energy that he could muster. He was a short, stout man with a thick neck and heavy jaws. As he talked, his face turned violently red and he swung his arms with the greatest gusto. His voice was deep and stentorian and filled the courtroom with blasting echoes. When he became excited and spoke rapidly, he squealed like an enraged stallion. Perspiration came easily to his face and he was continually mopping his fleshy neck and wide forehead with a handkerchief.

"From the defendant's own admission and from the autopsy performed by the state, we know that this man, this faithful servant of the people, was struck down with an axe or hatchet. Now, I want you to consider, gentlemen of the jury, what this implies. How much strength does it take to swing a hatchet with sufficient force to break a man's skull? The head of the game warden was not cut open; the bone was broken. With an axe not a great deal of strength would be required; the weight of the instrument would add greatly to the force of the blow. But if we are to put any reliance on the defendant's story, we are to believe that the instrument was a hatchet, not an axe. I think we are safer to disregard the defendant's story entirely; we have more reliable information. We know, for one thing, that Indians are not in the habit of carrying an axe with them, no one traveling on horseback in the mountains is apt to carry an unwieldy axe, a short-handled hatchet of fairly light weight is handier. But it takes strength to swing a hatchet with any effect.

"Now then, consider. How much strength is there in the arm of a sixty-year-old woman? That is a point well worth considering. Do not let that point escape you when you are arriving at your decision. This brazen young man has audaciously asserted that his sixty-year-old mother swung the hatchet that killed the game warden, a faithful servant who gave his life in the pursuit of his duty.

"Let us review another point in this young man's ingenious story. According to his own testimony, at the moment before the shooting occurred, the defendant was standing on the game warden's left, the mother was facing the game warden at some distance, as much as twenty-five feet, the defendant admits; Louis was only a little to the right of the game warden and halfway between the game warden and the mother. When the game warden shot, and don't forget, gentlemen of the jury, that in all probability, he shot in self-defense—"

"I object!" the defense attorney rose to his feet and revealed a tall, gray-headed man, straight backed, with an open, youthful face. He spoke without flourish, but his voice carried the deepest conviction and sincerity. He was slow of speech.

"Your Honor, I object to mentioning the motives of the two dead men. We have no evidence bearing on the matter, neither defense nor state. I do not think my opponent has a right to make an emotional appeal to the jury without evidence to support his view."

The judge sat motionless, his elbows on the desk before him, his shoulders slightly pointed upward. He cleared his voice with a dry, hollow cough.

"The objection is sustained," he said and spat tobacco juice into the cuspidor at his feet.

The Hungry Generations | 311

Once more the scene was resumed. The defense sat down calmly. Archilde, sitting next to his lawyer, had experienced an exultant sensation when the objection was made, and carried. Now his eyes returned to the florid, perspiring prosecutor who had turned purple during the interruption. He continued with the same malicious intonation.

"I have just recalled to your minds the defendant's account of the relative positions of each person prior to the shooting. Now consider this. After the shooting, the game warden is said to have stepped forward and bent over Louis, who had fallen to the ground. The positions of the others did not change and how does this place them? Why, the defendant was off to the left and at a *little distance behind* the bent form of the game warden! The mother, mind you, was almost *directly in front!* That, gentlemen, is the defendant's own admission. And yet, he asks us to believe that this aged woman was agile enough and quick enough to move around behind the game warden and strike him a blow in the head. In other words, she moved out of his direct line of vision and stepped up from behind, crossing in front of the defendant to do so. She did not *throw* the axe; there would have been a more plausible element in the story if she had done that. No, we are asked to believe that she became invisible for the moment and passed without the slightest noise to the game warden's back where she dealt him a mortal blow with a light hatchet. In justice to our intelligence, I do not see how we can be expected to believe such a fabrication for even a moment.

"The defendant, meantime, was standing a few paces behind the unfortunate man and to his left. To move from his position to the victim as he bent over the brother required but an instant. It was not necessary for him to exercise ordinary caution. He moved so quickly that his victim was taken unawares; he did not have time to act even if he did hear the defendant approach. In a second it was over with. The man, who in a simple, human gesture had stooped over his fallen enemy, was done to death.

"That, I submit, is an account more in keeping with the circumstances. There you are not asked to ascribe to an aged, rheumatic woman the agility of a youth of twenty with the strength of a grown man in her withered arms. What the defendant asks you to believe is, in all truthfulness, a *physical impossibility!* The true story, as I have suggested, is simpler, more in the nature of men and women as we know them.

312 | D'Arcy McNickle

"There are other factors that bear me out. I do not ask you to base your decision on a single supposition. What we know of the defendant's subsequent movements, taken from unimpeachable testimony, must stand in itself as damning evidence. He has not sought to deny what follows; in fact he had no ground on which to base a denial. But he has tried to cover his motives with a high and mighty righteousness that those who know him find inconsistent with his character. Let me recite to you once again his actions following the murder.

"What does a man do when he commits a crime? He attempts to conceal it. Crime falls into two classes; it is either premeditated or it is committed on an impulse, that is, without forethought. In the former case, a criminal plans how he will conceal his deed beforehand. He arranges an alibi or makes his plans for a quick getaway. In the impulsive crime, the concealment is carried out afterward. That is all you need to know about crime to understand the present instance. The murder that we are attempting to explain was probably unpremeditated—we seem to have no evidence to the contrary. All right. Did the defendant act as we might expect him to act? Did he attempt to *conceal* his victim? He most certainly did! He resorted to a cold, inhuman act that can only be matched by one other fact in point of viciousness, and that is the murder itself. Any man who could dig a shallow trench and crush a fellow mortal into it, where for all he knows his victim may become torn to pieces by coyotes, at any rate left there in the mountains beyond the knowledge of his friends and family, unblessed by his church, any man who can commit such an act, *can commit murder!*

"He has tried to hide behind his mother. That is the reason he gives us for not having brought the body to a civilized grave and for withholding information when he knew that the whole community had become aroused over the missing man and had sent out search parties even in the midst of winter. He hesitated to involve his mother. But why should his mother have become involved! What had she to do with it? You know the answer! I know the answer! His mother had nothing to do with it! Who was he shielding then? *Himself!*

"How do we know this? Is this a guess? Consider. What did he do as soon as his father died, which, very fortunately, occurred only a short while after the murder? Why, exactly what any criminal proceeds to do.

The Hungry Generations | 313

Having concealed his act, the heavy snow aiding him, he sought to complete his defeat of the law by leaving the country. We are told that that he was under a sort of probation, having given his word to return if notified. I'll not stop now to question the regularity of such an act—neither will I attempt to criticize the authority that forestalled a complete investigation at the time. Certainly a grave injustice has been done this humble servant of the people and his family, who have suffered want and humiliation as a consequence. Let us not overlook our duty now and carry the injustice even further. Do not be afraid of the decision you must make—if it means that a life must be taken to expiate the murder so coldly, so inhumanly committed—do not hesitate to declare yourselves of that opinion.

"The defendant left the country, to all intents and purposes, beyond the arm of the law. And don't forget that he lied to his Indian agent—he has admitted this himself, and the agent has testified that he did so. He tells us next that he entered Columbia University in New York. All right—did he take a degree? No. He tells us that his preparation was not adequate; it was impossible for him to continue. Let us examine that statement a little further, gentlemen. Many of you sitting in this jury box are self-taught, self-made men. Have any of you, at any time in your lives, been confronted with what seemed at first glance an impossible barrier? Of course you have, you all have. What did you do about it? Did you drop your hands to your sides and give up? If I know anything about manliness, you didn't! How did I get through school? By scrubbing floors and washing dishes in a restaurant—and I don't mention my case as in any way unusual—there are hundreds of young, red-blooded American boys doing the same today. The defendant's statement that he couldn't finish his college course because he wasn't prepared is utter nonsense. It would have meant extra work, it would have meant sturdiness of character and strength of will—I think we are safe in assuming that he doesn't possess these things. Else why should he have run away? Why did he give up and go where he could live more at his ease? If there is another answer, it hasn't come out. I have been painstaking in my questions on this point, but nothing further has been vouchsafed.

"In Paris, we are told, the defendant studied the violin under one of the famous French teachers. How he got admitted to this man's classes we don't know, but since he had plenty of money with him, it is likely that he didn't have difficulty. Those of us who have traveled in Europe know that the American dollar is the only card of introduction necessary in most situations. But here again, we must ask the question, what was the defendant's purpose? Did he have any serious reason for studying the violin? Was he gifted? No one has ever heard him play. His own answer to my questions were, you will admit, amusing. Artists, he decided, didn't amount to much, or some such words he used. At any rate, he gave up the study of the violin. It would have required a good deal of work and hard study to have been able to play a decent tune—and he didn't have the perseverance. Everything that he has attempted stamps him lacking in character. He is just such a person as you expect to find when you examine into the lives of those people who have wronged society. It never fails but that they are lacking in some basic trait that makes for the backbone in a community and draws the line between the normal and the subnormal man. It has often been observed, and each of us have seen examples of it in our lives, that the one thing that makes for a sound, wholesome man is a love of work—a willingness to get in and dig. We have all seen men go to the bad because they lacked this quality—and here we have a fresh example of it! Here we have a young man who has lied and admits it, who has acted in an underhand manner, who has failed repeatedly to complete a simple task when he had every encouragement, every opportunity to do so; he is also cold-blooded, brutal, witness his burying a murdered man in a shallow grave in the mountains; he is ungrateful, witness his refusal to share his legacy with his family and his rebuff of the man who had been for many years a close friend and benefactor of his father. Such a man, I submit, would not hesitate to murder if he thought it necessary.

"As a last link in a chain of damning evidence, I will now recall to your minds the action of the defendant when he returned home three years ago. He made the statement, previously, that he had not spoken of the tragedy in the mountains because he did not wish to involve his mother; it was for this same reason that he lied to the agent. According to his version it was the aged mother, rheumatic, close to sixty years old, who had committed the murder. All right. He returns home; his mother is dead. Does any word pass his lips to solve the mystery that the state

The Hungry Generations | 315

has spent hundreds of dollars on in an attempt to clear up—or for that matter, to ease the anxiety of the murdered man's family? Not a sound does he utter. He lives here among us for three years as if he were one of us. It was only through the eternal vigilance of one of the foremost citizens of our county that the matter was brought to light. The defense has tried to vilify Mr. Moser and to attribute questionable practices on his part in obtaining the information. Close your ears to arguments of such a nature. When a cause that a man defends is lacking in virtue, it is natural to find him throwing mud at the righteous. Truth will prevail.

"I have a final word to add. The defendant is an Indian breed. He is one of a family of boys who have been repeated evildoers; they have been a constant drain upon the goodwill of the state. For some reason, we have always dealt leniently with this class of offenders. We have labored under the theory that we are under debt to the Indians and we have permitted them privileges that we deny to ourselves. I think it is high time we questioned the wisdom of such a course of action. If the Indian is to form a part of our state, he must learn the duties and the qualities of a citizen. How is he to get this knowledge? By granting him special privileges and dealing leniently with him when he defies our laws? Is that the way we treat our own children when they disobey our wishes and wander from the straight path? Or hasn't our axiom always been 'Spare the rod and spoil the child'? We come from a race of sturdy Pilgrim fathers who knew the virtues of discipline. They built for us a great nation on that very principle. Let us not give over their work into the hands of a race undisciplined in either spirit or mind. Let us be stern in our justice—but righteous, always. That is the duty laid upon you, gentlemen of the jury."

Such were the words of the prosecutor. They fell upon Archilde's ears like claps of dismal thunder. The bold, loud voice crashed upon him in endless waves of sound, now making his face grow pale, now making him sick with the cruelty of the words, now driving a blinding, seething rage through his body, top to bottom, like the blood that coursed through his veins.

The lawyer for the defense rose to speak.

Chapter Seven

A quieter voice drifted across the courtroom, striking softly on the ears of the audience, melting into the walls of the room, like water on a quiet lake. A gentle man, he was not lacking in a subtle, persuasive tone. In the days when he had talked with Archilde in jail, he had come to understand him well. As he gave his speech that afternoon in the warm courtroom, he looked often at Archilde and made the jury follow his eyes as he built before them the figure of a different sort of man.

"My gentlemanly opponent, the prosecuting attorney, has laid a great case before you, an almost perfect case. The prosecutor is an able spokesman and he has not spared his talent. He has made, as I say, an almost perfect case. He made one error; otherwise there might have been no possible response to make to his charge. He made one serious error: he assumed that the defendant was guilty. He built his argument upon that basic idea, like a pyramid with its sharp point resting on the ground. It is only necessary to knock the point from under and the structure will crash. It shouldn't take long to see this done. I ask for a few minutes only.

"The physical facts that the prosecutor called to your minds don't amount to much. He has a great talent, I've already admitted, and he developed these physical facts with strong, impressive words. For he is skillful that way. What was the nonsense he said?

"Well, how much strength does it take to swing a hatchet? A hatchet weighs twelve ounces. It has a very hard head made out of steel,

The Hungry Generations | 317

much harder than bone. Could an old lady swing it? Who was the old lady? She was an Indian squaw. She thought she would like to go on a hunting trip with this young son, so she jumped on a horse and they rode for three days into the mountains. Have you known many old ladies like that? When they stopped, she made camp, chopped wood, fished, and went tramping through the woods to skin the game—only the defendant missed his shot. Do you suppose she could swing a twelve-ounce hatchet? That was a very good point the prosecutor made, but he should have applied it to some other case.

"Now the matter of where the people were standing. I don't know if you understood him very well through his explanation, but what he meant to bring out was that the defendant was standing a little ways behind the game warden. Have any of you heard the defendant admit anything of the sort? I haven't, unless I was asleep. No, the defendant has said over and over that he didn't know exactly where he was standing or what happened. I tried to figure that out too and I asked the boy a dozen times before the trial to try and recall that scene. He has never been able. When he came to, he was leaning against a tree—twenty-five feet away from the two dead men. His mother, however, was sitting on the ground looking at her son, Louis. After that she pulled her shawl over her face and began to lament. That is all the defendant has told us. The prosecutor has made up the rest of his story—for he is skillful that way.

"Let me take you on a little side trip and have a look at something the prosecutor didn't discuss at all. Who of these two people, mother and son, would be likely to have a motive for killing the game warden. Who, on the spur of the moment, would have a blind, thoughtless urge to avenge—a brother the death of his brother—or a mother the death of her son? Well, let's see what we know about the defendant and his family.

"The prosecutor made a special point of reminding you that the defendant was one of a family of lawbreakers—his brothers have all had their day in the courts—some in the penitentiary. He neglected to point out that this particular member of the family has never before had his conduct questioned. In fact, he made no distinction whatever between the defendant and his brothers. That distinction is very real. There was no love between Archilde and Louis. The defendant has brought this out in his answers to questions and it was also disclosed by Agnes, his sister.

Only a few weeks before the shooting affair Louis asked the defendant to help him hold some horses that he had stolen. The defendant laughed at him and called him a fool. The defendant was never, at any time, on friendly terms with his brother; his mother and sister were the only ones he cared for.

"There is another way to illustrate this distinction. Many of us knew Max Leon in the old days. If there was ever a man who was ashamed of his sons—who hated his sons—Max was the man. We know that he had some reason for his hatred. His youngest son, the defendant here, was no exception. Until he was twenty years of age, his father had scarcely spoken to him—then a change came about. Leon began to inquire of his daughter what the defendant was planning to do—even told her that he intended to let the defendant have his ranch—if he was willing to accept it and go to work. The defendant actually started to work that fall, helping with the harvest. You can imagine how Leon felt about that—none of his sons had ever done a lick of work around there before. They all gambled and drank. Archilde did none of these things—he had gone to school, not as much as a white boy of his age—but much more than you would expect, living as he did without the encouragement of his family or associates. An Indian boy is brought up under influences that we don't begin to touch with all our laws and government provisions. Yet, this boy was avoiding those influences almost by himself.

"The prosecutor said, more elegantly than I can express it, that work is the first virtue. The defendant found that out by himself. He did not have it solemnly expounded to him one warm day in spring after he had returned from Sunday school—as happened in my case—as probably happened in the prosecutor's case. But he found out about it, through instinct or somehow, and that fall he went to work in his father's harvest field. And did Max respond to that show of willingness? He certainly did. He willed over his entire fortune and estate to the boy, with provisions to care for his mother and sister. To his other sons he left not a smell and directed the defendant to ignore them also—'unless they changed their way completely'—his very words. All these things have been brought out in the course of the trial. The prosecutor ignores them; he makes a blanket charge against the defendant and does not pick out the points that make the story convincing. Yet, the prosecutor is a shrewd man, and a capable lawyer. Perhaps he knew where the danger lay when he was analyzing this business for you.

"There was no love between the defendant and his brother Louis. What were his emotions when he saw Louis shot down by the game warden? He was appalled by the action, growing out of a misunderstanding on the game warden's part, that had ended so tragically. He was dumbfounded and stood motionless in his tracks. But how about the mother? Did she feel the awfulness of the situation? Was she a creature of thought and deep feeling? She spent the last years of her life lamenting that her sons were cast away from her. When Louis came sneaking to her house, she was wont to supply him with food and whatever she had that he wanted. When he was shot down before her eyes, what were her feelings? Did she resent it bitterly and with blind passion? If you have noticed the defendant, you must be struck with how few of the Indian characteristics he has; his father is present in him. But the mother was a full-blood—simple in her hate and love; quick to avenge a wrong; loyal to her race and her sons. There is your motive.

"The prosecutor brings out in solemn, damning tones that the defendant lied to his Indian agent, ran away, and even after returning kept his mouth shut, although his mother was dead and the dead game warden lay in an un-Christianed grave in the mountains. Is that so hard to understand? Was that criminal? Was he anxious to have it known that his mother had killed the man, whether she were alive or dead? Here's what we haven't inquired into—a thing too that we can't very well present evidence about—how much did that boy suffer or debate with himself before he lied to the agent, who, by the way, was the best friend he had, or went away? How many times has he thought of that man buried in the mountains? You have all looked at the boy as he sat in the witness chair, you've heard him speak: has he the manner of a man who's been thinking criminal thoughts for the past six years? Look at him again, think about that; he's the best evidence I can offer on this point.

"He went away, he lied to his agent, he came back and kept his mouth shut—because there was nothing else for him to do!

"The prosecutor deplores the fact that the defendant didn't stay in college to finish his degree work. He hints that other boys are lustier, more red blooded, more determined in their ways of life. I'll give the prosecutor ducks and drakes and wager that right at this minute the defendant can beat him in an examination in history."

The prosecutor came to his feet like a rocket issuing from its gun. He came up so quickly, in fact, that his feet seemed to leave the floor. He was violent in his rage and the veins at his temples throbbed rapidly.

"Your Honor! I object to irrelevant, personal matters being brought into the case. The defense lawyer is repeatedly speaking in an off-handed, injudicious manner that should not be tolerated. He is presenting a modicum of evidence and a mass of impertinent, idle opinions!"

The judge cleared his throat and rapped on his desk.

"Objection overruled!" he said dryly and spat again into the cuspidor behind the desk.

Once more the defense lawyer began to speak and the audience, stirred for a moment out of its rapt attention, settled back with smiles and titters. Again the spell of a soft, persuasive voice drifted down upon their ears.

"I was bringing out the point that, contrary to the charge, the defendant has studied—in the east—in Paris—and at home. In his house he has a library that won't be matched in many homes in this county. More than that, he knows a thing or two—as I meant to suggest by my allusion to a contest. Evidence has been produced to show these facts. I can't imagine how the prosecutor missed them. As to the matter of the degree, it is possible that the defendant does not place the value on it that the prosecutor or I would—or such as young fellows of his own age, brought up in different circumstances, might value it. We're not measuring generalities here, we're dealing with a specific, living man and to pass judgment on his innocence or guilt we must understand his individual character and upbringing. To say that all men should cherish a college degree—and scrub floors to attain one—is to express an impertinent, idle opinion!

"The defendant is innocent. Of all the witnesses who have testified concerning his character, only one has mentioned him in an unfavorable light, that was Mr. George Moser, the storekeeper. Who is this Mr. Moser? The prosecutor warned you that I would attempt to vilify him; in a word, he said I would throw mud. We all know that the prosecutor is a shrewd man, and when he warns you beforehand of a thing, there must be a reason for it. Why was he afraid that the one supporter of his

The Hungry Generations | 321

characterization of the defendant would be attacked? Was it because he knows that it is the practice of all lawyers, good or bad, to throw mud at witnesses who present contrary evidence? Or does he know that there is something questionable in Mr. Moser's attitude and behavior? Who is this George Moser?

"He came to the country twenty years ago, stone broke. He got a job with George O'Brien's freighting outfit, but he couldn't drive a horse, and the first time he took an outfit out, he had a runaway and scattered his wagon all over the prairie and almost broke his neck to boot. Old George gave him a job keeping books then and he was better at that. Finally, O'Brien gave him a little stake and set him up in a little store. Things went along better then, and at the end of five years, Moser went back east and came back with a wife. In a few more years he was lending money and taking mortgages. They say he'd take a mortgage on anything from a straw stack to a pair of false teeth and he got a reputation of being mighty quick on the collecting end. He began to own land, stock, houses, and crops. When things were booming and the country was still young, he didn't hold on to these things long—he always found a buyer as quick as he could. But he had a slump a few years back, as I guess we all know without any character witnesses. You couldn't get change for a four-bit piece this side of the Divide. We all suffered, and George Moser along with everybody else. He was collecting on mortgages faster than ever, and before long, he was just about the biggest landowner up in this part of the country. But he couldn't sell an acre. Like every merchant and every bank in the country, he became land-poor. They had the land and the stock, but no money—and there was no place to get money.

"There was one man had money—that was Max Leon—he played a good game. He sold his herds of cattle and buffalo just when the squeeze started. Moser became real friendly with old Leon in less than a year. The daughter has told us that, for a while, he was calling at Leon's ranch almost every week. He had him appointed a director in the bank—I'm a shareholder in that bank and I remember the incident well. But old Leon died and left all his money to his son, the defendant. Whether he approached Leon or not we don't know, but he did come to the defendant and tried to unload his sack of grief on his shoulders. He went so far as to say that the defendant's father had promised verbally to buy his interests in the store and bank. The defendant wasn't in the mood to buy anything and told him so. Moser never got over that. He's been on the defendant's trail ever since. I'll not take any more time on this score. The Indian agent has testified that Moser got Leon's outlaw sons to come back, and he went to the agent himself to demand their allotments back, explaining that they couldn't speak English well and had given him power of attorney. He has also challenged the validity of Leon's will to make the defendant share his legacy with the sons Leon wouldn't recognize.

"This is the man who has testified on behalf of the state and has condemned the defendant's character in no uncertain terms—and he is the only witness who has presumed to do so. I do not need to explain why he has taken the attitude he has, the facts explain themselves.

"Now then, I have a little surprise for the prosecutor. But just a word before that. Who gave information leading to the arrest of the defendant? Why, Mr. Moser. Where did he get his information? Three people in the world had the information—three only. They were present at the death-bed of the defendant's mother. She called them there. They are, Agnes, the defendant's sister, and Mike and Narcisse, his two nephews. These were the three people and there were no others. Then how did Moser get his knowledge? Listen to this. During the month preceding the arrest and informing—Mike, the youngest nephew, was presented with a saddle, bridle, chaps, spurs, lariat, Stetson hat, two silk shirts, and cigarettes. By an error on the bookkeeper's part, these things got charged on the books and the defendant received a bill for them. Shortly after that, Mr. Moser turned his information over to the authorities—but in doing so, he twisted things about somewhat. Today, gentlemen of the jury, you will hear the story as it should have been told in the first place. Today you will hear the deathbed confession of the defendant's mother, the person who killed the game warden with an axe!"

Exclamations and quickly drawn breaths filled the courtroom. There was a sound of people moving in their seats and sitting erect to watch the witness stand. There was a break in the proceedings as Agnes, the first witness, was called.

Chapter Eight

Thus the trial came to a close. Archilde walked from the dusky interior of the jail into the bright sunlight and shook the lethargy from his limbs. There was no exultation in his mood.

The Indian agent's little Ford car was standing in front of the courthouse. Archilde got into the front seat and a moment later Parker came out of the courthouse and took his place at the wheel. They drove through the quiet, shaded streets and started for home. They were both silent during most of the four-hour trip.

Climbing the long hill that gave access into the southern end of the valley, Parker said:

"Go home now, Archilde, and rest. Don't do anything for a week or two. I have had your first crop of alfalfa cut—it was a little thinner than it should have been as Tom didn't give it enough water. Your grain is coming along fine. So take it easy."

Archilde did not answer. He was tired of the human voice that day; he had heard too much of shouting, threatening, and blaspheming. He had given too many answers explaining his thoughts, feelings, actions, and ambitions.

When they entered the little town Archilde told Parker to stop in front of Moser's store. The road leading to his ranch passed at one side of the store. Archilde started to get out.

"No," Parker said, "I'm going to drive you home."

Archilde smiled faintly.

"Don't bother. I need exercise badly. Come and see me soon." He turned away.

Moser's house was behind the store, placed in the midst of a fine lawn with tall poplar trees around it. It was the only well-kept and the most pretentious house in town. It was painted yellow and white with an old-fashioned mansard roof whose shingles were stained a dark red. Archilde experienced an unexpected passion as he walked in front of the house, and he could not keep his eyes from gazing stealthily toward the front door. The place seemed to be deserted. Archilde continued his way up the dusty road. His clothes were wrinkled and soiled.

It was past noon and the sun shone high overhead. Summer had come in all its heat and roadside foliage during his absence. Glancing upward to the mountains, he saw that all but a few streaks and patches of snow had been melted away. The bare rocks stood out purple and brown in the glaring midday heat.

The countryside was deserted. Once or twice, as he walked along, he saw a solitary figure standing in a green field—irrigating alfalfa, no doubt, but he passed no one along the road and he heard not a sound. Butterflies of many sizes and colors—white, brown, and pale yellow—rose and fell along the road way. Grasshoppers scattered from under his feet, hopped a few feet, rose again as he approached, and finally spread their wings with a crackling sound and flew beyond the fence that bordered the lane. Honeybees crossed the road, going from one field of clover to another, or bearing their freightage homeward. There were only a few birds who broke the stillness with a sharp note or two. It was too hot for song.

A figure appeared as the road turned out of a grove of cottonwoods and underbrush. At first he was indistinct, but gradually he grew familiar to Archilde's eyes. He was an old man, an Indian, bareheaded, a dirty shirt that had once been yellow, a faded blanket that had once been red. Because it was warm, he had taken the blanket off his shoulders and folded it waist length. With one hand he held the blanket up and with his other hand he clutched his cane—a sawed-off billiard cue. Now he was quite close and Archilde saw him plainly. His hair was quite gray and yellowed with dirt; it was braided in two braids that hung down his shirt front. In his ears were large pearly shells, suspended on small brass rings. His eyes were sightless, the lids blinking continually and a thin moisture lurking in the corners. This was Blind Michel, who wandered the valley from end to end, in all weathers and at all times of the year. Sometimes he had an old black dog, but usually he was alone. Some called him the "Wandering Jew"—which meant nothing to him.

"Hello!" Archilde said. Michel stopped and faced the speaker. He raised his cane to indicate his greeting.

"Hello," his voice was thin and weak. His withered, deeply furrowed features relaxed and a smile broadened his mouth. His eyelids fluttered faster.

"Arsheel, eh?" he asked.

"Eh." The rest of the conversation was in Indian. "The sun is hot," Archilde said.

"Yes. For many days yet there will be no rain."

"You are going to town."

"Yes. I will see my sister. One son is bad. His horse kicked his head."

"That is bad." Archilde gave him a cigarette.

"It's good to come home, eh?"

"Yes. The police gave me up."

"Well, I will go now."

"Why don't you get a horse, Michel? Your people have lots of horses. You walk a long ways."

The old man's eyes flickered and he smiled. "No. I walk. A blind man trusts his own legs. So it is best."

"That's good, Michel! Well, come to my house and get some meat sometime."

The old man went down the road again, bareheaded, dirty, his moccasined feet shuffling softly in the heavy dust. Once more Archilde turned his face toward the mountains and home.

The world was such a place that not even a blind man looked otherwhere for help than in himself. All bounty, all strength, lay there.

The road on which he walked was familiar. The fence posts along the way were not unknown; the hollows and high spots met recognition in his eyes. Now, as he came nearer his goal, his blood began to quicken. He had not expected it, he had not looked forward to the first glimpse of his fields, but as he mounted a rise after crossing a dried creek bed and saw his green land, the round hill beyond his house, he could scarcely breathe, so choked was his breast and so hot his blood. His eyes dimmed. A little later he entered his own domain. A lane had been cut through one corner of a pasture section. Off to his right a little ways was the bedraggled, stained teepee and weather-beaten shack of his brother Pete. Lean, mangy dogs barked viciously as he passed.

Home again! A few flies buzzed within the screened porch. Agnes and the boys hadn't come home yet. He sat down in the wicker chair that had been the favorite of his father. The wild cucumber vines had climbed the height of the porch and their shade was pleasant. He tossed his hat aside and leaned his head back; through the unbroken stillness he heard the quiet murmur of the creek behind the house. A rooster crowed drowsily.

As Archilde sat there with half-closed eyes he felt his strength mounting bit by bit. The far corners of his world began to press upon him, faintly and indistinctly at first, but resolutely, like water washing in small wavelets to a river's edge. The blood within his body grew yet warmer. He hadn't looked forward to the homecoming; he did not know that there was magic in the earth beneath his feet. The hill beyond the house lay like a great dog fawning and crouching at his side. All this world would be his—when he had recaptured it again. He must march out soon and make a survey of everything, asserting his command once more. What had the chickens and hogs been living on? Had Tom milked the cows right? How was the water running in the fields and pastures? His was a large and complicated world; everything seemed to depend on what time of year he bred his cows.

As he sat in jail, shame and sorrow seemed to have eaten his bowels away—he sat with a green pallor over his face and movement almost gone from his limbs. It had seemed then that the pillars of his manhood had been blasted asunder and he sat amid the ruins without a whole purpose in his body.

"Come," the agent had said. "You mustn't sit here! The judge has allowed you bail. You must come home and wait for your trial!"

"Leave me be!" Archilde had growled. Go home and sit like a toad, blinking his eyes at the sun with nothing to do but wait? No, he did not care to do that. If his body broke out in sores, he would go and hide until they healed, wouldn't he? So he preferred to sit in the shadow of his cell until there was no more ulcer in his breast. It was in his blood, that when an ordeal faced him, punishment, torture, recrimination, he should stand up to the judgment without flinching; he should take the full measure of his enemy's wrath. Now that he had gone through the fire he stepped forth unshaken, undeterred.

The earth lay unfolded before his eyes; bright and fierce were the arms of the sun that held it fast and blew a furnace breath over the trees and hills. Archilde gazed over his wheat fields and his eyes caught a suggestion of golden haze dancing over the tall, green stalks. The grain was beginning to turn and in a few weeks more the harvesting would begin. The time of fulfillment was at hand.

Soft, shuffling steps approached the side of the house. Archilde turned and saw old Tom coming to greet him. He wore the same clothes, looked the same as he had for twenty years or more; a flat-crowned, broad-brimmed hat, the band that had once been white was stained black with perspiration and dirt, he wore his blue serge coat that had been given him long ago and which he never removed for heat, work or—possibly—sleeping. His moccasined feet were small as a woman's. When he looked up at Archilde, his brown, furrowed face beamed for a moment; it was the warmest expression he could register.

"Eh!" he grunted in salutation.

"Eh!" Archilde replied and came down from the porch to shake hands. "How's it go?"

"It's good. They let you go, eh?"

"Sure. They made lots of talk—but nothing happened." The old man was silent for a moment. Archilde squatted on his heels to roll a cigarette and the old man sat down too, taking the sack of tobacco when Archilde passed it to him.

"Mike got you in trouble, eh?" Tom asked.

"That's so. But he was all right at the end. The lawyer told him to speak the truth and he did—so it was all right."

Tom paused again. "He was bad. But Agnes talked to him for a long time. Many days she sat down by him and talk. I guess she made him good again. While you was in jail, he irrigated—cut hay too. Agnes is good talker."

328 | D'Arcy McNickle

Archilde was speechless and smoked his cigarette for a long time. "That's fine!" he said at last. A little later he asked: "What does Pete do?"

"Pete is getting blind. The Indian doctor comes to see him."

"Does he drink all the time?"

"Sure. At night he sings down there with his old woman."

"Does Mike go to see him?"

"Not much now. They had a fight. Mike kicked his old woman in the belly, and Pete chased him away with an axe. I guess, Mike won't go anymore."

"Good! I'll go and look at the wheat."

He walked along the edge of his wheat field letting the tall wheat stalks slip through his open hand. The hardening beards scratched at his perspiring flesh and set his hand to tingling. The first blades near the ground as well as the bottoms of the stalks were tinged with yellow. The ground was dry and hot with tiny cracks appearing everywhere. A hot breath lived amid the wheat stalks and kept them in a tremble.

The alfalfa was ready to be cut at once. It stood high and green and in luxuriant tangles. The purple blossoms were rich in color and subtle perfumery. Seeing his wheat so near to ripening and his alfalfa all ready for the sickle sent repeated electric shocks through his blood. His body became more and more agitated. He was ready to start at once! Unintentionally, he drew off his coat and tie; the heat was growing insufferable. He walked back to the house with long, swinging steps; his shoulders swung in unison and at times he gesticulated with his hands. There was work to do!

His cows were standing in a group under some alder trees by the creek. They were sleek and plump.

At sundown the family returned. They had driven to the county seat in the delivery truck, and now they were just getting back, Mike driving, Narcisse at his side, and Agnes and Annie sitting on sacks of hay in the back. The car came up the road slowly and, instead of coming to the front of the house, turned into the barnyard, stopping near the horse barn. Archilde paused a moment at the side of the house and then walked forward and a soft expression was on his face.

Mike and Narcisse were loath to get out; they nudged each other to make a start but neither moved. Agnes and Annie climbed out through the back and moved around with cramped limbs. They said nothing. Archilde walked toward them.

"So you got back, eh?" When he stepped forward and shook hands with first Agnes and then Annie, he was not expecting their faces to remain blank and their lips dumb—but so it was. They stared at him and drew their hands away slowly when he had given them a second shake with a warm grip and a broader smile on his own face.

"Well, now we're all here again!" he said.

He went to the front of the car.

"Come Narce and Mike! We'll shake hands!" The two boys climbed from the seat and one at a time stepped forward, Mike coming first.

Agnes and Annie went to the house and the two nephews stood beside Archilde awkwardly for some time, smoking and scraping the ground with their feet. Presently Mike said:

"Arsheel, we gotta go behind the barn!" and twisted his legs together. Archilde broke into a loud laugh, and the boys turned and ran.

Chapter Nine

The sickle of the mowing machine whirred loudly on the air. Archilde swayed in his seat as the machine rolled steadily over the earth's unevenness. His two fat mares swung along with slow and measured steps, switching their tails and lathering where their harness straps hugged their bodies and where their fat thighs rubbed. When he turned a square corner, the idling cogs in the gear mechanism clicked sharply. The odor of the wilting hay hung heavily in the air. Old Tom was raking in a nearby field. Farther away Mike and Narcisse were bunching the windrows, stopping at times to roll a cigarette and spit on their hands. A second mowing machine followed behind his own. The sun beat down fiercely, drenching man and beast with sweat. Crows flew overhead from time to time with lazy wings. Smoke and haze lurked in the mountain canyons and on the horizon; fires were burning in Idaho and the forests to the north.

Archilde, as he rode the machine across his meadow, watching the lush grass billowed by the dividing board, was warmed and cheered by the spectacle of peace and harmony that had followed the trial. Harsh words and threats were no longer necessary when he spoke to his nephews; they had been given a scare and now there was nothing they would not do around the house or in the field. The agent had already come to visit on the morning of this very day and spoke jovially of better times to come. Nor could he forget that the judge had shook his hand after the trial and commended his stolid qualities that would, no doubt, make him a splendid citizen. "I commend you!" were the judge's words and as Archilde passed through the corridors packed with people, everyone paused to let him pass and smiles and pleasant words met him on every hand. The atmosphere lingered on in the actions and looks of the people near him. It seemed that Agnes cooked better meals, and Annie kept her dark eyes on him at all times in her stealthy way, bringing what he needed before he asked and speaking oftener than had been her habit. His cows were fat and milking heavily, his hay was heavy and there would be a good harvest. It was no wonder that rapture filled his breast and bright images floated through his head.

But he was not fooled. He knew the pleasant days would pass and strife would come again. He did not know on what hand or how soon the shadow of discontent and malice would fall, but he knew it was near. While with one mind he was happy for the kindness of those who had helped him, he was inclined to resent their charitableness; it overemphasized the incident and put everyone in a glowing frame of mind from which they would soon react. He was not particularly pleased that the judge had shaken his hand, and although he resented the harsh words of the prosecuting attorney, he was actually upset by much of what the defending attorney had uttered. Nothing could make him feel as silly as when flattery was offered him.

So he discounted the soft words and was already looking to the horizon for the first storm clouds to appear. His brother Pete sat before his squalid shack like a big frog. At night his friends came with whiskey and they sat around singing and crying at the [bleak?] moon. Big Blase was coming over the mountains in another month, he had heard, and they were going to put their case before the Indian council. The appeal of the will contest would be brought to court soon—if Moser was thinking of continuing his support. Archilde did not forget Moser's words of long ago: "You're a damn Indian and you'll never be anything better!" Now Moser's wife was sick, near death, it was said, and some new bitterness would probably grow out of that. Archilde did not hate Moser; he spat on the ground when he thought of him and frowned—but put him out of his thoughts at once. Someday yet he would give him a poke in the jaw!

Mike and Narcisse would be kicking over the traces again, he told himself. They were working hard today, but who knew what they'd be doing tomorrow? One thing he knew, he'd waste no words on them hereafter. They could make their own choices and his shoe would be ready to boot them through the door the first time they strayed too far. He was standing now in the footprints his father had left twenty-five years ago. Already he had said in his mind: "If they will not live on my terms—then they will get out and stay out!" As for himself, he would live in his father's house and bring to pass such of the dream as he had caught from the old man—and his own in its time.

Hereafter, they would live a stringent life who lived with him. His goal was set and he would not be deterred. What he asked of himself, he would ask of others on the same terms. So, in a word, the story of Archilde's life had only now begun. How he would live out his days was to be a greater problem than his approach to life and possibly a less happy one. But a man had been made from a stick.

Another day ended. In a bath of effulgent light the men unhitched their horses and started for home. Long shadows went before their horses and roseate colors tinged the round hill beyond the house. Coolness and relaxation came to man and beast. Rest and ease lay ahead.

Archilde was riding the plump back of one of his mares; one team was ahead bathing him in dust. Old Tom plodded behind, driving his horse before him, his blue coat and flat hat bobbing up and down. Mike and Narcisse were farther behind, playing a game as they walked along. The colors deepened in the sky, the smoky haze adding to the miracle of sunset. The chains of the harness jangled. Archilde hung his head, enjoying his feeling of peace.

Then, of a sudden, certain words came into his mind, words such as he had never used before. One by one they pressed into his brain, each one breaking in a shower of light as when rockets end their flight and expire in bright flame. Each word had the breath of fire, but it had also the strength of cold metal. These were the words he spoke:

Clouds out of water!
I have seen my dream of power
Walking the clouds of water!
He was a valiant god, a red warrior.
He buckled to his breast a bright robe

And strode over the tops of hills,
Walking the clouds of water!

And his own ears were astonished. But deeper than his outward senses there was no astonishment. There was strength beneath that surging and charging in a rush to the light. It was a dream of power and nothing less.

That night as he lay in bed he heard life pounding in his ears for many hours. The opened windows rattled in a fresh wind that had come up and he heard the trees move and saw them swim against the dark sky. Sleep would not come. He knew that Claudia was at that moment on her way to visit him. Her letter was waiting for him when he came from the field.

I will be with you three days after this reaches you, I have figured it out. Now I have hinted for three years, but you never come. So I will then. The taxi is here and I am leaving for the train. I will stop in Kansas City. Will you be pleased to see me? And will I be pleased? Only wait!

That was the note that she had written. The phrases galloped up and down his mind, striking fire against his closed eyelids. He lay in bed and dreamed, but sleep he did not, until dawn came. Then he slept and a cool wind passed over his outstretched form.